P9-CRT-455

ALSO EDITED BY ANDREW BLAUNER

Our Boston: Writers Celebrate the City They Love

Central Park: An Anthology

Brothers: 26 Stories of Love and Rivalry

Coach: 25 Writers Reflect on People Who Made a Difference

The GOOD BOOK

Writers Reflect on Favorite Bible Passages

Edited by

Andrew Blauner

SIMON & SCHUSTER

New York London Toronto Sydney New Delhi

Simon & Schuster
1230 Avenue of the Americas
New York, NY 10020

First Simon & Schuster hardcover edition November 2015

Book design by Ellen R. Sasahara

Manufactured in the United States of America

1 3 5 7 9 10 8 6 4 2

Library of Congress Cataloging-in-Publication Data

The good book : writers reflect on favorite Bible passages / edited by Andrew Blauner. — First Simon & Schuster hardcover edition.
pages cm
1. Bible as literature. I. Blauner, Andrew, editor.
BS535.G66 2015
220.6—dc23 2015010157

ISBN 978-1-4767-8996-5
ISBN 978-1-4767-8998-9 (ebook)

Contents

∴ Other ∴

The Good Book: An Introduction

Adam Gopnik

How shall we sing the Lord's song in a strange land? And how should we read the Bible in a secular age? At a time when this odd, disjointed compilation of ancient Hebrew texts and later Greek texts has lost its claims to historical truth, or to supernatural revelation, it would seem to some that we might simply let it fade, read, until it becomes one more of those texts, like Galen's medicine or the physics of Aristotle, that everyone knows once mattered but now are left quietly to sit on the shelf and wait for a scholar.

As history and revelation its stories have long ago fallen away; we know that almost nothing that happens in it actually happened, and that its miracles, large and small, are of the same kind and credibility as all the other miracles that crowd the world's great granary of superstition. Only a handful of fundamentalists—granted that in America that handful is sometimes more like an armful, and at times like a roomful—read it literally, and, though the noes may not always have it in raw numbers, the successive triumphs of critical reason mean that they have it in all educated circles. (Believers may cry elitism at this truth—but the simpler truth is that when the educated elite has rejected an idea it's usually because there's something in the idea that resists education.)

And yet. The Bible remains an essential part of the education of what used to be called the well-furnished mind. Not to know it is not to know enough. Most of what we value in our art and architecture, our music and poetry—Bach and Chartres, Shakespeare and Milton, Giotto at the Arena Chapel and Blake's Job among his friends—is entangled with these old books and ancient texts: we enter Chartres and see the Tree of Jacob, and we need to know that this is the line of the inheritance of Jesus. We queue for hours to see the Sistine Ceiling, and our hearts stop at what Michelangelo's hand has done all the quicker if we see the sublime text in our mind as we look at the picture with our eyes—"and God made two great lights; the greater light to rule the day, and the lesser light to rule the night: he made the stars also." We listen to Bach's *St. John Passion*, and it means nothing if we do not know what a passion was, and how this one horribly unfolded.

Though our search for the spiritual needs no help from the supernatural—it is fully accounted for by human sensibility—still, it does need help. The philistinism of the "new atheists," the meagerness of their aesthetic responses, is the one fair reproach against them; the human content of the art and music of the past too often seems duly "appreciated" by them, as a tiresome obligation, rather than really known and felt, as an irresistible temptation. The past dependency of our whole civilization on a scaffolding made from scripture is a low stile that they leap over lazily, with a shrug, rather than a high one, demanding a huge leap of, well, non-faith.

Yet some other part of its appeal lies beyond its history in art and architecture, lies rather in our daily bread—our continuing need for guidance through the harsher perplexities of earthly existence. The Twenty-Third Psalm remains as stirring for those who take heart simply at its image of a shepherd's care as it does for those who think the Lord exists to exercise it. No, modern people are drawn to faith while practicing doubt, as our ancestors confessed their doubts while practicing their faith. Each of us engages, casually or self-consciously, with the idea of faith and the fact of doubt—and so there is a vein of modern literature, philosophical and poetic, that will always remain a chronicle of how we read the Bible. The shuttle between the arguments made by liberal doubt and the magnetic pull of the art made by belief is not one that can be avoided by thinking modern men and women, and it turns, always, to the question of scripture, and how it's read. How do we reconcile the power of the prose and the passions described—the wisdom of the Psalms and the beauty of the Song of Solomon—with the plainer but truer truths of a civilization of rational inquiry? That fugue of doubt and faith, experienced as argument and art, is the music of our lives.

But how *do* we do it? How, we may ask as we propose to embark upon reading, do we go on reading scripture in a secular time? There seems something dispiriting about merely reading for "effect," or for "pleasure." Some may recall that in *Goldfinger,* Bond carried his Walther PPK in a hollowed-out book called *The Bible to Be Read as Literature.* The mordant joke was that, once we read the Bible only for pleasure, we might as well use it to inflict the more glamorous kind of pain: after faith goes, nothing but vodka, bullets, and a void. If the Bible is to be read as literature, as something more than a joke, or an antiquarian oddity, how is it to be done?

As usual, to answer the question of what we should do, it is best to look at what we *do* do. There are, in place already, four pervasive methods or styles, shared by modern people, for reading the Bible (all illustrated, often overlapping and hybridized, in these pages).

There is first of all the *aesthetic* habit of reading—we read and dissect the books and verses of the Bible because they tell beautiful stories, stirring and shapely. We read the good book because it is a good book. We explore the stories because they are transfixing stories, dense and compelling. The beauty of the Song of Songs, or the nobility of the account of creation in Genesis, or the poetic hum of the Psalms—these things are beautiful as poetic myths alone can be. That they were best translated into our own language in the highest period of English prose and verse, in Shakespeare's rhythms and vocabulary—conceivably with his hand at work, and certainly with hands near as good as his—only makes them more seductive. (Even when more modern translations are not as good, they often echo the King James Version.) These are good tales and great poetry, and we need not worry about their sources any more than we worry about which level at that endless archaeological dig in Turkey is truly Troy. We read them not as "myth" but as fiction—we read them as we read all good stories, for their perplexities as much as for their obvious points.

Nor is an aesthetic reading—the idea of the Bible fiction as narrative—an aesthetic idea alone. It is itself a view from *within* faith, meaning that the best way to save the faith is to admit its fictions. The theologian Hans Frei is often associated with this view—that the force of the Bible is exactly the force of stories of a particular kind, and that discovering that scripture can be storytelling is not a limiting case, but what gives scripture power. We do not, Frei points out, need to believe in Pierre and Natasha to, in a real sense, *believe* in *War and Peace*—to believe in its picture of human affairs, its vision of history, its knowledge of what was once called the human heart. To ask if Pierre existed, or to track down partial Pierres and early Pierre literature in Russian history, is to miss the point of *War and Peace* entirely. To say that the Bible's stories are good stories is to say that they are *sustaining* stories: tales we tell ourselves in order to live. The story of Job's suffering, defiance, and faith, or the story of Esther, like the passion of Jesus, is applicable as Tolstoy or Tolkien is applicable—they need be neither true nor heavy, academic allegories. The recognition that fiction is not a synonym for falsehood but another way at the truth is in itself powerful and helps us read on.

Next, there is the *accommodationist*, or moral-metaphorical way of reading. This is different from the aesthetic or literary reading because, instead of asking us to be stirred by scripture for its narrative complexities, it asks us to be stirred by the Bible as enduring moral inquiry—the accommodationist seeks to translate the gnomic knots of the Bible stories into acceptable, contemporary, and even universal ethical truths. It is the kind of reading that shows how, in texts that might otherwise seem obnoxious or alien to a modern mind, enduring moral teaching can still be found. Thomas Jefferson's famous version of the Gospels—the miracles left out, the humane teachings left in—is of this kind. In another way, in our own era, when the scholar Elaine Pagels reads Revelation for us, she both untangles its real first-century history and finds in it a convincing larger allegory of the long, bending arc of justice. It belongs to its time, but still has much to teach ours. In this way, we continually recast, through subtle rereading, a tribal or schismatic or merely difficult text into a universal one. If at times this may seem merely to turn brutal injunctions into liberal mysteries, at others it clears away the encrustations of time and the barnacles of old rhetoric and lets us see the real yearnings for justice and freedom that enlighten the book. That the slaves in the American South, being told of the Israelites begging to be let go from bondage heard in that story the echo of their own plight shows how powerful the right kind of "accommodationist" reading can be—how far-reaching the metaphors, how strong the morals.

Then, there is the *anthropological* habit of reading. This style insists on intellectual detachment, on a sense that the Bible is an extraordinary compilation of truths about how we imagine miracles—that the miracles are imagined does not diminish what they tell us about that imagination, or about mankind. We don't read scripture to hear good stories or learn good morals. We read to learn about human history, and human nature. How do laws get made? How do dietary restrictions work? Why? How does order come from warfare? Or, looking at the New Testament, the anthropological-minded reader asks: What is the nature of charismatic leadership? Academic in origin, the anthropological view need not be merely academic in practice. By seeking to use the holy text right at hand, it tries to enlarge our views of how we make ideas of holiness.

And finally, there is the *antagonistic*, or frankly hostile manner of reading. We read holy books in order to show why we need none. We read to fight back. Nor is this habit merely antagonistic. Without strong oppositional readings, how can we ever make sense of texts at all? Indeed, much classic Talmudic reading, though not heretical, is often best described as antagonistic in this sense: fed up with the stolid apparent meanings of the verse, it searches for a meaning that wiser men can live with.

Now, all of these kinds can and do crossbreed. I irregularly attend a Unitarian church in New York where the sermons are almost always exercises in amiable accommodation—the hard texts must mean something else, and it is the job of the clergyman to show us what. (Bar mitzvah readings in the Upper West Side are of this kind, too. The thirteen-year-old draws his or her day's text, often with an eliminationist or brutally tribal accent—God reneged on a promise, or took pleasure in a mass slaughter— and must make it, under the watchful eye of a worried woman rabbi, into an acceptable NPR editorial.)

Aesthetic, accommodationist, anthropological, antagonistic—any good reading of a biblical text will include elements of *all* of them. When we read, say, the Book of Esther, we are fascinated by the dramatic history of Esther, Jewish queen in a foreign court, a tense story of a woman torn between loyalties (aesthetic), while we also search for a moral to be plucked from the tale of suddenly renewed loyalty and awakened conscience (accommodationist); and while we may resent the history of massacre and countermassacre (antagonistic), yet we end with thoughts on how surprisingly mixed and multicultural ancient civilization really was (anthropological). Good books have many levels, and good readings take many kinds.

Yet we cannot pretend that this is not a book without a complicated hero, God—two heroes, really, counting his son as the hero of the second part—and that the way we imagine a Deity is inescapable from the way we feel about his book. The images of God that appear in these pages are as various as the styles of the book: there is an evil deity, vengeful and psychopathic, a sublime creative one in Genesis, a narrowly rule-giving one in Deuteronomy, and an argumentative one in Job.

If the variety proves, to the anthropological or historically minded reader, how complex and historically conditioned the idea of the Deity is—Simon Schama has recently given us a clear sense that monotheism was never monolithic—for the common reader it suggests more. It suggests that we need not regularize the idea of God to contemplate it. The most recent attempt to "save the phenomenon" among desperate theologians has been to remove the Deity entirely from his creation, moving him backwards from the fields of biology and geology, where we know no sign of him can be seen, into a metaphysical background where at best he blinks mysteriously, like a distant star.

This is, of course, as a historical claim about belief, absurd. As any reader of the book can see, this is not what theologians have "always" believed; it is all they have left. But can this big, foggy, metaphysical idea of God, immunized from all empirical examination, still somehow do the things he does in his chronicles: make moral rules, choose up sides in battle, much less sanctify temples and dictate complicated rules for how many hooves the food you eat has to have? Logically, no. No one has remotely succeeded in finding a way for him to do this, because no one can. The obviously anthropomorphic sky-God of actual practice and empirical interference can never be subsumed into the metaphysical and removed God, untouched by it.

But things that defeat logic can often invite imagination, and as a fictional creation the idea of the Deity remains compelling exactly in its—in his—plurality. We need neither believe nor doubt as we read, but remain suspended in that ether of scruples, credulity, and wonder where all good reading really takes place.

A deeper point remains. No moral idea worth preserving has been lost as the idea of God has diminished. Indeed, many moral ideas—of inclusion, tolerance, pluralism, and the equality of man, and the emancipation of women—depend on the diminishment and destruction of a traditional idea of an absolute authority Deity. But nor have moral ideas worth saving been gained *simply* by diminishing the idea of God. Atheism is a fact about the world, but humanism is a value that we make. Supernaturalism needs the cure of sanity. But humanism needs humility.

There is, in truth, really, nothing at all complex or mysterious about the relation between "soulfulness" and science. There is a huge range of human inquiry, questions of meaning and purpose and value and morality, that are too complicated or variable or ever newly folded to be subject to scientific investigation properly so called. Attempts to make a science of affections, or an evolutionary psychology of art, always end by being fatuous. There is no science of siblings, much less a science of sonnets. These games are too mutable, their terms too changeable, their goals too open to creative tinkering to sit still for confident predictive generalization. From the indisputably hardwired human need to find mates to make more humans we can deduce the polygamous court of a polygamous king and the marriage of Leonard and Virginia Woolf.

And no philosopher of science has ever disputed this. Karl Popper, mistaken for a positivist, insisted throughout his life that his famous criterion of testability was only a criterion of science, not of rationality, much less of meaning, and that, as he wrote, the specificities of a single smile would never be susceptible to science.

But the persistence of the metaphysical has nothing in common with the intercession of the magical. The alternative to science is human sensibility. It lies in poetic description and singular witness—the manifold distinctions of philosophy and the thick observations of psychology. An argument for intellectual pluralism is hardly an argument for divine intercession. Existence is itself miraculous. But that water is amazing, and wine a miracle, does not alter the truth that water has never become wine except by people stamping their feet on grapes, a process we know. Our lives are fully accounted for by our lives, our minds make our meanings, and the argument goes on forever.

The paradox in our history has been that the renewal of humanism has come about most often—and the most arresting questions asked of it—by reexamining the old stories, and asking them new questions. This act of replenishment—in W. H. Auden's Christmas poem, in T. S. Eliot's austere retellings, in Christina Rossetti's Victorian Christmas carols, or in Pasolini's and Scorsese's passion stories—is the kind that makes the Bible live. Rabbi Ismar Schorsch, of the Jewish Theological Seminary in New York, once supplied a simple idea: that the Bible is a universal book, with a chapter for every part of human experience—lust, desire, renewal, rage, pedantry, and inexplicable suffering, a book of mourning and a book of passion and many books of pain. Such a book is still worth rereading.

Every myth system has some quiddity essential to it. The beauty of Greek myth is that it understands that contradiction is character, and makes that understanding come alive in ways human and dramatic: Love, Aphrodite, makes an unhappy marriage to Work, Hephaestus, but a gloriously orgiastic relationship with War, Ares. The wild man, the Centaur, is the great teacher. Wisdom springs fully born from the head of Power. Each man secretly wishes to marry his mother, and each of us wants to stare at our own image in the pool.

The special virtue of the biblical myth is its recognition of the ineluctability of human suffering and the possibility of human speech: from the first chapter, the metaphors of the Bible speak to our knowledge of mortality, and they do so by offering us a still-unrivaled cast of characters. They show us recognizable people making recognizable cries. Moses and Aaron, brothers at war; Saul and David, flawed king and pure protégé; David and Absalom—"would to God I had died for thee"—Esther and Solomon and poor cowardly Peter and Jesus himself, arrogant and humbled. No book has ever had more men and women within it. A desert religion, a dark universe of pain into which the light of justice or mercy occasionally breaks, and in which we find small shadowed stations of poetry or nativity to comfort us. Made by men and women, the Bible is populated by people. That's what makes it, and leaves it, an open book.

THE OLD TESTAMENT

Who Is the Snake in the Garden of Eden? A Thought Experiment

Genesis 2–3

Avi Steinberg

There are many drawbacks to growing up in a community of religious fundamentalists. (Right-wing summer camps, for example, don't tend to be quite as fun as liberal-minded ones.) But there are also some benefits to fundamentalism: reading the Bible as nonfiction is, in my experience, one of them.

At the Orthodox Jewish schools in which I was educated, we were taught that the Torah—that is, the first five books of the Hebrew Bible, from Genesis to Deuteronomy—was written by God himself (dictated to Moses). And, what's more, those books were, we were taught, a sober factual report of history: every character in the story was a person who really lived and breathed, and every event described in the story, we were told, actually happened.

It's hard to describe to people who didn't grow up with these beliefs what it's like to read the Bible in this odd way, what it's like to believe that the accounts of Noah and Abraham and Moses are as fact-based as today's *New York Times*.

To the uninitiated, this type of literal-minded reading can seem simplistic: Can't a story be "true" even if it isn't factually true? Is *Moby-Dick* less great because Ishmael is a fictional person and not a guy who actually lived and boarded a whaling ship in the nineteenth century? Doesn't insistence on the historical realism of a text miss the point of a story?

Perhaps. But what if we could have it both ways, a powerful piece of literature that was also all factual? The Bible after all was intended to be taken as factual, and even though its literary worth may not depend on its historical accuracy, can we deny that it would be much more thrilling to the imagination if these sensational stories all turned out to be fact? Wouldn't that make it a work of singular interest?

Even after I left the Orthodox fold, and read the text in a variety of different and less pious ways, I began to realize that there was something missing. Not believing in the realism of the story had created a kind of barrier between the text and me. Even though I could read Hebrew, it was as if I was no longer able to read the story in its original language; in losing faith, something was lost in translation. Even though I maintained that a critical approach to the biblical text was the intellectually honest position, I had to admit that something important had been lost in my personal experience of reading those stories: the energy, the drama, the electrifying sense of immediacy that comes from the knowledge that *this really happened*. All of that was gone. This wasn't simply a loss of religious faith; it was a loss of literary faith. That paradise of true belief in a story was lost—or, at least, it seemed to be lost. Was it somehow possible to regain it?

During my former life as a religious reader, I'd learned that the text as nonfiction yielded the opposite of simplistic interpretations. On the contrary, the project of harmonizing religious faith with common sense and rationality required an obsessive degree of careful thought, a compulsive impulse to reread more deeply. One of the unique properties of reading a text in this manner is that it forces a reader to work a bit. A reader must actively mine the story for plausibility, for verisimilitude, where another reader wouldn't bother. When reading the story of the Garden of Eden, most people are perfectly content to accept it as a fable, or an allegory. Just as nobody is bothered by the realism of Kafka's talking dogs and chimps, or by Aesop's tortoises and hares, no reader is bothered by the talking snake in the Garden. Why should it bother them? These things happen every day in the world of fiction.

Nor is a secular reader bothered that the creation story in general is riddled with contradictory details. In one chapter, Adam and Eve are described as having been created together. In the next chapter, Adam is created first and Eve is fashioned out of his surgically removed rib. To the secular reader, there's a simple historical reason for this contradiction: when the Bible was being compiled there were different versions of the story floating around in different documents. A scribe, or group of scribes, simply cut two versions of the story from two documents and pasted them into the Bible (possibly as a clever effort to attract the fans of each version).

But to the religious reader, who believes that the text emerged more or less whole from the Cloud of Glory, the theory of multiple documents doesn't quite suffice. To the religious reader, both narrative versions of the creation must somehow reflect a single set of facts, and the (apparent) contradiction was intentionally placed there for artistic purposes, to create the effect of layered meanings. In the case of the two dueling creation stories, the contradiction perhaps speaks to the contradictory nature of humans, how they were at odds with themselves from the moment they were created: sometimes they are coupled and sometimes they are individuals, sometimes their natures are in sync and sometimes they are in opposition to each other and to their surroundings. The human is a creature who wants to be a creator, a mortal who aspires to be a god. In short, if you believe that Adam isn't just a character who appears in different literary documents but an *actual* person, with thoughts and emotions and clashing motivations, you are compelled to see him that way in the text. To the religious reader, the story's inconsistencies show Adam and Eve as they really are: creatures of contradiction.

If you read the story as literally true, there is a greater need to account for strangeness, to puzzle out its mysteries. Religious reading, in my experience, demanded more of me. It required a great deal of clever literary maneuvering and creativity, an elevated degree of alertness and commitment and activity. It was an ambitious way to encounter a story, and it yielded results that were as brilliant and innovative as any secular reading. Ever since I left the fold, I've wondered if it was possible to recapture that unique mode of reading.

And so I decided to do a thought experiment: I would reread the story *as though* I believed in it. I would work on the premise that everything in the story has to make logical sense—as much as possible—and that it's more than just a tall tale; it's a chronicle of true events that happened in *our* world. Without actually becoming an Orthodox believer again, I could adopt the reading style of a believer.

In doing my thought experiment, it was only natural to begin with the story of the Garden of Eden—and not only because it's the opening of the book. In a text whose story lines are deepened through the ceaseless repetition of themes, Eden is the Story of Stories, the narrative upon which every other story in Genesis, and beyond, is structurally modeled. It wasn't an accident that the Gospels, that late addition to the biblical library, imagined its story as another rendition of the Genesis narrative and its protagonist, Jesus, as a second Adam. The story of Eden is the key to understanding many other stories in the Bible, and in western literature.

The challenge, however, is that Eden also happens to be one of the more notoriously difficult stories to imagine in realistic terms. Any thought experiment in literary realism must address the veracity problem posed generally by Genesis, with its six-hundred-year-old heroes and its mysterious passages (e.g., just who are those "daughters of men" who mate with the "sons of gods"?). But the story of Eden is especially weird, and its basic meaning is hard to figure.

True, most Bible stories are weird—but few are quite this baffling. Later in Genesis, for instance, when Jacob and his mother plot to hoodwink Jacob's brother, Esau, by hoodwinking the aging Isaac, we immediately grasp the realism of that situation: it's an inheritance plot, an all-too-familiar family drama. Even though the characters are nomadic shepherds living in the Land of Canaan in the year one billion B.C.E., we easily recognize the human story there.

But where's the realism with the slick-talking Snake and the blissfully naked Adam and Eve romping around their garden? The setting itself is mystifying; it doesn't seem to be happening on our planet. What is going on in this story? Even if we assume that it indeed happened, as per the thought experiment, *what* is it exactly that happened?

And, who is this Snake? To answer this question, the Christian tradition developed an entire prequel-like backstory to the Garden of Eden narrative. Without some kind of explanation, the Eden story hardly makes any sense: What, after all, motivated this Snake character to be such a troublemaker? The answer, according to those Christian readers, can be found in an untold history: there was a war in heaven, an armed rebellion against God led by a dissenting angel, who was then cast out, along with his fellow rebel angels, and subsequently became a devil who set up headquarters in the underworld, plotting revenge. The Snake, then, was actually this devil-angel in disguise, on a secret mission to sabotage God's plans. Eden, in other words, was just one battleground in a larger war between God and the fallen angels, a battle in which humans are mere pawns.

It's a great story. But it's not a very enlightening read of Genesis. The Satan backstory only highlights the gaping hole at center of the Eden story in the biblical text: Just who is this Snake and what motivates him? Without much to go on, Christian readers can hardly be blamed for filling in the narrative gap by inserting an elaborate backstory. But that gap remains a gap.

Can we discern a true human drama in the Garden of Eden, a real story, or is it just a one-note moral allegory, or merely fodder for comic-strip punch lines? Is there a story in Eden, like the conflict between Jacob and his brother, that feels as real as a family drama?

As soon as we accept the premise that the Snake is real—as per my thought experiment—that he really said those things to Eve, the weirdness of this detail immediately demands that we make sense of it. When we're forced to find realism in Eden, a story suddenly emerges so clearly that it's surprising we didn't see it there the whole time, hiding in plain sight: the Snake and Adam are brothers.

The story of the Garden of Eden is as dramatic as a family conflict because it *is* a drama of family conflict. The Snake isn't secretly a devil out to take vengeance on God, but rather the conflict in the story is exactly what it says it is: an encounter between one character named "the Snake" and the other named "Adam" (or, to be closer to the Hebrew, *the* Adam—translation, "the human"). These two characters, the Human and the Snake, share the same father, and yet one is favored and the other is not. One has been given the mantle of leadership and the other has gotten nothing. This is the source of a conflict.

Like all brothers in the Book of Genesis, Adam and the Snake quarrel over an inheritance: Who will be given the right of dominion? Adam is given this right by their father, the Creator, but the Snake believes that he, the Snake, is more worthy, and he sets out to prove it.

Fraternal conflict, the fight over which son is favored, is the central recurring motif in the Book of Genesis. According to the usual reading, this motif begins with Adam and Eve's children, Cain and Abel, and the cycle of fraternal strife repeats with Isaac and Ishmael, then Jacob and Esau, and concludes with Joseph and his brothers. I would suggest, however, that this motif starts earlier in the book, at the very beginning, with Adam and the Snake. As it turns out, Eden is the first and archetypal instance of brothers at war.

And, like other brothers in Genesis, they are joined together as opposites. Like Jacob and Esau, the soft-skinned tent dweller and the hairy hunter, the Snake and the Human are twins, two sides of a single principle. We meet these twins in twin statements. In the first, we see that "the two of them were naked, the man and his wife, and they were not ashamed." The Hebrew word for naked is *'arum*. In the very next sentence, almost as a non sequitur, we are introduced to a new character: "Now the snake was more shrewd (*'arum*) than all the living-things of the field . . ." In two consecutive verses, this word *'arum* is used to describe the main characters—but the meaning of this single uncommon word is completely different in each verse, indeed opposite. The humans are naked, *'arum*; everything, including their motives, is out in the open. They are guileless. But in the next sentence, in connection with the Snake, the word *'arum* means shrewd, sly; the Snake is a trickster who keeps his intentions hidden. Adam and the Snake are brothers because they share a single father, and they are twins because they both embody a single word, a single quality, the two-sided coin of *'arum*-ness.

Note that it doesn't say the Snake is evil or immoral. He possesses shrewdness, which is a skill set and not a moral value. In other Bible-era sources, the Snake of Eden is shown in an explicitly positive light. In a Gnostic version of the Bible, for example, the Snake in Eden is celebrated as the knowledge-giver, a role associated with the snake gods in Near Eastern cultures and perhaps later hinted at in the Bible itself, in the Book of Numbers when Moses fashions a copper snake in order to heal the people from plague. The snake gives knowledge and medicine to man.

Even though the Hebrew scribes might be trying to satirize the Near Eastern snake fixation—a cult of worship associated with the serpentine-shaped Nile River—perhaps a trace of that heroic role for the snake migrated into our version of the Bible. Even if he's shady, he might still be gallant. In the ancient world, the trickster type can indeed be a hero. Odysseus is praised for his clever ruses. Because he's a noble person and our hero, we relish his deviousness, just as we cheer for Robin Hood.

Jacob, later in the Genesis story, is a fine example of this kind of heroism. Jacob lies and cheats. He swindles his brother, his father, his uncle, whomever. And for his wiliness, Jacob is rewarded with the distinction of being the father of the nation. Jacob, in fact, is suggestively linked to the Snake of Eden by dint of his name: in Hebrew, the name Jacob, or Ya'akov, is derived from the word *'eikev*, which means heel—this because Jacob is born tightly grasping the heel of his twin brother. This same word, *eikev*, is invoked in the memorable punishment meted out to the Snake at the end of the Eden story: "upon your belly shall you walk and dust shall you eat . . . [humans] will bruise you on the head, you will bruise them in the heel (*eikev*)." Jacob, a heel bruiser like the Snake, is a crafty hero, skilled in the art of domestic intrigues.

The Eden Snake is shrewd in precisely this manner. Just as Jacob offers delicious stew to his starving brother and, dressed in a disguise, gives juicy morsels of grilled meat to Isaac, their father—all part of an elaborate scheme to steal an inheritance—the Snake offers Adam and Eve a delicious treat. And his intention is the same: he believes that Adam is laughably unworthy of this honor. When it says that the Snake was "more shrewd [*'arum*] than all the living-things of the field," the story's narrator is actually communicating the Snake's point of view, for this shrewd quality of mind is the Snake's own political claim: he, the Snake, has the sole right to rule over man, and everything, because he is smarter than all. Shouldn't the ruler of the earth be the most intelligent? It's certainly a fair claim. With lawyerly precision, the Snake demonstrates that Adam is the original emperor without clothes: a fool and an impostor, not a king.

Whoever he might be, the Snake is something more than a snake. He's a complex character, torn by mixed motives, who seeks justice while also indulging in petty ambition; he is tormented and ultimately undone by his wounded nobility. He is, in other words, as human as Adam. To read the Garden of Eden as a theater of conflict between siblings might seem odd, but it actually brings the story in line with the rest of the Book of Genesis.

When we start with the premise that these stories describe actual people, we are given the ability to see them as precisely that. Was the Snake real? If you believe that he was, you will be motivated to look for him. And what you will find is a vividly real character looking back at you.

Noah

Genesis 6–9

Charles McGrath

I was raised a Catholic, and Catholics in those days weren't really Bible people. For all I know, they still aren't. Bible reading, I understood then, was something that Protestants went in for, and look where it got them. We had missals and faithfully took them to Mass: fancy little books with leatherette covers, gilt-edged pages, a little red tassel for keeping your place, and even some text printed in red—the rubrics. But if there was a Bible in the house, I don't remember ever seeing it. Selections from the New Testament—the Gospels and the Epistles—were read aloud in church every Sunday, but the Old Testament we mostly knew from hearsay. Moses and the tablets, Daniel in the den, Joseph and his coat, Solomon proposing to hack the baby in two—these were familiar stories, like folktales almost, but not texts to be pored over. We grew up with the sense that the Bible was such a dense and forbidding book that amateurs weren't entirely to be trusted with it.

I first heard the story of Noah from my father, who was mildly obsessed with it. I'm not sure why exactly. He loved boats and was unhappy in his work, beset by money problems, so perhaps the notion of forty days afloat appealed to him—secure and self-sufficient in a brand-new wooden vessel, and not one made of fiberglass, which my father detested—followed by a complete reboot in which you could start your life all over again. My father was not a literalist, exactly, but a man of very practical imagination, and many of the other details in the story bothered him. How could Noah build such an ark with just his three sons? Without power tools it would have taken them decades. How did they herd all those animals, and once the creatures were all on board, what prevented them from eating each other? What did Noah and the crew do about the prodigious amounts of manure that would have piled up? This one bothered me, too—until I saw the recent Darren Aronofsky movie *Noah,* in which the animals are put to sleep after a few whiffs of some very righteous dope that Noah burns in a censer. That seems as good a solution as any.

The one detail my father never questioned, and the one that seemed to appeal to him most, was God's placing the rainbow in the sky as a promise that he wouldn't do this kind of thing again. If we were driving in the car and happened to see a rainbow, he never failed to bring this up. God will never again destroy the world by flood, my father would explain, though he once suggested that didn't necessarily mean God wouldn't let a nuclear war happen.

I didn't begin to read the Bible on my own until I got to college, began studying seventeenth-century English literature, and fell in love with the King James Version, not the most accurate of translations, perhaps, but still a grand monument of English prose. I hadn't read the Noah story in years, but went back not long ago after watching the Aronofsky movie. Who were those creatures that looked like Transformers made out of boulders? I wondered. How had I missed them? (Because they're not there, it turns out.) What mostly struck me this time was the sublime bleakness of the poetry. Here, for example, is a description of the flood:

> And the waters prevailed exceedingly upon the earth; and all the high hills, that were under the whole heaven, were covered.
>
> Fifteen cubits upward did the waters prevail; and the mountains were covered.

> And all the flesh died that moved upon the earth, both of fowl, and of cattle, and of beast, and of every creeping thing that creepeth, and every man:
>
> All in whose nostrils was the breath of life, of all that was in the dry land, died.

The repeated *h* sound in that first verse, the doubling of *creeping* and *creepeth,* that wonderful phrase "all in whose nostrils was the breath of life," the way the syntax holds off that emphatic *died* until the very end—this is verse that really enjoys the destruction it's talking about, and prolongs it even, just to enhance the pleasure. It reminds me a bit of Wallace Stevens in "The Auroras of Autumn," where you feel the thrill of extinction, of losing yourself into nothingness. Despite that rainbow ending, Noah's is really a very dark story, in which God stays his hand not because he has changed his mind about mankind but because he realizes that we're just incorrigible: "And the Lord said in his heart, I will not again curse the ground any more for man's sake; for the imagination of man's heart is evil from his youth."

If you study the text you discover even more oddities and perplexities than my father imagined. For one, there's the gopher wood from which the ark is built. What on earth is gopher wood? As my father would surely have pointed out, gopher wood, whatever it is, doesn't sound very seaworthy. Then there's the presence of two competing versions of the story, like two radio stations interfering with one another. In one the flood lasts 150 days, not 40, and Noah is instructed not to lead the animals in two by two but rather to round up seven of all the "clean" beasts (a strange recommendation, if you think about it, since it means one will be left without a mate and thus unable to be fruitful and multiply) and just two of the others. Finally, there is the mysterious character of Noah himself, who is practically a cipher, and that strange detail, coming seemingly out of nowhere, about his getting drunk after the flood and being discovered, naked and asleep, by his son Ham, who, unlike his brothers, declines to avert his eyes. They never told us about that part when I was growing up. Torah scholars may have fretted over it for centuries, but historically Catholics were just embarrassed. In the Middle Ages, when the Noah story became the subject of mystery plays, it was Noah's wife, and not her husband, who turned into a sot. In Benjamin Britten's charming children's opera *Noye's Fludde,* inspired by those medieval plays, she's a gossip and a shrew, so busy chatting with the neighbors that she has to be dragged onto the ark.

But maybe she can be excused, for her husband is clearly not much of a conversationalist. In the Bible he never opens his mouth, and this, now that I think of it, may have been another point of connection with the story for my father, who was a man of very few words. Noah is clearly one of those biblical figures, like Moses and Abraham, who is meant to stand for Jewish exceptionalism—singled out by God and entrusted with delivering his people from extinction. And yet, unlike Moses and Abraham, and for that matter the Russell Crowe character in the movie, Noah isn't heroic or even very personable. His role is one of mute, unquestioning obedience. Build an ark? Okay, whatever you say. Round up all the animals, the beasts of the field, the fowls, the creepers that creepeth? Got it, no problem. "Thus did Noah; according to all that God commanded him, so did he."

After all those labors, his drunkenness is perhaps understandable. Elsewhere the Bible is pretty tolerant about wine, and there's no sense in Genesis that the mere growing and fermenting of grapes is itself a crime. Noah's sin is that he passes out, and somehow sheds his robe in the process. But what are we to make of Ham's apparently worse offense—that he sees his father's nakedness and, unlike his brothers, doesn't walk backwards into the tent and cover it up? Some scholars and commentators have suggested that looking upon nakedness is a euphemism and that what Ham really does is masturbate his father, or sodomize him, or even castrate him. As interpretations go, these seem extreme, and yet the Noah story is clearly pervaded by a sense of sexual shame and disgust. Though not explicitly labeled as such, the offenses that cause God to repent that he ever made man seem to be sexual in nature. The text says the sons of God "came in to the daughters of men, and they bare children to them," and that "God saw that the wickedness of man was great in the earth, and that every imagination of the thoughts of his heart was only evil continually." God's earth itself is corrupt, it says later, because "all flesh had corrupted his way upon the earth."

I remember, as a boy, being shocked by the accidental sight of my father's penis, white and hairy, and a few years later being grossed out at the thought that my parents must at some point have had sex together. And maybe that is Ham's only crime: a shameful awareness of his father's sexuality. Whether he and his offspring deserve to be cursed for thinking those thoughts is another matter, and it seems even harsher that God would wish to destroy his own creation—to drown the entire world—because of sexual longings that he instilled in men to begin with, and that are intrinsic to the process of fruitful multiplication that the Noah story elsewhere goes on about at such length.

In the end, God proves by far the most interesting and complicated character here. He's a father disappointed in his children and, as fathers often are, of two minds about what to do with them: wipe them off the face of the earth or give them another chance. He's also a creator who seemingly takes no pleasure at all in his creation. Noah alone has found grace in God's eyes, we're told, but the text doesn't dwell much on that. His grace seems to consist mostly of tractability. Until the rainbow shines across the sky, the world of the Noah story is a colorless and unlovely one, and you sense that God, like my own father all those millennia later, is antsy, dissatisfied, and yearning for a reboot himself. He wants to wipe the slate clean and start over again—until he realizes that it will never be any different, because mankind will never change: "the imagination of man's heart is evil from his youth." An interesting, seldom-noted point about the rainbow is that not only is it a covenant with mankind, it's also God's reminder to himself that he can never succumb to such feelings of irritation and nihilism again. The world may be irretrievably corrupt, but when Noah builds an altar and burns a sacrifice there is a sweet savor. "While the earth remaineth," we are reminded, "seedtime and harvest, and cold and heat, and day and night shall not cease."

Like so many stories in the Bible, the Noah story is partly about fathers and sons—about the burdens of patrimony and about filial duty and expectation. Back when he told me the Noah story, I had yet to disappoint my father. But in time I failed to live up to his expectations—in part by becoming the sort of person who would prefer the King James Bible to the Catholic one. I in turn held his expectations against him, and wished his imagination could be less practical and a little more elevated. Still hoping for a reboot, another chance, he died young (unlike Noah, who lived to be 950), before we could get over being disappointments to each other. Probably the worst thing I ever did to him was try to shake his faith. There was no God, I told him, and the Bible was made up by men. There wasn't a word of truth in it, especially the parts promising an afterlife. He thought about that for a moment and then said I didn't know what I was talking about.

Abraham, Isaac, and Us
(and Hagar and Ishmael and Trayvon and Michael Brown, too)

Genesis 22

Michael Eric Dyson

The story of Abraham being commanded by God to offer his son as a burnt offering as proof of his love for the Almighty has always bothered me. It's not that I think that God doesn't have the right to put those of us who believe in God to the test. After all, I'm a university professor who tests his students all the time, even if the stakes aren't nearly as high. One might think by the horrified reaction of some of them that I was asking them to sacrifice their firstborn. That's a curious sight to see since most of them aren't yet parents.

To be fair, many of my students have been victims of a culture of high-stakes testing in our public schools that has got way out of hand. The debate about what we take to be standard, and about the standards we observe in the pursuit of solid education, is plagued by racial injuries and cultural scars that have never fully healed. In many schools across the nation, the stakes are too high when standardized tests are used to determine promotion to the next grade, or what courses one might take, or what curriculum might be followed, or even if one graduates from school. I spent many days in Florida with activists arguing that the Florida Comprehensive Assessment Test (FCAT) was unjustly used to block the high school graduation of black and Latino students who failed the test but successfully completed their course work. Testing is never devoid of social forces and political choices that test our commitment to equality and justice for all children.

God's tests are steeped in politics, too, and a fair bit of philosophy and theology as well. That's especially true in the case of Abraham, who believes he heard the voice of God tell him to sacrifice his only son. How does Abraham, or any of us, ever really know that we've heard God's voice and not our own desires or fears, our own hatreds and suspicions, or our own intuitions and dreams dressed up as divine will? How do we know we're not merely sanctifying our social norms or deifying our political instincts when we say that God is telling us to believe or behave a certain way?

Take, for instance, trying to decide between moving to Michigan and moving to Minnesota for work. What roles do my racial identity and political ideology play in how I discern God's will? Does God work within my biases to protect me from exposure to ideas that I find harmful or distasteful, while upholding my preferences and validating my experiences? Is that why few black pastors feel called to white churches in Maine, or why few white churches in New Hampshire extend a call to black pastors, despite Martin Luther King, Jr., immortalizing their "prodigious hilltops" in his famous "I Have a Dream" speech? Does the divine will merely track human intention, and how do we know the difference between the two?

One answer to this question subscribes to the notion that there is a transcendent truth that eclipses the limits of our human understanding. Many believers seek to avoid the quicksand of subjective ideas of truth and goodness by endorsing an objective point of reference to ground their moral beliefs and ethical practices. These believers get nervous when they think that what they say or do lacks the seal of divine approval or the signature of godly intention. Oddly enough, many believers think that the Bible offers them unqualified access to transcendent truth. I say oddly because if there's any book that's proved to be the product of its time and place in history, it's the Bible. The scriptures capture ancient folk fighting for meaning in a world that either oppressed or inspired them, or sometimes both; we see glimpses of the humble trading places with the exalted and stories that show how power can be both redeeming and corrupting.

David, for instance, rises from shepherd to king by slaying a menacing giant, only to arrange the murder of a loyal soldier and steal his wife while leaving his kingdom in shambles. The Bible scolds injustice in the mouths of the prophets, yet amplifies it in the throat of Paul, whose *Haustafeln* (Household Codes) reinforce the social inequality of women as a way to reassure the Roman Empire that Christianity wouldn't undermine the social order. The Bible is in heated conversation with the culture that shaped it, at times as a faithful mirror of its virtues and biases, and at other times as a window onto a liberating social landscape.

The Bible's complicated cultural status makes it impossible to conclude that the scriptures offer an ironclad version of transcendence that resolves clashing views of truth. The Bible is intimately bound to those clashes; its words are used to support one truth claim or another in vastly different communities with greatly opposed theological, moral, and political agendas. Even if the transcendence police break down the front door of faith and arrest theological interlopers, enough dissenters will escape out the back door to challenge the Bible's link to truth.

The only meaningful interpretation of transcendence we might propose is to strip the term of its philosophical and theological orthodoxy and offer instead a more forceful definition. Truth can be described as transcendent if it illumines the time and place of its emergence as well as other places and periods. Truth's transcendence is not pegged to its authoritative reflection of an unchanging reality that everyone would agree on if they had access to it. Truth happens when we recognize the expression of a compelling and irrefutable description of reality. Truth is not irrefutable because it appeals to ideals that escape the fingerprints of time and reason. Truth is irrefutable because it is morally coherent and socially irresistible.

That's why Martin Luther King, Jr., and his comrades could challenge the transcendent truths of white supremacy and black inferiority, truths seen by their advocates as true for all times and places, and truths that were rooted in religion and reason. But King and company offered a more compelling version of truth that ultimately proved to be more reasonable, more morally coherent, and more socially irresistible than the tribal truths it sought to displace. They didn't prove their vision of truth was superior by appealing to a transcendent truth that rang through the universe as self-evident, even though King spoke of black folk enjoying "cosmic companionship" in our struggle for equality and justice. Rather King and his companions worked to show that they had a more edifying grasp of truth—that their moral vision was clearer, their ethical energy more uplifting, their description of democracy more meaningful, and their alliance with other truth tellers more cogent than those who bonded around the moral and legal justification of oppression. Thus, irrefutability is provisional, and may change with the appearance of other compelling views of truth that are rooted in reason and affirmed by morality. Such is the case, for instance, with gay marriage: traditional views of marriage that rest on religious and social orthodoxy are slowly giving way to superior versions of the truth that support gay and lesbian domestic intimacy and family values.

Closely yoked to the idea of a transcendent truth, of course, is biblical literalism, a plague that has often robbed Christianity of its liberating power and inspirational appeal. Believers who turn to the Bible for a transcription of God's thoughts, word for word, have arguably done more to harm the reputation of the Good Book than a million heretics. I suppose the fear that some misguided soul would hear God telling him to sacrifice his children is a major reason I've worried about the meaning and interpretation of Abraham and Isaac's story over the years. Scores upon scores of mentally ill folk have done just that, telling us that God instructed them to drown, stab, shoot, or otherwise murder their offspring. Instead of reading this story metaphorically, as one that asks human beings to clarify the priority that God holds in our lives, too many folk afflicted with demons seek to purge their spirits by spilling the blood of innocent children. The tragedy is that literalism fails us when we need it most, when even naysayers to the doctrine wouldn't mind being wrong for once. Alas, no angel descends to keep many fathers from slaughtering their children in the name of God; no lamb is caught in the bush to exchange for the sacrifice of a child.

The story makes it clear that Isaac was an unwitting victim of religious sacrifice. He trusted his father to protect him, like millions of children around the globe expect their fathers to do. Isaac had no idea that the man who had crept into his centennial before fathering the only son he had with his wife, Sarah, would be the one who thought he must kill the future he had helped to make possible. The tragedy was doubled because Abraham had already lost one son, Ishmael, the child he fathered with his slave Hagar, whom Sarah had forced Abraham to cast out with his mother in a fit of pique, making certain that Isaac was his father's sole heir. (One can't help but note that too many children of the oppressed, who are the legitimate heirs of American freedoms for which black folk bled and died, are treated as outcasts, their rightful share of equality divided among members of the majority culture, who are viewed, with all the protections it brings, as the as sole heirs of our national bounty.) Now all of Abraham's plans would go up in smoke on an altar whose components Abraham compelled Isaac to tote on his back, making his son the vehicle for his own destruction.

In retrospect, I'm sure that as I got older I read this story through my own pain and suffering. My father believed, like many other black fathers do, that God dictated not the sacrifice but surely the punishment of his children. Brutal measures of corporal punishment feel like symbolic sacrifices of one's children, a snuffing out of their self-esteem, a mortal unbodying of their fragile, vulnerable flesh.

The indictment of famed football player Adrian Peterson by a Texas grand jury for reckless or negligent injury to a child—he subsequently pleaded no contest to a misdemeanor charge of reckless assault—set into relief the harmful disciplinary practices of some black families. Peterson used a "switch," a slim, leafless tree branch, to beat his four-year-old son, raising welts on the youngster's legs, buttocks, and scrotum. This is child abuse dressed up as acceptable punishment.

While 70 percent of Americans approve of corporal punishment, black Americans have a distinct history with the subject. Beating children has been a depressingly familiar habit in black families since our arrival in the New World. As the black psychiatrists William H. Grier and Price M. Cobbs wrote in *Black Rage,* their 1968 examination of psychological black life: "Beating in child-rearing actually has its psychological roots in slavery and even yet black parents will feel that, just as they have suffered beatings as children, so it is right that their children be so treated."

The lash of the plantation overseer fell heavily on children to whip them into fear of white authority. Terror in the field often gave way to parents beating black children in the shack, or at times in the presence of the slave owner in forced cooperation to break a rebellious child's spirit. Black parents beat their children to keep them from misbehaving in the eyes of whites who had the power to send black youth to their deaths for the slightest offense. Today, many black parents fear that a loose tongue or flash of temper could get their child killed by a trigger-happy cop. They would rather beat their offspring than bury them.

If beating children began, paradoxically, as a violent preventive of even greater violence, it was enthusiastically embraced in black culture, especially when God was recruited. As an ordained Baptist minister with a doctorate in religion, I have heard all sorts of religious excuses for whippings.

And I have borne the physical and psychic scars of beatings myself. I can't forget the feeling, as a sixteen-year-old, of my body being lifted from the floor in my father's muscular grip as he cocked back his fist to hammer me until my mother's cry called him off. I loved my father, but his aggressive brand of reproof left in me a trail of uncried tears.

Like many biblical literalists, lots of black believers are fond of quoting scriptures to justify corporal punishment. Many Christians often cite what they think is a verse of scripture that supports beating their children, "Spare the rod and spoil the child." But that is a line from *Hudibras*, a mock epic poem penned in 1664 by English poet and satirist Samuel Butler to ridicule the Puritans. To be sure, there are plenty of scriptures that bolster corporal punishment, particularly the verse in Proverbs 13:24 that says, "He who spares the rod hates his son, but he who loves him is careful to discipline him." And Proverbs 23:13–14 says, "Withhold not correction from the child: for if thou beatest him with the rod, he shall not die. Thou shalt beat him with the rod, and shalt deliver his soul from hell."

But in Hebrew, the word translated as "rod" is the same word used in Psalms 23:4, "thy rod and thy staff they comfort me." The shepherd's rod was used to guide the sheep, not to beat them. Of course, the Bible, in Exodus 21:20–21, accepts slavery, in part by referring to the death of slaves by the same rod used to beat children. "Anyone who beats their male or female slave with a rod must be punished if the slave dies as a direct result, but they are not to be punished if the slave recovers after a day or two, since the slave is their property."

The passive acceptance of slavery and the ringing endorsement of child beatings are flip sides of the same biblical coin; the same literal interpretation of the Bible that justifies beating a child justifies enslaving her as well. In the end the believer is faced with a choice to worship either the Bible or the God who inspired it. Arguing for biblical literalism in the case of punishment—although certainly not in the case of slavery, as one is often forced by biblical literalism to pick and choose which verses really do apply—casts the black Christian in an uncomfortable role of supporting his own oppression.

Many believers—including Peterson, a vocal Christian—have confused the correction of children's behavior with corporal punishment. The word *discipline* comes from the Latin *discipulus,* which means student or disciple, suggesting a teacher-pupil relationship. Punishment comes from the Greek word *poine* and its Latin derivative *poena*, which mean revenge, and form the root words of *pain*, *penalty*, and *penitentiary*.

The point of discipline is to transmit values to children. The purpose of punishment is to coerce compliance and secure control, and, failing that, to inflict pain as a form of revenge, a realm the Bible says belongs to God alone. Yet secular black culture thrives on colorful stories of punishment that are passed along as myths of ancient wisdom—a type of moral glue that holds together varying communities in black life across time and circumstance. Black comedians cut their teeth on dramatically recalling "whoopings" with belts, switches, extension cords, hairbrushes, or whatever implement was at hand. Even as genial a comic as Bill Cosby offered a riff in his legendary 1983 routine that left no doubt about the deadly threat of black punishment. "My father established our relationship when I was seven years old," Cosby joked. "He looked at me and says, 'You know, I brought you in this world, I'll take you out. And it don't make no difference to me, cause I'll make another one look just like you.'"

The humor is blunted when we recall that Marvin Gaye's life ended violently in 1984 at the hands of his father, a minister who brutalized him mercilessly as a child before shooting him to death in a chilling echo of Cosby's words. Perhaps comedians make us laugh to keep us from crying, but no humor can mask the suffering that studies say our children endure when they are beaten: feelings of sadness and worthlessness, difficulties sleeping, suicidal thoughts, bouts of anxiety, outbursts of aggression, diminished concentration, intense dislike of authority, frayed relations with peers, and negative high-risk behavior.

Equally tragic is that those who are beaten become beaters, too. And many black folks are reluctant to seek therapy for their troubles because they may be seen as spiritually or mentally weak. The pathology of beatings festers in the psychic wounds of black people that often go untreated in silence.

Adrian Peterson's brutal behavior toward his four-year-old son is, in truth, the violent amplification of the belief of many blacks that beatings made them better people, a sad and bleak justification for the continuation of the practice in younger generations. After Peterson's indictment, the comedian D. L. Hughley tweeted: "A fathers belt hurts a lot less then a cops bullet!" He is right, of course, but only in a forensic, not a moral or psychological sense. What hurts far less than either is the loving correction of our children's misbehavior so they become healthy adults who speak against violence wherever they find it—in the barrel of a policeman's gun, the fist of a lover, or the switch of a misguided parent. Far too often a literal interpretation of the Bible has tragically reinforced violence against loved ones and prevented Christians from embracing the emancipating elements of the stories we read.

Ironically, the siege of biblical literalism keeps us from identifying with the son of Abraham who, like many black children, is referred to, though not by name, and certainly not heard from. Hagar was the slave mistress of Abraham, just as Sally Hemings was the slave mistress to Thomas Jefferson. Hagar's son, Ishmael, was prophesied by an angel to become "a wild donkey of a man; his hand will be against everyone and everyone's hand against him, and he will live in hostility toward all his brothers." That angel's message delivered Isaac but damned Ishmael. That reality rings true today.

There are still few angels to deliver the children of the socially disposable and despised. Isaac is kept from death by divine intervention; Ishmael is condemned to bitter circumstances with no relief in sight. There are far too many Hagars in our time who are social outcasts: single black mothers who bear the stigma of shame and disrespect, who scrap for every single resource they can muster to provide for children who are marked for tough and brutal lives. Our present-day Ishmaels are prophesied, or stereotyped, as failures, when in truth they enjoy few of the privileges of the Isaacs in our culture. The same drug use by contemporary Isaacs that leads them to be lightly admonished about their bad behavior leads our Ishmaels to be harshly reprimanded and sent to prison. The same adolescent pranks in school that land the Isaacs of our time in the principal's office land our Ishmaels in detention or lead to outright expulsion. And far too frequently the Isaacs of our age are free to grow into fruitful adulthood while our Ishmaels are harassed and policed to death.

Our present-day Ishmaels, and our young Hagars, too, suffer the wounds of persistent and subtle racial injustice. The nation's foster care system, like most other institutions in America, reflects the racial dynamics that plague our society. Although black children are only 15 percent of the U.S. population, they make up 27 percent of the children in foster care. Not only are black children more likely to be reported, investigated, and relegated to foster care, but once they are there, they face prohibitive barriers: black children are far more likely to endure longer placements in out-of-home care, are on the short end of comprehensive services, and reunify with their families far less than white children. In Los Angeles County, for example, 8 out of every 100 children are black, but 29 out of every 100 children are in foster care. When black children in Los Angeles County are placed in foster care, they are trapped there 50 percent longer than children of other races. More troubling is the fact that black children are mistreated by family members and die at a higher rate than children of other races.

Young Hagars are also targeted by the epidemic of sexual abuse in our communities: 60 percent of black girls are sexually abused before they turn eighteen, while 40 percent of black women suffer sexual assault in their lifetimes. Their suffering is compounded by the virtual silence that clouds the issue and the reluctance of black female victims to seek counseling. Black women are raped at a higher rate than white women yet are less likely to report it. Then, too, the myth that they are "fast girls" has made black girls who are victims of sexual exploitation wary of coming forward. As long as the culture at large, and black culture in particular, perpetuates stereotypes of inappropriate black female sexual desire, black girls and women will endure their sexual suffering in silence. Although "hashtag activism" has been widely assailed as a virtual substitute for substantive social action on the ground, it can have helpful, even therapeutic, results. Such was the case with #fasttailedgirls, the idea of *Hood Feminism* cofounder Mikki Kendall, a topic that trended nationally on Twitter as survivors of sexual abuse detailed their hesitation to speak up for fear they would be labeled "fast tailed girls." From the pulpit to the playground we must educate our communities and fight vicious stereotypes of black women as Jezebels and loose women who bring harm to boys and men.

But the battles over our children don't end there. Sixty years after the Supreme Court ruled in the *Brown* decision that blacks should receive the same education as whites, educational disparities between the Isaacs and the Ishmaels of our nation loom larger than ever. Black and brown students are less likely to gain access to advanced math and science courses and experienced instructors. Black students, even preschoolers, are more likely to be suspended than other students. That's not the entire story of educational inequities: 25 percent of high schools containing the greatest percentage of black and brown students don't offer Algebra 2, while a third of such schools don't offer chemistry. As our civil rights groups, and other bands of activists, advocate for broader social justice, and the fuller participation of black folk in our society, these educational disparities must be targeted to ensure that the next generation of Isaacs thrive.

Even more proof of the failure of biblical literalism can be seen in how elements of Isaac's and Ishmael's stories are conflated in narratives about the social suffering of black youth. Our Ishmaels, like the biblical Isaac, are unwitting victims of sacrifice. Our nation's political fathers have left our black youth vulnerable, convinced, like Abraham, that they are listening to the voice of God when leading our youth to their downfall, saddling them with vicious beliefs about their own lack of worth in a culture that doesn't prize or respect them. Trayvon Martin and Michael Brown are but the most recent examples of our national failure of will to protect our Isaacs from sacrifice. Trayvon deserved the dignity of normalcy. He deserved the protection that comes with the presumption that one is a regular kid, a child with no malicious intent, one who will experiment his way to adulthood by making the same immature choices many children make when they pose as rebels on social media or smoke some weed. And, like any red-blooded youth, Trayvon deserved the right to defend himself when recklessly pursued, and then shot to death, by a cowardly bully masquerading as a community savior named George Zimmerman.

Michael Brown was an unarmed black youth who, like many Isaacs, made mistakes (on the day of his death he was caught on tape rough-arming a store clerk and stealing some cigarillos from a convenience store) but didn't live long enough to regret them. Brown was gunned down in the street by a relentless, and apparently remorseless, policeman named Darren Wilson. The officer fired several shots into Brown's body, including one into the top of his head as he was bent downward. A friend of Brown's who witnessed the killing said his friend pleaded with Wilson, "I don't have a gun, stop shooting," to no avail. After Zimmerman shot Trayvon, his killer claims that Trayvon's final words were "Okay, you got it." If true, what could Trayvon have meant by "it"? That Zimmerman had the presumption of innocence on his side despite being out of order in pursuing Trayvon? That Zimmerman had the right to kill any black youth he wanted because their negative images flooded the culture? That Zimmerman had the advantage because he brought a gun to a fistfight that he provoked?

Trayvon Martin and Michael Brown both perished as unwitting victims of sacrifice on the altar of an American history that has exploited and expelled black youth from school—and from existence. Uncaring political fathers have repeatedly compelled black youth to carry the instruments of their own demise, such as unjustified reputations for wrongdoing, on their backs. Or, in turn, they see, like so much of society sees, what is on their backs, and their faces, and their bodies—their black skin—as cause for suspicion and death. (How, indeed, can we distinguish God's will from cultural suspicions and racial intuitions? The question has far greater existential weight when asked in relationship to black bodies that have been deemed threatening and perishable in our culture.) The black *New York Times* writer John Eligon summed up the harmful view of black youth in a sentence that was published the morning of Michael Brown's funeral: "Michael Brown . . . was no angel." In sharp contrast, the *Times* ran a concurrent story that praised Brown's killer, Darren Wilson, as a "well-mannered, relatively soft-spoken, even bland person." It may as well have called him an angel.

There is another sense, however, in which Eligon's phrase is quite fitting: "no angel" showed up to save Brown, or Trayvon, or thousands of other black youth. Even though it had been drilled into the collective unconscious of black American youth that no ram would be waiting for them in the bush, that no angel would deliver them, Michael Brown's and Trayvon Martin's last words were, tragically and paradoxically, a stubborn belief that the lamb might come, that it should, somehow, be in place, or that their last-breath attempt to snatch hold of its wings might make the angel descend to their aid. Their final words were gasps of protest at the horrifying, and unjust, absence of help, and also the undying affirmation of a crude optimism, equally unjustified, that they shouldn't perish this way; that, by surrendering to their victimizers, they'd done what was necessary to live past the rage of an armed assailant who sought to impose his one-man judgment—his steely, bullet-riddled narrative—on their lives and bring the story of their youthful existence to a violent end in the barrel of a gun.

As a sign of how even bad stories feature glimmers of hope, Eligon also offers us, in the same piece that disparaged the youth, a heartening glimpse of Michael Brown's theology of divine intervention:

It was 1:00 A.M. and Michael Brown, Jr., called his father, his voice trembling. He had seen something overpowering. In the thick gray clouds that lingered from a passing storm this past June, he made out an angel. And he saw Satan chasing the angel and the angel running into the face of God. Mr. Brown was a prankster, so his father and stepmother chuckled at first. "No, no, Dad! No!" the elder Mr. Brown remembered his son protesting. "I'm serious." And the black teenager from this suburb of St. Louis, who had just graduated from high school, sent his father and stepmother a picture of the sky from his cell phone. "Now I believe," he told them.

Sadly, Brown's budding belief was killed and left to fester in the same body that lay prostrate on the street for four hours after his death. If Michael Brown is Isaac, and his father, Michael Brown, Sr., is Abraham, imagine the suffering the father endures as he realizes he was unable to keep his son from being sacrificed, that no angel spoke to rescue his son from peril, that no lamb was exchanged as his son was sent to his bloody demise.

The story of Abraham and Isaac offers us a powerful lesson about the tests of God, and what we do with them, and our own tests, and how we sometimes abuse them. The story opens the possibilities of a broader view of truth, and the contrasting perils of biblical literalism. It highlights the virtue of rescuing narratives from the grasp of the powerful, and the parochial, as we read them to rescue in ourselves the excitement and vigor of fresh interpretation—and an uplifting, if sobering, application of the Word to our words, and to the worlds we make of them.

Above all, Abraham and Isaac, and Hagar and Ishmael, too, remind us that Trayvon Martin and Michael Brown, and countless other black youth besides, are daily sacrificed on the altar of unmerited suspicion and fear of black identity, pushing them into early graves. We must be the angels our children seek. We must keep them from destructive discipline at our own hands. And we must shield our children from death at the hands of those who think, bizarrely, often in veiled manner, though sometimes in fatally explicit terms, that they are doing God's will to kill them.

My Father's Commandments

Genesis 23

Jane Leavy

My father abandoned organized religion on the day of his bar mitzvah. He ascended the bimah ready to chant his Torah portion and join the generations of thirteen-year-old Jewish males who had successfully negotiated this ritual passage to manhood. Alas, he had memorized the wrong portion.

Talmudically speaking, reading out of order is not an option. So, he never became a bar mitzvah. As an adult, he never joined a synagogue. As a parent, he never sent me to Hebrew school. As a result, I didn't get invited to a lot of bar mitzvah parties.

Apart from a semester abroad as an exchange student in a Belgian convent during my senior year in high school—they called me La Juive—I remained biblically challenged until I took a course in the Gnostic Gospels with Elaine Pagels in college. She was not yet the rock star of biblical studies she has since become. I was shocked to learn that my father had read her book and knew her work well. It was my first intimation that the failed bar mitzvah boy had morphed into something of a biblical scholar. We talked about the Old Testament, too. He said: "The Ten Commandments are the basis for all western jurisprudence"—a statement I took as gospel.

By day, he was Morton L. Leavy, Esquire, "Morty Baby" to his showbiz clientele—writers, directors, producers, lyricists, and actors who never wrote, directed, produced, limned, or appeared in a flop. His client list included everyone from Robert Graves to Meat Loaf to me. When you retained Mort Leavy, you got undivided attention and unequivocal, familial support. "You've done it again!" my mother declared more than once at opening night parties for shows that closed the next day.

The writers Joan Didion and John Gregory Dunne, whose representation meant most to my father, credited the longevity of their marriage in part to an inability to decide who would get Mort in a divorce.

Arthur P. Jacobs—ApJac Baby!—producer of the Planet of the Apes movies and *Doctor Dolittle*, phoned every night just as we sat down to dinner even though we never ate at the same time twice and knew Morty Baby would always take his call.

My father was the son of a bookie and rumrunner named Abraham. As a towheaded toddler he served as his father's decoy, stationed on the rumble seat of the Model T as the hooch-laden car sailed through customs at the Canadian border. He was the prettiest baby in an Asbury Park, New Jersey, parade and the youngest man to graduate in the class of 1934 from City College in New York. "At 18 He Heads CCNY Class Of 2,000 at Commencement," a headline in a New York broadsheet declared. "He wants to be a lawyer and has intentions of entering Harvard in the fall."

He went to Columbia Law instead and got a part-time job working as a magician's assistant for a Broadway review called *Continental Varieties*. His job was to translate audience requests for a Belgian Svengali who swore he could turn water into anything potable. One night someone demanded sauerkraut juice and my father couldn't think of the word. The next day they made him stage manager. In that capacity he was tasked with presenting a bouquet of long-stemmed roses to the French chanteuse Lucienne Boyer, who closed the show every night with "Prenez Mes Roses." First day on the job my father forgot to remove the thorns. She clutched the bouquet to her breast and screamed.

That was the end of life in the footlights and the beginning of compassion. He would make his career in entertainment law, looking after the legal rights and fragile psyches of artists.

He practiced law parallel to the ground in a gray leather Herman Miller chair, whose springs had long since lost the battle with his girth. His round mound of renown rose above his Herman Miller desk like the Rockies emerging out of the plains. Entering his office, you heard a patriarchal rumble emanating from somewhere beneath the horizon of the cluttered desk. Phone tucked beneath his chin, hands gesticulating with either-ors, he perfected the art of the schmooze in the service of attaining the best possible deal. Done: he popped up, a beaming Jewish jack-in-the-box in a Turnbull & Asser shirt. "How ya doin', baby?"

John Gregory Dunne testified to his bona fides in an August 1983 *Esquire* essay called "Big Deal," detailing the particulars of a failed motion picture deal for John le Carré's book *The Little Drummer Girl,* in which my father represented all the principals, including the author; the director, George Roy Hill; and the prospective screenwriters Didion and Dunne: "It is not all that unusual a situation. There are only a handful of good entertainment/literary lawyers, and they are constantly balancing the conflicting concerns of clients who work with each other, who wish to work with each other, who detest each other, sue each other, marry and divorce each other."

Or, as my friend Dan Okrent, creator of the off-Broadway hit *Old Jews Telling Jokes* puts it: "No conflict, no interest."

Dunne continued:

> Morton Leavy is short, round, and benign; he looks, as I have often told him in the fifteen years he has been our attorney, like a Jewish Dr. Doolittle. He is so scrupulous that my wife and I once felt free to leave the country when he agreed to referee a negotiation she was having with her publisher and one I was having with my publisher. The twin negotiations—each for a new novel—needed a referee because my publisher is married to my wife's publisher, a situation further complicated by the competitive strains between

my literary agent and my wife's literary agent, each of whom wished to negotiate a better deal than the other. I might add here that Morton Leavy was most aware of these strains as he is also the attorney for both my literary agent and my wife's literary agent. We told him to keep the peace between the two of them, that we did not wish to be played off against each other, but that we also wanted the best deals possible.

Morton Leavy's success as a referee was such that the only real difference between my contract and my wife's contract was that she would receive fifty more free copies of her book when it was published than I would when mine was. Both my publisher and my wife's publisher called Morton Leavy a son of a bitch, which he took as praise for a job well done.

I can't remember which client gave him the pair of brass balls that sat proudly on his desk, but they now sit on mine.

Though largely deaf and mostly blind, he continued to practice law until his death at age eighty-seven in 2003, two weeks after breaking his hip while getting up from the table where Arthur P. Jacobs had interrupted so many dinners. When the paramedics arrived to take him to the hospital, he was lying on the brick floor dictating the particulars of a contract.

After his death, I inherited the contents of his library. The client collection, lovingly arranged in alphabetical order with unanimous inscriptions of praise, diverted me from grief. The big names and bright lights had always been more interesting than the hundreds and hundreds of volumes devoted to biblical law and archaeology, which had come to occupy more and more space in the den without my noticing. In the breadth of this collection, I first discovered the extent of his passion for the subject and how little I knew about that part of my father's life.

I had never talked to him about the conferences he attended and addressed. I had never read the papers he wrote and delivered. I never learned what Torah portion he should have memorized. I never asked him to elaborate on the Ten Commandments.

I kept the most precious volumes, among them a 1902 edition of *A Dictionary of the Bible*, a set of four vellum-bound, gold-embossed books with hand-painted endpapers made to look like a peacock's feathers—blue, green, and mauve. I donated the rest of his books to my synagogue and promised myself that one day I would delve into the legal files he had crammed full of notes and marginalia.

A decade passed. The vellum binding cracked and split. The books on the shelf in my living room that I dedicated to my father's collection remained undisturbed.

With the invitation to contribute to this volume came an opportunity, finally, belatedly, to honor my father.

"Sure, I'll do it," I said.

I would dig through his notes and his papers and find in his blocky, angular masculine hand the part of him I had ignored. I would be my dad's archaeologist.

Two months of digging through the attic, the basement, and the climate-controlled storage unit where I keep my children's baby clothes produced only disappointment and the unhappy reminder that memory is unreliable. I had kept none of his papers.

I turned to the Internet. A month of online sleuthing produced only a citation for a 1985 paper he had delivered to the annual meeting of the Biblical Law section of the Society of Bibical Literature, added in 2013 to Brigham Young University's database: "Customary Law in Biblical Narrative: Genesis."

Neither BYU nor the Society for Biblical Literature could locate the paper. My dad preceded the digital age. The best they could do was provide an abstract, in which he argued that in biblical narratives, specifically the trials and tribulations of the patriarchs, you find the rudiments of common law: rules governing transactions between people as opposed to the covenant between God and his people.

I ransacked his books, looking for evidence of his exegesis. I found it scribbled in the margins of his edition of E. A. Speiser's translation of Genesis. Specifically: Genesis 23. He had dissected the chapter, diagramming in the endpapers examples of common law he had found throughout the book. Among them: personal vengeance, human sacrifice, homicide, slavery, status of the sojourner, witnessing, covenant, sale of real property, divorce, adoption, inheritance, birthright, and polygamy, all of which except, I think, the last, he dealt with in his practice.

The chapter concerns the death of Sarah and Abraham's purchase of a burial site for Judaism's matriarch. As Torah portions go, this is a major anticlimax, coming as it does immediately after the "Ordeal of Isaac," a biblical showstopper in which God demands that Abraham sacrifice his firstborn son. How many Rosh Hashanah sermons have been devoted to that harsh test of faith?

After the harrowing narrative of father and son, the boy carrying the wood for his own immolation to God's appointed destination, the father tying up the son and laying him on the altar above the wood he had carried, the poised knife, the intervening angels, Chapter 23 is dry kindling. But, in it, my father found meaning not just in the evolution of jurisprudence but also in his own legal practice.

Sarah gets short shrift in Chapter 23. Her death at age 127 merits one paragraph. Mourning and bewailing are confined to two short sentences: the extent of it must be taken on faith. The rest is a negotiation between Abraham—"a stranger and a sojourner"—and the children of Heth for a burial place for Sarah.

You have to consult commentaries and apocrypha, Louis Ginzberg's *The Legends of the Jews,* to get the whole story: how Satan tricked Sarah into thinking that Abraham went through with the sacrifice of Isaac and then acknowledged the falsehood, causing her to drop dead with joy. How Jewish.

In Ginzberg's account, "a great and heavy mourning" ensued. Abraham had "great reason to mourn his loss for even in her old age Sarah had retained the beauty of her youth and the innocence of her childhood." One hundred and twenty-seven years old and still a looker.

The biblical account also omits salient details about the burial plot Abraham sought for her in Hebron in the land of Canaan. The Cave of Machpelah was also the final resting place of Adam and Eve, chosen by Adam—no innocent—because he feared his body might be used for idolatrous purposes. God assuaged his fears by stationing angels at the entrance to deter trespassers.

This was not what interested my father. He focused on the polite give-and-take between the parties, strikingly modern in the niceties that camouflaged the bottom line. When Abraham, a resident alien lacking the right to purchase property, first asks for a place to bury his wife, the natives offer him any parcel he wishes. Abraham declines, asking them to bring forth Ephron, newly made the chief of the children of Heth, who also happens to own the Cave of Machpelah and the field it lies in. No fool, Ephron offers to gift Abraham the cave but insists that he must take the field as well, which some commentators read as a shrewd move to avoid having to pay taxes on the whole tract.

Ephron makes the grand gesture, knowing full well that it is a deal Abraham cannot accept, thus freeing him to ask his full and exorbitant price—four hundred shekels of silver. "What is that between you and me?" he asks the patriarch.

Though God had already pledged the Promised Land to Abraham and his seed, it is not yet theirs. He needs clear title, and he needs witnesses to the deal, essential in a world where nothing was written on paper and codes of law had yet to be established. That, some scholars believe, explains the presence of legal transactions in biblical narratives such as Genesis 23. Locating the particulars in an oral tradition vouchsafed that precedents would be established, acknowledged, and accepted. Abraham counts out the silver at the current merchants' rate.

It figures that my dad would focus on a passage that features the patriarch in the art of negotiation because that was his art, too. In the study of biblical law, he found a portion of the Torah that made sense to his logical, lawyerly mind, and assuaged a sense of intellectual inferiority he once confessed over dinner. To find the meaning of Chapter 23 was to find meaning in his career.

Yes, he went to the opening night of *Hair* in New York, Paris, London, and Budapest—or was it Prague? Yes, John Gielgud came to dinner and politely ate the My-T-Fine chocolate pudding I, at age five, prepared for dessert. Yes, John le Carré camped out on the trundle bed in our guest room between books and marriages.

But my father harbored a desire to be taken more seriously as an attorney or at least to be seen toiling in Serious Law, to engage in the rigors of legal debate as practiced at the highest levels and argued in the highest courts. That was not an option for a nice Jewish boy getting out of Columbia Law in 1937. He envied the practice of my former husband, who dealt with "matters," not people.

I think I know how he felt. The desire to be deemed capable of more than the froth of sportswriting is one reason I welcomed this assignment.

But, absent my father's guidance and scholarship, I floundered. I doubted. Seized by a crisis of faith, I called Elaine Pagels for counsel. She gently reminded me that the Old Testament is not her area of expertise.

Just as I resolved to abandon the task, I heard my father's voice, as if from above, taut, not quite righteous, but brooking no nonsense. "*Writers write.*"

That was the advice he offered every whiny author, including me, who called to complain of writer's block. My father's commandment was an injunction as well as a statement of fact. After all: in the beginning was the word.

He Who Struggles with God

Genesis 32

Alec Wilkinson

I cannot separate the Bible from my father. In the middle of his life, he became a Christian Scientist, I don't know exactly why. The questions one might ask of the dead pile up, and it is only one question I might ask him. He worked in an office on a high floor of a building in New York City, and from things he said later I pieced together the impression that he had begun to feel deeply anxious when he had to pass an open window. In addition, he had painful headaches.

Our family might have been better off if he had taken a more worldly approach, if he had occupied a couch in an analyst's office, say, but maybe not. Some people can't take self-examination and collapse instead of get better. Or shed their old lives for new ones, the way some people survive car wrecks that kill everyone else. More than the Catholics or the Episcopalians (there were no Baptists in our town that I was aware of, and Judaism was far too mysterious and challenging an engagement for my shallow father), the Christian Scientists promised wonder working in response to hardship and suffering, at least that was my understanding as a child. They had very few metaphors. No one talked about streets paved with gold or mansions waiting in heaven. They insisted on the need for unshakable faith, and the recognition that a person was constantly being tested. The version of God I remember from my father's Sunday school class was a mixture of Old and New Testament forms—part crazy man out of control, a psychopath, as Harold Bloom has written, and part reformed divinity. The Christian Science Church also flattered the vanity of the practitioner by giving him or her the sense of having taken up a modern form of worship, one without Latin or candles or men in robes who claimed obscure knowledge and swung pots of smoke. Its appeal was similar to the appeal of Zen for a more refined crowd, the sense that you saw through the pretensions and knew that God didn't stand behind chants and funny hats, he stood behind faith. Christian Science riddles were not about trees falling in the woods when no one was around but about how, after being prayed for, someone had risen from his or her deathbed and returned to life. My only intersection with Christian Science as an adult was receiving from a friend a copy of *Science and Health* given to her by J. D. Salinger, who had written notes in the margins concerning the pages he thought applied to her circumstances. Letters from Salinger with religious advice are so common, I learned, that collectors shun them.

The Christian Science church occupied a Victorian house on a street of other old houses in a neighborhood that had once been prosperous. The service took place in what I think would have been called the parlor, which had a bay window. There were no pews; the practitioners sat on folding chairs, as if for a meeting someone had called to deal with an emergency. The service had no splendor, no sense of long-lived ceremony or comfort. You were made to feel, in a plainspoken way, that, if you fell short of the necessary faith, you would pay for it with your well-being. You would get sick or become crippled from polio and God would turn his back on you.

Part of my father's spiritual practice was to read from the Bible and from *Science and Health* early in the morning, before leaving for the train that took him to the city. One morning when I was five or six, I woke early and, wandering downstairs, feeling the house was empty, saw him on the couch at the far end of the living room. A book was open on his lap, and the light from a lamp beside him hid his face. A friend of mine once said, "Your children never want to see you scared." I wasn't aware that my father was scared, but I had the feeling that he was doing something, not illicit, perhaps, but solitary and obscurely desperate, and I was unsettled. He kept the books in a drawer in a table beside his bed, and I used sometimes to open the drawer and look at them, especially the Bible, with its softbound leather cover and marbled end pages, and wonder what he used it for—what it did for him, that is, what secret did it contain? When he learned that his headaches were the result of hypoglycemia, he stopped taking me to the severe old house and giving me coins for the collection plate.

The Bible is, among many other things, a catalog of antique miracles and a plan for moral behavior. Nearly every page contains a story about how to behave or how not to. Only Dante, perhaps, spent as much time thinking of consequences as the writers of the Bible did. The stories, the admonitions, the dramatic scenes must have seemed less opaque in ancient days. One was reading an account of one's time in the language of one's culture. One knew the references. The world was full of mysteries and enigmas, and the darkness was so overpowering and forbidding and spooky, and it was so dangerous to be a stranger, and only the towns and cities were safe, if they were safe at all, and the violence was so sudden and furious and liable to be fatal that the dramatic episodes and the miracles must have appeared to credulous people simpler and more straightforward. Their understanding of the world was such that large portions of their thinking were ceded to supernatural beliefs and explanations. It is no observation of my own that the biases of various cultures between the days of the Old Testament and ours have given us a version of the text that has striven to preserve its majesty. And it is a majestic book, of course. The greatest book of all time, at least for western civilization. Beautifully written, concise, stirring, pointed, and with a reach of human feeling that it took Shakespeare to rival. Even so, of course, it is an elderly text, and who knows what the people who assembled it intended. A means of preserving their legends? An attempt to find a boundary between reality and exaltation? We feel an intimacy with its stories and characters that is partly a literary sleight of hand—the result, that is, of the language's having been modernized, even in the King James Version, which is much closer to our time than to the one in which the Bible was written. I feel fairly sure that the people who use the Bible today as a text to punish homosexuals and women who seek abortions would be deeply alarmed if they were to come face-to-face with the people who wrote it and the ones who appear in it. Blood-loving savages and primitives is what they might seem like to a closed modern mind.

It's an enlarging book, of course, the way Shakespeare is enlarging, and Dante and Tolstoy. I can read the Bible partly as history or as a key to the states of mind of ancient people or as a guide to the complexities of belief. Perhaps it is my own shortcoming, but I can't read it as a magic book, although I feel a good portion of it involves the attempt to find form for the magical. It can make you feel in the company of holy people and holy events and people struggling to absorb the parts of life that are elusive and demanding of attention and regard. It can reduce you to a state of wonder. Too many people, I think, believe it is a compendium of practical advice. I regard it as a work of art, a repository of human knowledge. A description of the terrible struggle to remain completely alive in a harsh period.

The passage that recurs in my life is that of Jacob wrestling the angel. For many artists it is a metaphor for the struggle of subduing one's talent so that it collaborates with one's ambitions to create. I encountered this version first in a letter written by the novelist William Maxwell to his father. Maxwell was trying to explain why he lived as he did. His father was a businessman in the Midwest, and deeply concerned that his son who loved reading might never find a way of earning a living and might end up living off his friends. His father was of the generation that settled a relative's debts if the relative couldn't, even if settling the debt ruined you. The standing of one's name, especially in a small town, was as important to them as almost any other moral point in life. He had probably never met another writer. The most famous writer of the period would have been Hemingway, and Maxwell, who was recessive, was as far from being like Hemingway as it was possible to be. Maxwell wrote his father that he regarded his task as being like Jacob's in refusing to let the angel go until he blessed him. He never sent the letter. I am guessing it might have been enough for him to spell out the terms for himself. He might also have thought that his father wouldn't entirely understand and that the letter might only make matters between them more complicated. There is no longer anyone I can ask.

Shortly before Jung died, he was interviewed by a writer from *Good Housekeeping,* who asked what his idea of God was. "To this day God is the name by which I designate all things which cross my willful path violently and recklessly, all things which upset my subjective views, plans and intentions and change the course of my life for better or worse," Jung said. I tend to see Jacob's encounter in similar terms.

Jacob's circumstances are probably familiar enough that I needn't describe them, but, briefly, Jacob is returning from twenty years of exile in Mesopotamia to Canaan, where he was born. He is traveling with his family, and in the morning he is to meet his brother, Esau, and his soldiers. Either he would be killed by Esau or he would shed his past as a devious brother and, by an act of maturity, atone and make peace. After crossing the Jordan River, Jacob sends livestock to his brother, hoping to appease him. Later, in the middle of the night, he sends his family and his possessions ahead. He is alone when he feels a man lay a hand on him, and they wrestle until the sun begins to rise and the figure, an angel, a messenger from God, that is, says, "Let me go, for the day breaketh." Jacob says, "I will not let thee go, except thou bless me."

The approach of day suggests that the encounter is a dream. Angels did not walk the earth in biblical times any more than sea monsters lived in the oceans in the Middle Ages. Antique darkness was of a richness we can only imagine in our light-soaked world. The night in the desert must have seemed like something you could touch and feel the texture of, like a piece of cloth. It was possible then as now to imagine demons and angels in the flickering light of a torch or a campfire. It may have been simpler then for the imagination to roam—the world man invented, and his explanations for it, was closer to being new; the barrier between conscious and unconscious thought may have been less defended—so perhaps Jacob had a vision. Extremes of feeling that distort reality are not uncommon these days, either. The psyche has a boundary past which it is not safe to travel, but people do. The quest, I think sometimes, is to live as close to it as one safely can, but I am aware that this might easily be regarded as a romantic notion. Even so, I believe that somewhere near it is where the elements of the self that are divine reside. They arrive sometimes as intimations and epiphanies after one has prepared the ground for them, or they can disrupt one's thinking and insist on being heard.

Jacob's having crossed a river suggests that he is on the far side of a boundary. The encounter is forced on him, violently and abruptly. He must wrestle, as I see it, with the temptation to remain as he was, with the task of enlarging himself against the resistance within him to a more serious purpose, his calling to establish Israel. He must subdue a fierce and unruly part of his nature in order to possess it, instead of having it rule him.

My hope in life is eventually to be wise. Wisdom, so far as I can tell, is the capital one collects from years of endeavor and failure, of sadness and joy, from an attentive engagement with life, that is. The melancholy element of this arrangement, of course, is that each advance is exchanged for an hour or a day or a year in one's life. My father remained all his life a child, so his example is not useful to me, although I endeavored for years to enact it, having only that model. I used sometimes, though, to sit at the table at Thanksgiving or Christmas, with my brothers and their own families around me, and my father at the head of the table, and think, in biblical terms, that he was a false patriarch. I have grown to want not to be like him, not to replicate his behaviors or his charm or his self-engagement. One can regard Jacob's struggle with the angel on Maxwell's terms, as the artist's challenge with his talent and the strife of finding words or images for things only partly or faintly perceived. Such an interpretation seems fitting to me, but not exclusively so. I have spent a good part of my life trying to reconcile the way I was raised, and the person I was raised to be, with the person I hope to be, which has involved facing thresholds that the psyche insists be crossed. The crossings are often forbidding, at least to me, and require faith and can only be managed by means of a struggle. I expect to run out of time before I finish.

Deuterogeniture, *or* How I Killed My Grandmother

Genesis 48

André Aciman

The airport terminal at JFK is filled with passengers waiting for the Varig flight to São Paulo. It's a cold Saturday evening in February, and the waiting area is brimming with excitement as passengers my age mill around, laughing and speaking loudly, some necking before boarding, others busy saying good-bye to boyfriends or girlfriends. Carnival is days away, summer has just started in Brazil, and the girls are wearing light clothing despite the chilly weather in the waiting area. Meanwhile, my father and I are standing, speaking to his mother—my grandmother—who is sitting in a wheelchair waiting for the flight to Brazil. She has run out of options and has reluctantly bowed to move in with my uncle, her other son. She is not pleased at the prospect of being so entirely dependent on him in a country the customs and language of which she knows nothing about. She senses she'll be abandoned in São Paulo, and, I can tell, she is already trying to muffle stirrings of something bordering on terror. She is not showing it, of course, but you can read it on her face. At the advanced age of ninety-four she has no option but to yield to what both my father and his brother consider the best outcome given her age and her need for more space than the cramped and cluttered bedroom she's been occupying in our apartment on the

Upper West Side. So, she'll put up with my uncle, the way she put up with living with us, the way she was resigned to renting a maid's room on a high floor in Paris before moving to the States, or to spending a few months in Rome with her younger brother and his live-in mistress.

The three of us are tense. I feel for her and dread what awaits her in Brazil. I may not be sorry to see her leave New York, but I hate goodbyes, and this may very well be our final farewell, though I banish the thought each time it crosses my mind. My father is already speaking about this summer, when we plan to visit her at my uncle's summer house on the resort island called Campos, not far from São Paulo, or so we're told. But, even if I want to believe we'll travel to see her, I know my father has no intention of visiting Brazil. Nor do I. The two of us pretend, for her sake. She nods quietly, but the old lady has her wits about her and knows that this short interlude at the airport may be the last time she'll ever see me. She already misses me and on impulse slaps me hard on the arm, as though I'd misbehaved. I feel guilty. She is angry. She should be. There is nothing to look forward to. Why love anyone, why even live? she says.

Soon an announcement is made in both English and Portuguese. It's time. One of the airline attendants comes over to us and offers to wheel my grandmother to the plane. She does not object. My father asks the attendant for a few moments, then turns to his mother: "I want you to bless him," he says, indicating me. This is a first. I had no idea that my father believes in religious practices, much less that he would ask her to bless me in public. But it is clear to me now that, without saying anything to me, the two of them know that we'll never meet again. She asks me to come closer and, in front of all the young people my age who have already slung on their backpacks and have started singing a rock song everyone's been playing recently, she places her right hand on my head and begins to mutter a prayer in both Hebrew and Ladino. I wished she hadn't done that. I want it over and done with, but she is dragging out the prayer as if she means every word of it. I am so embarrassed. Everyone is staring at us. I roll my eyes, hoping they'll notice. I even smile in an effort to scoff the whole thing away, to show I'm merely putting up with the old lady's antics. She then gets ahold of my head and with both hands brings it to her lips. She asks me to live my life well.

I don't know what this means—living my life well—but I am both moved and mortified by the spectacle. I want the attendant to wheel her into the gate area and just take her away. My father and I stand there while she is being escorted through a narrow passageway. For an instant I catch myself hoping she'll turn in her seat and look back; but she's been complaining that her neck is so stiff she can scarcely turn her head. She doesn't even try. No one weeps.

I've always wondered why my younger brother did not come to the airport with us. They had said good-bye earlier that morning, which was good enough for the two of them. He had never been her favorite. I was, probably because I was the older of the two. Yet it was he who, over the months during her stay with us in New York, had been far kinder to her than I. I would lose my patience with her and in the end didn't want her around me or asking questions all the time as a way of endearing herself. My brother was more tolerant, and made it a habit every evening to buy a pint of ice cream, which she loved. Eventually, she stopped seeking me out. She could tell I didn't want her around and had enough tact not to try to win me over. My brother became her friend. Yet she loved me more, and I, too, loved her, certainly more than I knew. I never saw her again.

The scene at the airport came back to me while I was rereading the Book of Genesis one day. I had forgotten the story, but as I reread it, it suddenly resonated with me when I saw the similarity between my grandmother's blessing at the airport and Jacob's blessing of his two grandsons before dying.

Jacob is old and about to die. His son Joseph, who, after being sold into slavery by his brothers and then rising in the world under Pharaoh, rescued his father and his clan of brothers from famine by billeting them in Egypt. Now, seeing his father about to die, Joseph brings his two sons, Manasseh and Ephraim, to Jacob and asks him to bless them.

According to *The American Heritage Dictionary*, a blessing is the act by which one "invoke[s] divine favor upon" or "confers well-being or prosperity on" someone else. It would have made perfect sense for Jacob to place his right hand on the head of the firstborn and his left on that of the second born. But, despite his failing eyesight and Joseph's attempt to redress what he perceives as a mistake on his old and blind father's part, Jacob knows exactly what he is doing. He is gifted with prophetic vision and knows that a hand cannot redress or undo what divine will has ordained. Ephraim's younger brother "shall be greater than he, and his seed shall become a multitude of nations." Jacob is merely submitting to the will of God.

What grants blessings their peculiar power is that they are usually given by people who are either very old or on the point of dying—in other words people who are no longer tied to the things of this world and who already have a foot elsewhere. Jacob is a patriarch, of course, so he is endowed with divine foresight. My grandmother, too, was edging her way to the hereafter; she knew it, which is why there was nothing perfunctory about her blessing. It's as though for a blessing to have any effect or persuasive power vis-à-vis eternity it needs to be administered by someone who does not stand to benefit from it and who is already paying the ultimate price: death. There is an implicit "covenant" here: by paying the ultimate price one ensures that the blessing will not fall on deaf ears. My grandmother might as well have said, *He will live his life well if I pay with my life.*

Blessings are pledges we exact from the Almighty. No less than are curses. Once a blessing or a curse is uttered it cannot be retracted or annulled, because once the Almighty or Jove heeds us and grants what we ask, he cannot and will never go back on his word. There are many myths where a curse is mistakenly uttered, but, once out in the world, it can no longer be countermanded or taken back. It will seek out its victim, find him, and strike him down. A blessing is no different. Once it has been given, there is no taking it back. Of all people in the history of mankind, Jacob should know this. He stole his older brother's birthright by duping his blind father, Isaac, into blessing him instead of Esau. Even after Isaac realizes he's been bilked by his crafty son, he knows that the blessing is now set in stone and that there is no voiding it. What we ask for may sometimes come to haunt us—or, as in the case of curses, may totally backfire.

My grandmother always repeated the story of a neighbor who cursed another neighbor with blindness only to find her darling, youngest son turn blind a week after. She was punished for wishing something so evil that when it backfired it hit her where it could inflict the most pain. She could have asked to have the curse lifted and visited on her eyes instead, but apparently she never did. On the other hand, there is the story of her father, my great-grandfather, who, when he heard that all four of his sons were inducted into the Italian army during World War I, asked the good Lord to return all four of them safely, in exchange for which he would be happy to lay down his life. Sure enough, as family lore has it, the very day after the fourth son returned, my great-grandfather fell sick and soon after died. My grandmother was surely thinking along the same lines. If I was going to live my life well, she would need to forfeit hers.

When the price is death, then, maybe, maybe the gods listen. A blessing or a curse uttered by someone willing to die for it is how we hope to turn a mortal dictum into a divine fiat.

The point in all this is that the human mind believes—but always provisionally—that in the course of a lifetime it can negotiate a couple of good deals with Providence. There may be a price to pay and there are no freebies, since Providence always exacts something in return, which is why we offer sacrifices and make sacrifices. *I will give this up if you give me that. I will forfeit going after that, if in return I can continue to hold on to this.* But because the logic of divine Providence is not only ironic but frequently counterintuitive, we also know that it may be unreliable enough to bring about something other than what was asked for. *You didn't ask well.* Or *You asked too much.* Or *You asked too soon.* Or *You didn't think through your request. You turn to me only when you need me. Be happy you got what you got. Now off with you before I change my mind and take back the little I doled out and give it to someone else, preferably your rival.* History is full of instances where a genie will grant three wishes exactly as they've been requested, knowing full well that all three will be taken back because the requests were not thought through. History is also filled with examples of oracles answering life-and-death questions with such inscrutable pronouncements that mortals always end up misreading them and paying a price.

To obviate the miscarriage of our requests, we are forced to play reverse mind games with the mastermind-gamester himself.

In blessing me my grandmother was doing something that is traditional the world over. I was the firstborn, my brother wasn't. I was the privileged one, he wasn't. He turned out to be kinder, but I was the chosen, not he. And yet in blessing me, the firstborn, my grandmother was doing something that goes against the Jewish tradition.

Let me explain.

When Jacob decides to bless his grandson, he blesses not the obvious person—the older son—but the younger one. Yes, we know he has a prophetic vision and that Ephraim and not Manasseh is to be the one from whom will issue "a multitude of nations." But why would God fumble this way and break the rule of primogeniture? After all, the worst and final plague that God visits upon the Egyptians is the dying of the firstborn, not the second born. That would never have softened Pharaoh's heart.

One could point to another example of the importance of the firstborn in the case of Tamar's twin sons, the first of whom puts his right hand out of his mother's womb and then withdraws it, but not before the midwife ties a scarlet band around his hand (Genesis 38:28–30).

Or to frame my question otherwise: Why would anyone think that God chose the younger over the older, when one knows that it is the older who is the more privileged of the two? And yet, to baffle the very foundations of primogeniture, the Old Testament teems with instances of reverse primogeniture, what one could call *deuterogeniture,* which favors the second born, not the first. Cain is the firstborn, but God favors Abel; Shem is younger than Japheth, yet Shem begets the Semites; Isaac is younger than Ishmael, Jacob younger than Esau, Judah younger than Reuben, Moses younger than Aaron, David younger than all of his brothers, and Solomon younger than his own brothers. Jacob himself chose Rachel over her older sister, Leah, though he, the grand trickster of all time, is himself tricked by his soon-to-be father-in-law into marrying Leah and begetting children with her first. And as though to add a further torsion to these reversals, Rachel bore Jacob two sons, the elder called Joseph but the younger Benjamin. Benjamin means son of my right hand.

Why then does Jacob or the authors of the Scripture favor the second born?

Here are ten possible reasons.

1. The younger is favored because he is the most vulnerable, and hence more easily harmed. He is not brawny; he is delicate, feminine almost, as Abel and Jacob are delicate. He is, after all, the child in the family.

2. The younger is favored as a way of saying to the forces of the universe—in this case God—that one is willing to settle for second best.

3. The second born is favored as a way of preferring Beth instead of Aleph. Which is totally counterintuitive. The very foundation of deuterogeniture is counterintuitive. But then it sets up counterintuition as a foundational metaphor.

4. Evil is averted by "hiding" the privileged firstborn behind the pretense of favoring the second born.

5. One may favor the second best as a way of questioning the very wisdom of primogeniture, which puts a premium not on the inner qualities of a son but on something as arbitrary and meaningless as the order of his birth.

6. One favors the second born as a way of asking for less than what everyone else might have wished, of not asking too much, of not appearing too greedy. In other words, asking less is a way of already negotiating. Asking less is reasonable, muted, humbler, and won't draw too much attention. Asking less averts punishment for aiming too high. One banks on the second best as a way of hedging one's aspirations, and therefore of hiding those aspirations. One favors the second best as a way of placating a donor who is capricious and frequently hostile enough to change his mind. One favors the second best because one does not trust the donor—though we also need to show we fear retribution for not trusting him.

7. One favors the second best as a way of distrusting appearances, of questioning first our obvious and impulsive choices, and of learning to set them aside. But it is also a way of saying that the hidden, the difficult to arrive at, the easily dismissible should always be preferred to self-evident and obvious choices. The moral was taught by Herodotus in his tale of Croesus, the richest man on earth, who had two sons: the firstborn, who had all the qualities one could wish for in a son who would one day inherit the kingdom; and a second son, who was mute and neglected. The first son dies in a hunting accident while the second ends up saving his father's life. Croesus, who, incidentally, was also guilty of misreading

the Oracle, should always have looked within, looked under. Signs are meant to confuse us. Thus one favors the second born as a way of passing a test meant to measure our ability to interpret providential signs.

8. One favors the second best as a way of avoiding the intractable mind game meant to trap our inferior thinking skills when pitted against those of the Creator himself. Reading his signs, reading his patience in even tolerating our desire to read his signs could be offensive to him, because the very suggestion that his signs are intentionally misleading or that we are even meant to suspect they are misleading may trigger his anger. The very assumption that God needs to speak in signs when we all know he invented language and knows all the languages—subjunctive, optative, absolute constructions, and all—can backfire. God does not need to speak with a forked tongue. This is insulting.

9. One favors the second best as a way of avoiding an infinite Minsk-Pinsk contest of readings and counterreadings, always with the understanding that avoiding such a contest, because one suspects it could be a trap—which already suggests that one is able to read God's intention to trap us—is itself dangerous. Ultimately, thinking that one is able to read his signs, or that one may have seen through his wiles and avoided the temptation to read his signs as a way of not stirring his wrath, can, in and of itself, backfire. Everything can backfire. Thinking that things can backfire as a way of preventing them from backfiring . . . can backfire. Avoiding thinking at all as a way of avoiding being punished for "thinking that things can backfire" can backfire—if only because it suggests that one has read God's desire not to be read at all. And this, too, is punishable. Trying to show that one is not fooled is punishable. Trying to

show that one fears one could easily be fooled—as a way of concealing that one may not really be fooled—is also punishable.

10. One favors the second born as a way of saying, I will pretend to favor the boy at my left but we all know I don't mean it. I will pretend not to know I am pretending, because if he knows I am pretending he will punish me, and my lineage will suffer. I must void my mind of double-dealing and of reverse mind games. But even trying to void my mind of this is a ploy, and if he gets wind of this—and how could he not, he is God after all—he will punish me and my lineage will suffer. And if it turns out that history will be stuck with my choice, then I must bear in mind that, had I jumped and favored the boy at my right, I would have been punished for not looking into things and, as a result, my lineage would have suffered just as much.

To repeat: counterintuitive thinking invokes infinite double-dealing, in the sense that bluffing at poker is potentially infinite. An impulsive first and obvious choice would have solved matters. But if one distrusts a Lord who has shown himself willing to play fast and loose with his chosen people, then one has to open up the possibility that everything that comes to mind must be rejected, but because everything that comes to mind must be rejected, this rejection is rejected, and so on and so forth.

Superstitious people are forever cursed with this kind of thinking. If thinking that taking the elevator to the right has augured a good day for me, then taking that same elevator every day, and avoiding the one to the left, might be a wise course. Except that in a universe where the deities that govern all things are perceived as whimsical and unreliable, these powers may feel I have grown overly confident in my ability to bring about a good day simply by taking the elevator to the right. So, out of an apotropaic desire to placate these deities and show that I am aware that as a mortal I have no control over how things turn out, I will decide to take the elevator to the left, knowing that by so doing I may forfeit having a good day but might also be rewarded for not being too greedy or presumptuous in my alleged ability to bring about a "good day." All this, of course, provided I never think and never allow myself to think that there is a reward awaiting me for forfeiting something that was to my advantage.

There is, in short, no good faith in counterintuitive thinking.

And maybe this is the time to say it: there is no such thing as a good, bad, or capricious Being out there. There is only a Being whom we project out into the ether and whom we distrust—but our distrust is no less provisional and capricious than is his benevolence or malevolence with respect to us. We contend and tussle with him as we tussle and contend with ourselves. It is like playing chess against oneself. That we are trapped in an infinite regress each time we try to reason with him or about him reflects our inability to understand that, whichever son we choose, or whichever elevator we take, and however much we would like to believe that our dictums can be transformed into fiats, we have absolutely no control and will never have any control over how things turn out.

But the very shrewd genie, whom we thought we had tamed by admitting we had no control over how things turn out, rears his head again, and with the wiles of Satan in Sir Thomas Browne or the wiles of self-love among the Jansenists, reminds us that the more we think we know his wiles, the more he is onto our own.

Superstitious people do not believe in God. They believe in something far more powerful but also far more mischievous and insidious. Even thinking, as I am doing now, in this laboriously captious manner, may risk upsetting him. Thinking in regressive forms turns us into satellites that have lost their orbits. All we do is spiral and spin, playing Minsk-Pinsk games, outwitting ourselves.

My grandmother blessed me for two reasons: because I was the oldest and because it was her way of saying good-bye forever. A blessing was all she had to give. There was nothing else. Though I didn't believe in blessings or in their power to help me live my life well, I have always thought that, of the two of us, she should have blessed my brother instead. He had given her all his love, his kindness, his compassion, his humanity. I did not. He was cheated.

When I heard that my grandmother had been operated on a few months later in Brazil and that there was a slim chance she might pull through, I found myself making a wish: let her live another few years, in exchange for which I would be willing to fail an exam. Better yet, I would fail a whole course, two if necessary. I had nothing else to give. I was basically parlaying with eternity, trying to strike up a deal. Eternity responded: what I was proposing was by no means acceptable enough. What else could I put on the table? I asked. How about Gail, it said. I had just met Gail and was in love with her and was pretty certain she was in love with me. I would have to give up Gail if I wanted my grandmother to survive.

No, I could not give up Gail.

In fact, a while later that summer, when things with Gail weren't going so well and Gail said she was not returning from Germany that year and was going to travel to Greece with someone she had just met in Munich, I found myself giving up my grandmother altogether if Gail could be returned to me.

My grandmother died that very week.

I lost Gail as well.

The Best Jew in the Family

Exodus 2

Cokie Roberts and Steven V. Roberts

As an interfaith couple who met more than fifty years ago—Cokie is Catholic, Steve is Jewish—we share the Old Testament as a sacred text. And we've always admired the women in those stories who display exceptional cunning, courage, and humor.

Take Sarah, who became pregnant with her son, Isaac, at age ninety. Genesis records her endearing reaction to her improbable motherhood: "God hath made me laugh. Everyone that heareth will laugh with me." Sarah was certainly not laughing, however, when her husband Abraham almost sacrificed Isaac on Mount Moriah to satisfy God's command. And while the Bible does not relate her comment when her husband came home, any mother has to believe it was some version of the cry "*You did what?*"

Then there is Esther, a Jewish orphan who became queen of Persia and saved her people from a genocidal plot hatched by the evil courtier Haman. She merits a whole book in the Old Testament and a major Jewish holiday, Purim, which celebrates her heroism. We focus on a far less famous figure, however, a woman named Zipporah, the wife of Moses, who receives only a few mentions in the Good Book. Call her the patron saint of interfaith marriages.

As related in Exodus, Zipporah's story begins with Moses, who was born in Egypt of Jewish parents but raised in the palace by Pharaoh's daughter. As he grew to manhood he despised the suffering of his fellow Jews, and one day "he spied an Egyptian smiting an Hebrew, one of his brethren." He killed the oppressor and hid his body in the sand thinking no one had seen the crime. But when Moses realized that his secret was out and Pharaoh was gunning for him, he fled to the land of Midian, across the Red Sea from Egypt in what is today Saudi Arabia.

The priest of Midian, usually called Jethro but sometimes Reuel, had seven daughters. When they went to the local well to draw water for their flock, they were harassed by a gang of unruly shepherds. Moses, who had "sat down" by the well, "stood up and helped them" by driving the shepherds away. When his daughters came home early from their task, Jethro asked why.

"And they said, An Egyptian delivered us out of the hand of the shepherds, and also drew water enough for us, and watered the flock." The grateful father admonished his daughters: "And where is he? Why is it that ye have left the man? Call him, that he may eat bread." The food and the company were apparently to the fugitive's liking. "And Moses was content to dwell with the man," says Exodus, "and he gave Moses Zipporah his daughter."

Zipporah was definitely not Jewish. Midian is far from Egypt, where the Hebrew tribes were living; and when the couple had their first child, a son, they named him Gershom, which means "a sojourner there." In explaining why he chose that name, Moses uttered the famous statement "I have been a stranger in a strange land." In other words, no Jews around.

Even more telling is the most noteworthy episode involving Zipporah. Jonathan Kirsch, who writes about biblical women in his book *The Harlot by the Side of the Road*, describes her tale as brimming with "mystery, mayhem and sheer baffling weirdness."

While the "stranger" was content to stay in Midian and raise the two sons he had fathered with Zipporah, the bondage of the Jews back in Egypt was steadily growing harsher and "God heard their groaning." One day as Moses was tending his flock on "the far side of the wilderness," the Lord appeared to him in a "burning bush"—which was miraculously not consumed by the blaze—and said, "The cry of the children of Israel is come unto me." Therefore, "I will send thee unto Pharaoh, that thou mayest bring forth my people the children of Israel out of Egypt."

Moses was dismayed by the assignment, but God reassured him, "I will be with you." So he packed up his little family and they set out for Egypt. But since Zipporah was not Jewish, and they had been living in a "strange land," the boys had not been circumcised. In Genesis, God told Abraham that circumcision would be "the sign of the covenant between you and me" and that any male who had not endured the procedure would be "cut off from his people." So this omission was a big deal.

Now comes the "baffling weirdness" part. God seemed to have second thoughts about Moses's fitness for the task of liberation. When the family stopped at a "lodging place" for the night, "the Lord met [Moses] and sought to put him to death." In response Zipporah sprang into action, "took a flint and cut off her son's foreskin and threw it at Moses' feet, and she said, 'You are indeed a bridegroom of blood to me.'" As a result, the Lord "let him alone" and Moses lived.

Like most Bible stories, this one is subject to many interpretations, but the implication is pretty clear. God was so displeased with Moses that he was ready to bump him off, and Zipporah realized at least one reason: his sons had not been circumcised. This non-Jewish woman perceived the importance of the covenant between God and her husband's people and performed the ritual without proper training or equipment. She never converted to her husband's faith, but she respected and honored a core principle of his tradition.

In our experience, that's exactly what partners in a healthy mixed marriage have to do: care enough to understand and embrace what's important to each other. Zipporah's lesson actually applies to all couples in all unions and for one simple reason. Every marriage is really a "mixed" marriage, especially one between a man and a woman. Anyone who's been married more than a few weeks knows that gender is often a much deeper division than religion. Even same-sex couples have to understand the broader principle her story teaches. Love your partner for who he or she is. Cherish your differences as well as your similarities. Most of us will never have to operate on our children with sharp stones. But all of us, in our own way, have to say to our partners in times of turmoil: I stand with you. We are in this together. As we wrote in our book *From This Day Forward*: "Marriage has enlarged our lives not encircled them. It has opened new doors not closed them. We are better people together than we are separately."

Zipporah's story is not just about religious differences but racial ones as well. She is often depicted as a woman of color. Some artists render her as a coffee-toned Arab in desert robes; others as a distinctly African woman with black skin, close-cropped hair, and a colorful headband. In the animated feature *Prince of Egypt*, released by DreamWorks in 1998, she is clearly several shades darker than her husband (although her voice is provided by the blond, blue-eyed actress Michelle Pfeiffer).

Zipporah's lineage is an issue to Moses's family after he returns to Egypt—no big surprise there. According to the Book of Numbers, his brother, Aaron, and sister, Miriam, "spoke against Moses because of the Cushite woman whom he had married, for he had married a Cushite woman." In some translations "Cushite" is rendered as "Ethiopian," but both versions have the same meaning: Zipporah is not one of us. In fact, in Israel today "Cushi" is an insulting term for a person of color.

In his novel *Zipporah, Wife of Moses*, Marek Halter takes that reference to "a Cushite woman" and writes that Zipporah was not a native of Midian at all and must have been adopted by Jethro. In Halter's narrative, "the color of Zipporah's skin sets her apart, making her an outsider to the men of her adopted tribe, who do not want her as a wife."

So in this version of the story, when they met in Midian, Zipporah and Moses were both strangers in a strange land. The name of their son reflects their common experience and their common belief: if you've been an "outsider" you know how it feels, and you know how important it is to make other exiles feel welcome.

When we met (at a conference in Ohio, not a well in Midian), between our sophomore and junior years of college, we were also strangers to each other's traditions. We've never faced the particular problem Zipporah encountered—our son was born in Beth Israel hospital in New York City, where circumcision was pretty standard—and we didn't know her story at the time. But we somehow sensed that, if we were going to make our relationship work, we had to follow her example. Not only did we have to love each other, we had to learn from each other.

We had to deal with our own Aarons and Miriams as well, people who "spoke against" our relationship, and, in those early years, reconciling our faiths and families often seemed like an impossible task. Cokie was deeply attached to her religious tradition (her mother was later the American ambassador to the Vatican) and the order of nuns the Society of the Sacred Heart, who taught her through high school. Steve was raised in an aggressively secular household, totally lacking in religious symbols or ceremonies. But his grandfather had fled the pogroms of Eastern Europe to become a Zionist pioneer in Palestine. He grew up in a largely Jewish neighborhood in Bayonne, New Jersey, and identified strongly with his tribal culture and community.

"In one sense caring so much about family and tradition made it all harder," we wrote in *From This Day Forward*. "We could not ignore who we were or what we'd been taught. Converting was never a possibility for either one of us and abandoning religion was also out of the question. But gradually we came to realize how much we shared. The labels were different but the values were the same. And since then, we've often reflected that Catholics and Jews make good matches. We're both really good at loyalty and guilt."

Two incidents before we were married reflect our long and sometimes painful struggle to find common ground. Cokie tells one story: "My reaction to all this was to be inclusive, to try to learn as much about Judaism as possible. I was in Cincinnati over Rosh Hashanah and one of the oldest temples in Reform Judaism, the Plum Street Temple, is there. I had no idea that tickets were required for services, so I went up to the door and the usher asked, 'What do you want?' I said, 'I want to come in. I want to go to services.' The guy said okay and he walked me down the aisle and said in this huge stage whisper so the entire congregation could hear, 'Here's one that came without her boyfriend.' It was not a good moment."

It was not a good moment, either, when Steve's father wrote him a harsh, five-page, single-spaced letter urging him to end our relationship. He mentioned how pleased he'd been to meet the friends his son had recently brought home and wrote: "Steve, visualize a family in which the father is of one faith and the mother and children are of another. Can there be the same kind of relaxed, secure atmosphere? Will a Catholic child be as comfortable bringing home his Catholic friends to meet his Jewish father?" Steve was always the "good son," who valued his parents' approval, and his father played on that: "You could not teach your Catholic children in the same way your father taught you." There was only one answer. Break up. "For I can see no viable solution, nor have you suggested any to me," he wrote.

But we did have an answer, a "viable solution." We showed him he was wrong. Instead of confronting Steve's parents, we courted them. We visited as often as we could. We introduced them to Cokie's family. We showed them that their fears were unfounded. We made it clear that Steve was not marrying the pope or a priest but one devoted Catholic woman, who loved their son—and them. We knew our efforts had succeeded when Steve's father finally admitted: "It would be a lot easier to oppose this match if it weren't so obvious that she's the perfect girl for you."

That was only the first step, however. The next test of tolerance was the wedding. Cokie's sister had been married in a Catholic church two years earlier, and Cokie's mother had always assumed her younger daughter would do the same thing. But when she heard that Steve had two living grandfathers, who would not be comfortable in a church setting, she immediately understood. So we got married in the garden of

Cokie's girlhood home (where we still live), after the Jewish Sabbath ended at sundown on Saturday, under a *chuppah*, a traditional Jewish wedding canopy. We had no trouble getting a priest—Cokie's uncle was a Jesuit and had to come—but finding a rabbi was far more difficult. In 1966 few if any rabbis would perform interfaith weddings, and Cokie's search for a cooperative clergyman proved frustrating and futile.

Just as Cokie's mother had compromised on the church issue, it was Steve's mother who solved the celebrant problem. In Jewish tradition, she pointed out, a rabbi is just a learned man, an elder of the tribe, so forget about some official figure and find an elder. Her suggestion: Arthur Goldberg, ambassador to the United Nations, former Supreme Court justice, and close friend of Cokie's parents.

It was a brilliant solution. Goldberg was happy to come. He said Hebrew prayers, quoted Bible verses, and made our Jewish friends and relatives feel welcome and respected. They were not strangers that night but honored guests. In fact the concept of an "elder" is such a useful solution to such a thorny problem that Steve has performed that role in a half dozen weddings, including our own son's. And he often quotes from the original text Justice Goldberg used that night. Zipporah would approve.

We were forced very young to decide what was important to us and what was not. Where we could make compromises and where we couldn't. We agreed that our family would practice both faiths, but as Steve has written: "Cokie was more committed to our agreement than I was. I came to realize that if you're a person of faith, you take all religions seriously, and she shouldered the task of making Judaism a part of our lives together. I was happy to go along but she was the driving force. We now joke that she is the best Jew in the family; she replies that there's never been much competition for the title."

Steve grew up with grandparents who read Yiddish newspapers, ate Jewish food, and told harrowing stories of escaping the Cossacks back in the Old Country. He was marked as Jewish by tradition and history. Cokie could not share that, so like Zipporah she turned to religious practice as a way of connecting to her husband's heritage. In *From This Day Forward* Cokie explained why: "We . . . realized that we had to create religious rituals for ourselves. Back home Steve knew he was Jewish because it was simply part of the culture. Now, if Judaism was going to be part of our marriage, we had to deal consciously and conscientiously with the religion itself. That was particularly true for me. I couldn't make any cultural claims to Judaism, so the religious rituals became terribly important to me."

The ritual that became most important to both of us was the Passover Seder, an evening meal that celebrates the Jewish liberation from Egypt with prayers, stories, songs—and lots of wine. The first year after we were married, Arthur and Dorothy Goldberg invited us to their Seder, but by the next year we were on our own. Steve's family never had a Seder and knew nothing about holding one. They didn't even own a Haggadah, the traditional book that contains the text of the service. But at Cokie's request, they gamely agreed to play host and found a few Haggadahs (free at the Safeway) published by Maxwell House, the coffee company. In later years, Steve's mother often said that the first Seder she ever attended was organized by her Catholic daughter-in-law.

It was just the four of us, and Cokie describes the scene: "During dinner Steve's twin brother, Marc, called to talk to his folks and when their father said he would call back later because we were mid-Seder, we could all hear Marc's amazed 'WHY?' at the other of the line. We could also hear the whispered reply: 'Because Cokie wanted it.' Well, that was certainly true. And by the next year, after we had moved to California, where we hardly knew anyone, it was clear that if 'Cokie wanted it,' she better figure out how to do it herself."

So she did. California was certainly a "strange land." We'd moved from an apartment on the West Side of Manhattan to a hilltop overlooking the Pacific Ocean in Malibu. But Cokie tracked down the closest synagogue and in the gift shop found *The New Haggadah,* published by the Jewish Reconstructionist Foundation. We still call it the "blue book," even though it's faded to dirty gray, and that's what we used for our first Seder Out West. But our friends were unhappy—it omitted some of their favorite passages and sounded too preachy in other places—so Cokie consulted a bunch of other Haggadahs, drafted her own version, typed it out on a portable typewriter she'd gotten as a high school graduation present, and printed copies on that glossy paper used by ancient mimeograph machines.

That's still basically the version we use today, with updated gender references. A few years ago we published it under the title *Our Haggadah*, but the subtitle is the important part, *Uniting Traditions for Interfaith Families*. Our guest list always includes many mixed couples, and in fact Steve's parents were often the only Jews in the room married to each other.

We were motivated to publish the book for many reasons. Over time we came to understand that Passover is the best pathway for "outsiders" in interfaith relationships to connect with Judaism. These rituals are usually held at home, so you don't have to join a synagogue or contribute to the building fund to participate. You can do it at your own pace in your own way. Moreover, Passover's message of freedom over slavery, of light over darkness, is a universal one that transcends religious doctrine.

The holiday is also intimately connected with Easter, making the Seder a comfortable experience for Christians and a teaching opportunity for Jews. This cannot be a one-way street. In any resilient mixed marriage, each partner has to respect the other's faith. And while Steve is hardly the "best Christian" in Cokie's family, he does read the Old Testament portion every year during Christmas Eve Mass at Cokie's old school.

In her introduction to *Our Haggadah*, Cokie points out how our two traditions are joined in the Passover celebration: "The most solemn week of the Christian year begins with Jesus arriving in Jerusalem to the hosannas of his followers who greeted him with palm branches as he entered the city to celebrate Passover. The gospel writers Matthew, Mark and Luke tell us that what Christians now call the Last Supper was in fact a Seder. The Passover meal, argues the *Encyclopedia of Catholicism*, 'celebrates God's liberation of the Jewish people and the continuing covenant with them. Such a celebration offers a model for understanding Christ's liberation of the world from sin through death.'"

We don't preach interfaith marriage, but we don't deny reality, either. Moses and Zipporah form a very modern couple who foreshadow by many centuries a growing contemporary trend. More than half of all Jews marry non-Jews today; one in seven American marriages is interracial. More and more young people are meeting and marrying a "stranger in a strange land" and raising their children to honor their combined heritage.

It was not easy for them and it was not easy for us. We all have our Aarons and Miriams who speak against those who marry outside the tribe. When we were based in Greece in the mid-seventies, we took a family trip to Israel, using a Bible to tell stories to our children about their two traditions. After Steve wrote an article about the trip for the *New York Times* travel section, he was deluged with hateful mail, most of it from Jewish readers, who were outraged that he should marry a non-Jew and desecrate the Holy Land with his half-breed children.

The most upsetting part of that whole episode was the intolerant reaction of ignorant people who presumed to know what our lives were like. We must be unhappy people and unsuccessful parents, they said, because we didn't follow their rules and their prejudices. Many readers fastened on the story Steve told about his grandfather Avram Rogowsky, who had lived in Palestine as a young man and worked on some of the first roads built in Tel Aviv.

They felt Grandpa Abe "must be horrified at his grandson's waywardness," Steve wrote in the *Times*, responding to the letters. But those readers got it exactly wrong. "Well my Grandpa Abe has had a crazy and colorful life, and now he's old and senile," Steve wrote. "He does not recognize people very often, even his own children, but he often asks for one particularly kind and charitable person, my wife, my Catholic wife."

Since we started writing and speaking about interfaith marriage many years ago, we've sensed an enormous change in the Jewish world. At first people would pull us aside and whisper in hushed voices that their children had married outsiders. Today many families and rabbis have had to adjust their thinking. They increasingly understand that, to keep these interfaith couples connected to the Jewish community, they have to be inclusive, not exclusive, welcoming, not hostile.

In Louisville, the president of one congregation started her annual report by emphasizing the importance of embracing non-Jewish spouses. In Atlanta, the Jewish Community Center described a grant they'd received to develop programs for the "strangers" who had married their children. At a Sabbath service in Florida the woman who spoke for the temple sisterhood was Chinese. The child who always sings the Four Questions at our Seder is also a champion Irish dancer, reflecting her mother's origins. One rabbi we know told us, "It used to be that when congregations interviewed rabbis, and asked if they performed mixed marriages, the answer they wanted to hear was 'no.' Today the answer they expect is 'yes.'"

Our favorite example happened at a luncheon in Boca Raton, Florida, when Cokie was made a life member of Hadassah, the Jewish women's organization. Zipporah would have appreciated the meaning of that moment. She, too, was the best Jew in her family.

Come On In, the Water's Fine

Exodus 14

A. J. Jacobs

My favorite biblical story isn't in the Bible. Not technically at least.

The story is about the parting of the Red Sea, but it's not the Moses-raises-his-staff account that we all know from Exodus and Charlton Heston. It's an entirely different version—either an embellishment or the true-to-life account, depending on your point of view—and it's found in the Midrash, a massive book of biblical interpretation compiled by rabbis over the centuries.

I first heard the story about ten years ago. At the time, I was writing a book about the Bible. I decided to write a book on the Bible because I was the ultimate biblical non-expert.

I grew up with no religion, the child of assimilated agnostics. As I say in the intro to that book, I'm Jewish, but I'm Jewish in the same way the Olive Garden is Italian. Not very. (No offense to the Olive Garden. Love your breadsticks.)

But I'd recently had a son, and I wanted to know what to teach him about religion and my heritage.

So I came up with a book idea: What if I learned about the Bible by living it? What if I tried to follow in our ancestors' footsteps and obey every single rule in the Hebrew scriptures for a year, from the Ten Commandments to growing a massive beard?

When I came up with the idea, I was torn. On the one hand, I was drawn to it. I knew it would be a fascinating year and I would learn a ton. I knew the premise had potential to make a splash. I could envision the cover photo right from the start—me in sandals, a beard, and a robe in the middle of my hometown, New York City.

On the other hand, I was terrified, and not just of the itchy facial hair. Would the project put a strain on my marriage? How would it interfere with my day job at *Esquire* magazine, a decidedly nonbiblical publication?

And most of all, I was nervous about the public reaction. My plan was always to take this project seriously—I really wanted to explore the Bible's meaning and relevance in modern times. But I knew it would be easy for detractors to criticize my approach as misguided. I wondered if true believers would condemn me for being irreverent. Would atheists slam me for being too gentle on the Bible? Would I be afflicted by boils?

To get advice, I asked an acquaintance for lunch. He was Rabbi Andy Bachman, later to become rabbi of Brooklyn's Congregation Beth Elohim.

I told Rabbi Bachman my doubts, and he told me a story from the Midrash. The story goes like this: When Moses was fleeing the Egyptians, he arrived at the Red Sea with his thousands of followers. Moses lifted up his staff hoping for a miracle—but the sea did not part.

The Egyptians soldiers were closing in and Moses and his followers were stuck at the shore. It was only a matter of time before every one of them would be slaughtered. Naturally, Moses and his followers were panicking. No one knew what to do.

And then, just before the Egyptian army caught up to them, a Hebrew named Nachshon did something unexpected. He simply walked into the Red Sea. He waded up to his ankles, then his knees, then his waist, then his shoulders. And right when the water was about to get up to his nostrils, it happened: the sea parted.

The point, said Rabbi Bachman, is that "sometimes miracles occur only when you jump in."

Rabbi Bachman's story remains the greatest pep talk I've ever gotten in my life. I did what Nachshon would have done. I jumped in and lived the experiment and wrote the book. (And, incidentally, did not get afflicted by boils, nor incur the wrath of either the religious or the atheists.)

Now, ten years later, I still think of Nachshon almost daily. He gives me courage. Before I embark on any project, I visualize myself just wading in. I think about Nachshon whenever I make a life decision, whether biggish (Should we get a dog? Should we send our kid to a new school?) or small (Should we try the new Vietnamese restaurant? Should I upgrade my smart phone?).

I'm enamored of the story for several reasons. First, I love that it's one of the most democratic stories you'll ever hear about the Bible. The hero isn't Moses, the one anointed by God, the patriarch known to generations. The hero is a little-known regular guy. The idea is, anyone can make a difference—you don't need to own a staff and have a personal directive from God.

I even like Nachshon story because it's pro-walking. Good things happen when you walk. After the book on biblical living, I wrote a book about health, and discovered the literal benefits of constant forward motion. As one doctor told me, sitting is the new smoking. It's terrible for you. I now work on a treadmill desk—I put my computer on the machine's ledge and stroll while I type. I'm not on a sacred mission, but still, I imagine Nachshon might approve.

But mostly I like this story because it's an ode to action, experimentation, and optimism. Nachshon was all about action. If Nike designed sandals several thousand years ago, they could have signed an endorsement deal with Nachshon. He lived their tagline long before it existed: Just do it.

He had optimism—almost delusional optimism. He believed that the water would part if he just plowed right in. Obstacles, he figured, will fall away.

I'm a big fan of delusional optimism. I think most of the great advances we've made as a species—going to the moon, curing diseases, inventing the waffle iron—have required some level of delusional optimism. Or consider our country. The Founding Fathers had some serious irrational exuberance to believe in a ragtag group of farmers defeating the greatest military might on planet earth. That's crazy talk.

I know I need delusional optimism every day. I'm not naturally bold. I think I was born pretty timid. I have to force myself to act like Nachshon, coerce myself to walk into that water.

Now, the Nachshon approach to life has its limits. Delusional optimism can be dangerous. Quite often, the sea never parts. The water goes above our nostrils and we drown.

So it's important to balance your inner Nachshon with your inner Moses—the part of you who hesitates, considers consequences, looks before wading. But for me, the fretting side comes naturally. It's the boldness that I need to work on. And for that, I thank the influence of the greatest wader of all time, Nachshon.

Desert Stories

Deuteronomy & Exodus & Isaiah

Kathleen Norris

The Bible has a way of reaching out and grabbing us when we least expect it. Even a snippet of a verse can stop us in our tracks. When I visited the memorial to Martin Luther King in Memphis, Tennessee, at the motel where he was murdered, I found a simple stone placed under the balcony made famous by the photos of King's companions pointing to the boardinghouse from where the shots had been fired. A plaque on the stone reads: "Behold, here cometh the dreamer, let us slay him . . . and we shall see what will become of his dreams." That is from the Book of Genesis, one of Joseph's brothers speaking, plotting to murder the family's favored younger son and leave his body in the desert. When I was a child, that story was my introduction to the notion of betrayal. I felt sure that my older brother would never do such a thing to me, but here was a story suggesting that it was possible.

Standing below that balcony at the Lorraine Motel, I found these ancient words taking on new life, revealing the terrible things we do to one another when we forget our common humanity. If we allow ideology and prejudice to take hold of us, we can forget that we are brothers and sisters under the skin. We find ways to kill each other, literally and figuratively. But the dreamers among us refuse to die. Their dreams, like seeds, give us a chance to grow into better people, a better society, and remind us that hatred does not have the last word.

* * *

Another time when I experienced the Bible in full voice was during my first visit to the Holocaust Museum in Washington, D.C. Close to the entry—after you pass through the metal detector, which unfortunately is a necessity there—you encounter a massive granite wall carved with a brief inscription: "You are my witnesses." When I read those words of Isaiah, I gasped, and had to sit down for a moment. Confronted by the prophet in that place, in the context of contemplating the Holocaust, I took those words to heart for the first time. I had read that passage from Isaiah before but had never felt it in my bones: "You are my witnesses." The Holocaust had just been brought to life for me. I could no longer tuck it safely away into the past, but had to accept that it is a present reality. I had to consider the ways I am being called to be a witness to cruelty and injustice here and now. Just four simple words.

And I think this is what the Bible is for. It is meant to keep reaching out to us and, despite our inattention and indifference and infernal self-absorption, every now and then hit us in the gut. Prophets like Amos, Jeremiah, and Isaiah challenge us in our complacency, reminding us of our calling to be God's witnesses, but also comforting us when we need it most, when we're in the desert and there seems no way out. In my book *Acedia and Me,* I talk about encountering a famous passage from Isaiah at an exceptionally difficult time, when my husband's life hung in the balance and our lives had been thoroughly upended. One morning, in a motel room in Bismarck, North Dakota, where we'd been stranded for an indefinite period in the dead of winter so that he could receive respiratory therapy, I found this passage in a Gideon Bible: "when you pass through the waters, I will be with you . . . when you walk through fire, you shall not be burned—for I am with you." And those words changed me; they gave me new hope. They reminded me to be grateful for my life, and that of my husband, to be thankful that he was breathing, with the help of supplemental oxygen, to be sure, but safe, a warm presence in our bed. I was grateful for the present moment for the first time in weeks. The desert of a bitterly cold North Dakota winter had just come into bloom.

The desert is a fact of life. We encounter it when the comfortable certainties of our lives are suddenly shattered: when we have a bad accident, or are diagnosed with a dire illness; when our loved ones die, or a spouse leaves us for someone else; when we lose a job that gave our lives meaning; when we fail miserably at something we had tried hard to make work. The desert stories in the Hebrew scriptures are meant to guide us through these times. The Books of Exodus and Deuteronomy hold up a mirror to us, teaching us about how, in the worst of circumstances, we can still find solace in God, and in each other.

These stories are about the desert experience of the people of ancient Israel, but studying them allows us to better understand the challenges we face in our own lives. This is a more difficult undertaking than it might seem. For some of us these tales will be so familiar that we take them for granted: the flight from Egypt with Pharaoh's army in hot pursuit, the parting of the Red Sea, the wandering in the desert for forty years (which if you've ever seen the landscape of the Sinai makes perfect sense—it has to be one of the most forbidding and confusing landscapes on earth, miles and miles of basalt and grit). As remarkable as these stories are, they can become like an old comfortable armchair in the corner, long past its time, and only vaguely useful.

For those less familiar with the Bible, it can be a challenge to find any relevance in this literature that comes out of a tribal culture, a warrior culture from thousands of years ago. But the human foibles present in the stories are all too familiar to us. These displaced people lose themselves in bickering, constantly carping at each other, at Moses—who had led them out of Egypt—and directing their anger and frustration at God. It's kind of depressing, and we might ask: What is all of this doing in a book of sacred scriptures? What possible meaning can these stories have for us today?

I believe that these stories contain the foundation of the Judeo-Christian heritage, and I am grateful that I learned them when I was a child. I loved the strange images in my children's Bible, of people in what looked like bathrobes crossing the Red Sea on dry land as the waters parted before them, and later being led by a cloud by day, and a column of fire by night. Those two images in particular appealed to me: they were wild, like nothing else in my quiet suburban existence, and that made them valuable, a great stimulant for my budding imagination.

I was attracted also by the never-ending miracles. When the people grow thirsty, God tells Moses to strike a rock, and water flows forth. When they are weak from hunger, God makes food appear out of the sky. These stories helped me to form an image of God as one who truly cares for us, and will do anything to help us in our need. And the starkness of that desert environment—one I could scarcely envision in the lush environs of Virginia, surrounded by dogwood and magnolia, with a honeysuckle bush in our backyard—made these miracles seem all the more significant. And that's where the spiritual impact of these stories kicked in, teaching me that it's when we are stripped bare, and all the usual comforts are gone, that God's love has the greatest chance to reach us, and change our lives for the better.

Nature itself confirms that the aridity of the desert contains the promise of bloom. As the naturalist Ann Zwinger has written, "Dryness promotes the formation of flower buds . . . flowering is, after all, not an aesthetic contribution, but a survival mechanism." This has been confirmed in my experience as I have grown older. It is in the harsh, inhospitable environment of the desert that I am most likely to pay attention to God, and my relationship with God has the best chance to grow.

But that spiritual insight came in later years. When I was a child, what I took away from the tales of Israel in the desert was not only wonder at the miracles God performed for his people but frustration and anger over the people's lack of gratitude. God had performed miracle after miracle for them, and still they griped and fretted and doubted so much that they began to worship idols instead of the living God, who had been with them all along their difficult journey. Over and over, they challenged and tested God—they whined and whined and whined. (I had learned early on, thanks to my wise parents, that episodes of prolonged whining did not end well for me. If nothing else, they were counterproductive.)

What was going on here? How could the faith of these people be so weak, so inconsistent? Every time they faced a dire need—protection, water, food—God stepped in and saved the day. But the impact of all those miracles wore off very soon. It was as if the people kept saying to God, as their gratitude faded, So what have you done for me *lately*? As a child I simply could not understand it—but of course as an adult I understand it all too well.

That's because I've come to recognize myself in these people of the ancient desert. Like them I have a well-developed capacity for ingratitude and forgetting that God's providence is there, even when I can't see it, and things are going badly in my life. It is all too easy for me to forget that, unlike my own fickle spirit, God's love is steady, and always present in my life. It's easy to lose hold of my trust in God. I've learned that the flame of faith burns high, like a pillar of fire, when things are going well for me, or if I've just come through a difficult time and have felt God's hand in my life. But I've also learned that my faith can quickly turn dull and listless, a distant memory instead of a living presence.

When I was a child, the story of God giving the law to Israel did not appeal to me nearly as much as the stories of miracles, but I did wonder why the commandment against idolatry was the first one given to Moses. I certainly wasn't worshiping any golden calves. And even after I became an adult, idolatry seemed remote from my experience, unlike the prime-time sins of anger, pride, lust, and greed. But I've come to see that idolatry is the first of the sins, because if you've broken any of the other commandments it means you've already broken that first one. You've made an idol of something other than God.

Human beings are inveterate idol makers. And in our desert weakness, when our trust in God falters, we find that we have plenty of options for doing just that: the infernal busyness of workaholism, the chasing after status and possessions, or money or power. We have addictions to all of the above, and also to television binge watching, video games, silly distractions on the Internet, and also to drugs that offer false promises of ecstasy. Heroin addicts will tell you that the drug takes all the pain away. You no longer care that your life is falling apart, because you can't feel it. But the consolations of our idols have a way of disappearing into the mist just when we are truly lost in the desert, and at our lowest point.

I think idolatry is the first of the sins also because it traps us so easily. Many things that become idols don't start out that way—they're not inherently evil: enjoying a TV series, for example, like *Mad Men*. What's not to like—a good script, superb acting. And that's fine, until you start organizing your life around the show's schedule, or refuse to take a phone call from a good friend while you're watching it. Or a glass of wine with friends over a meal: that pleasure becomes a very different thing when you're drinking a bottle a day in seclusion. Idolatry is all about taking things to extremes and, above all, refusing relationship. Our idols make it impossible to enjoy a proper relationship with God, with others, and with ourselves as people made in God's image. And that takes us back to the stories in Deuteronomy and Exodus.

The Israelites in the desert needed relationship as much as food and water. And when we read those stories in Deuteronomy—one monastery I know does this every Lent—they are meant to remind us that God's commandments are not a list of don'ts so much as a road map for the behavior that makes for good relationships, good community. Honesty, respect for oneself and others, and, above all, love. Taking a closer look at two of the stories from the Exodus, we can see that, in addressing our basic need for food and water, God is doing much more. God is teaching us how to be human.

The story of manna, in Exodus 16, begins typically with the people complaining to Moses and Aaron: "If only we had died by the hand of the Lord in the land of Egypt, when we sat by the fleshpots and ate our fill of bread; for you have brought us out into this wilderness to kill the whole assembly." Two things strike me about this. The people are saying that they would prefer the slavery they endured in Egypt to their present freedom, and also that their faith in God has been so shaken by hunger that they now believe God led them into the desert to let them die. The physical desert that they're in pales before this awful, stark desert place in their faith. To think that God means to destroy you: that is a truly terrible place to be.

The crowning glory for me in this episode is what happens when the bread from heaven appears at dawn one day—the Israelites say "What is it?" (That's the meaning of the word *manna*—what is it?) The people's faith has been so shriveled in the desert journey that they don't recognize God's providence when it is placed right before them. I hate to think how often that has been true of me. Not only do the Israelites not know what this blessing is, but, when they comprehend that it is nourishment, they don't know how to use it and begin to complain that they can't store this manna and hoard it: it's a grace to be savored in the present moment, on this day. Again, this sounds all too familiar to me.

When we look at the Meribah story in Exodus 17, we find that dread anxiety again, as the people ask: "Why did you bring us out of Egypt, to kill us, our children, and our livestock with thirst?" This question, repeated several times in the Book of Exodus, acts as a refrain in the desert journey. It's hard to believe that the people would prefer the slavery and abuse they suffered in Egypt to the freedom God has brought them to, but hunger and thirst do terrible things to us. We also have great difficulty when we feel lost, when our lives seem to have lost their purpose. It's easy to grow bitter and distrustful when we feel that we are wandering aimlessly.

When bad things happen to us, we do ask God: Why did you lead me into this desert? Because to die there is an option when things go wrong: to just curl up, feel sorry for ourselves, and withdraw from life. This can be a normal stage in the grieving process, a time-out, but eventually, with God's help, we move on and rejoin the human race. Fortunately for us, the Bible provides us with the answer to that question born out of such great desperation, and it does so repeatedly. In Exodus and Deuteronomy, God never seems to tire of providing life-giving miracles. We also have the gospel story of Jesus being led into the desert to be tempted, but not abandoned there. Both his knowledge of scripture and his absolute trust in God helped him through the ordeal. I've come to wonder if asking God if he led us into the desert to let us die isn't a sign of our trust, even the mark of a mature faith, for contained within it is the seed of an answer: God intends for us to live, and live fully. Our desert experiences are meant to help us grow, and to grow closer to God.

I suspect that we all have a manna story, a Meribah story, somewhere in our lives. I have several; the most recent is about my sister who died last year. She'd had an exceptionally difficult life. Brain-damaged at birth because of medical errors, she was just intelligent enough to understand what had happened to her. This made her angry and resentful, and she was doomed to be repeatedly frustrated in her desperate attempts to fit in with others. She suffered greatly as a young woman, nursing both great loneliness and great rage. But as my sister approached the age of sixty, she finally figured out that, for people to like her, all she had to do was be herself. She changed so much that I doubt people who knew her thirty years before would have recognized her. She'd gone from a woman harboring a load of rage to someone whose primary virtue was gratitude.

When my sister was diagnosed with terminal cancer, I was the angry one. She'd had such a hard time coming into this world, and now she'd have a hard time leaving it. I was angry at God, at the world, at everything. When I got home from the Cancer Center that day, I was greeted at my apartment door by the sight of two brilliant rainbows over Honolulu. I had just the strength to say, "Thank you." But I was still angry.

I was with my sister every day for her palliative radiation treatments, and we began plans for hospice placement. I accompanied her regularly to the three things she loved the most: to the movies—action flicks, romantic comedies, you name it—to my Episcopal church on Sunday, and, on Tuesdays, to a weekly art class at the Cancer Center, where she excelled at making vibrant paintings. One day she proudly painted flowers for a new grandniece, and a day later she was dead: the cancer had spread to her lungs, her breathing became labored, and her heart simply stopped. She was spared months of pain and misery.

I had doubted in God's providence, but there it was, right before me. A gift from nowhere, like manna. Water from the rock. And it was enough. I was no longer thirsting for my sister to have an easy death, because it had been granted her. I could be glad that her symptoms had just begun to manifest, so they weren't yet causing her much trouble. She'd been so happy right up to the end; she'd even reprimanded me that day, just twelve hours before she died, because I hadn't taken her to the movies in over a week! She'd been looking forward to *The Great Gatsby* film, and had struggled through the book in preparation. She had loved the party scene, and beamed when I told her that it was one of the most famous party scenes in literature. I told all of this to a nurse at the Cancer Center, who laughed and said, "Oh, that's so good: Becky was still herself."

This may be an odd form for manna to take, but I think one message of the Bible's desert stories is that you take what God provides for you. And you give thanks that you can recognize God's grace. Skeptics might say—well, this is one dramatic example—but what if her sister had entered hospice and endured that dreaded decline? Would that mean that God had abandoned her and her sister? I can muster just enough faith to answer that if God's providence hadn't come in the form it did, it would have come in another. And it would be up to me to recognize it and open my heart to receive it, and understand that God is close at hand, ready to lead me through the wilderness. For God never leads us into a desert only to let us die.

The Book of Ruth

Lois Lowry

I think it was probably 1985. The date doesn't matter, really, but I am trying to get my bearings here in order to tell this story. I know it predated e-mail, because I remember getting this information in an actual letter addressed to me in Boston, and that a photograph fell out from between the folded pages.

The photo was quite lovely, actually. It had been taken from above, from the sky, looking down on a fairy-tale stone castle, crenellated towers and parapets and all, surrounded by thick green woods.

I unfolded the letter, which had been addressed to me by my son Grey, a young fighter pilot, and chuckled when I read his first sentence. "I thought I'd show you my new digs," he had written. *Yeah, right,* I thought. He had just been reassigned to an air force base in southwest Germany, and I pictured him in the BOQ, tucking this stock photo into his letter with a grin as he wrote home to tell me of his new housing, probably something built from cinder block on the base.

But, as it turned out, he wasn't joking. He had taken the photograph from his F-15, he explained. His next paragraph began: "I met this countess."

Gulp. From this adventurous, outgoing, blue-eyed son, I had heard, from time to time: "I met this actress" or "I met this . . ." whatever. One of these young women had driven a convertible emblazoned, on its side, with the news that she had been crowned Miss . . . Well, I am not going to name the state. Pick any state.

Now, a *countess?*

And it was true. But she was not a playgirl, not nubile minor royalty with a penchant for yachts and roulette. She was a handsome, dignified widow with a gray chignon and a history of loss. The vast acreage of forests belonged to her family, and she had spent the preceding years—and no doubt a lot of family deutsche marks—restoring the castle from extensive World War II bomb damage, which had left it crumbling and ruined. Grey had met her at an official reception someplace. She had liked him. He was looking for a place to live. And the castle had a separate apartment within its walls.

It was while he lived in the castle that Grey met Margret, the beautiful young German woman he would eventually marry. In the States on a visit to meet his family, she endeared herself to us when, caught in a sudden rain in downtown Boston, she bought from a street vendor an umbrella that, unfurled, became a huge Red Sox cap.

And so, in 1987, we headed to Germany. The night before the wedding we sat in the immaculate kitchen of Margret's parents, who still lived in the tiny village—population five hundred—where they had grown up, met, married, and raised their two children. Their English was makeshift, and our German was even less than that. Martin, Grey's stepfather, hit it off with Johann, Margret's father, over schnapps; they laughed and clinked glasses and told jokes that no one really understood, though one in which the punch line included the phrase "horse's ass" seemed to leap the barrier. Her mother, Katerina, and I looked on and tried to fill in the linguistic gaps, sometimes with hand gestures. The wedding couple, both of them proficient in both languages, translated now and then, but mostly rolled their eyes at the sight of four middle-aged parents turning tipsy and maudlin.

The next day, dressed in our best, we sat in an ancient Catholic church and watched our children marry each other. The service was formal, in German, and long. I understood nothing of what was being said or sung. My mind wandered and I looked around. Beside me was Martin, who had mentioned casually the night before, in what had become a brief awkward moment, that he was Jewish. Hastily changing the subject, he had talked about leaving college in his freshman year to join the army during World War II. He had described being on Okinawa; the German in-laws-to-be recognized the name and repeated it solemnly: *Okinawa*.

And with that, our conversation had turned to the war years. Johann was younger than Martin, though not by much. "I was waiting to be seventeen," he said in broken English, "so I could join the army and get my gun."

"I was eighteen," Martin told him. "Infantry."

We sat there in silence for a moment.

"We were fools," they agreed, and poured another round. "We were all fools."

"I was just a little girl," I said. "Eight when the war ended and my father came home from the Pacific."

Margret's mother nodded. "I was nine. In this village. The Americans were coming. We were very scared."

We sat silently and gazed through the twilight out into the farmland beyond the narrow winding road that ran past their house. She was remembering, and I was imagining, being so young and so terrified. I recall wondering about the sound of the soldiers marching: their muddy boots, in unison. The rhythm of it.

"They hid us in the—I don't know what you call it." She gestured toward the floor of the kitchen. "Down there."

"The cellar," I told her.

"Yes. When the Americans came toward this village—down this road—they hid us in the cellar. All the village children. The door was closed. It was very dark.

"We were crying," she said. "They had told us the Americans would kill us."

None of us said anything. I was still hearing in my imagination the rhythmic thudding sound of the approaching soldiers, and picturing a dark basement filled with sobbing children. Martin had his forehead resting in his hands. Perhaps he was thinking of Auschwitz. Perhaps Okinawa. Johann sipped his schnapps, shook his head, and stared into the distance.

"When the door opened," Katerina went on, "the light came in slowly, like a"—she demonstrated with her hands: a triangle, a widening wedge of light—"and when I looked up, there in the doorway, in a uniform, was the first black man I had ever seen. There were other men behind him, but it was the black man I saw. He reached into his pocket and I thought he was reaching for his gun.

"I was so frightened I wet my pants." She laughed a little, embarrassed.

"What happened?" I asked.

"He turned to the other soldiers and he said—he said it in English, of course—'*Alle sind Kinder.*'"

I thought I understood the German. "They're all children." She nodded.

"Then from his pocket, he took candy and gave it to us."

I, an agnostic raised a perfunctory Protestant, watched her the next morning, devout and smiling, her lips moving slightly as she followed the familiar words of the German Catholic Mass. Johann's head was bowed. Martin, the nonpracticing Jew, sat silently. Grey, in his USAF dress uniform, and Margret, in billowing white organdy, stood before the altar, their hands clasped.

Near us was the countess, austere and patrician. Her eyes were moist. Grey had become like a son to her.

Suddenly, in the middle of the service, the organist played an introduction, and in a balcony at the back of the ancient church, a woman rose and began to sing in a clear soprano. She sang in English.

Wherever you go I shall go. Wherever you live so shall I live. Your people will be my people.

I found myself, inexplicably, weeping.

Later, back home in the States (my son and his bride by now on their honeymoon in Egypt), I looked around for a Bible. It was not surprising in a house in Cambridge, Massachusetts, that our walls were lined with bookcases. There were three or four shelves of cookbooks alone, and an entire floor-to-ceiling section designated for biographies and memoirs. Fiction was in the living room. Poetry—several shelves of it—was in my office, and nearby was an area that I thought of roughly as "reference"; it included the 1898 Sears catalog that I had found invaluable when I wrote a novel set in 1906. There, wedged in near *Roget's Thesaurus* and *Bartlett's Familiar Quotations*, was a King James Version. I opened it and read the Book of Ruth.

Parts of it felt familiar, and I remembered the days, long ago, when I had been a bored, reluctant Sunday school attendee at the Presbyterian church of my Pennsylvania childhood. The memorized Bible verses. The sweaty, crumpled little envelopes containing coins that I would have preferred to spend at the local dime store. The moralistic handouts filled with stories of worthy children doing good Christian deeds. The felt board! Yes, suddenly I remembered the felt board on which the Sunday school teacher, Miss Moody, adhered flat, poorly shaped illustrations—lions, a boy in a many-colored coat, a dove, maybe a rainbow—while she related Old Testament stories.

Despite its vague familiarity, I don't think Ruth's story made it to the felt board; not much about it would have appealed to children. It was mostly a lot of family chronology—marriages, deaths (so many deaths!), and remarriages—that necessitated traveling, apparently by donkey, and occasionally the acquisition of land. The passage that had so moved me at my son's wedding referred not to a marriage but to the loyalty of a young widow to her beloved mother-in-law. I noted that with interest, reflecting on the fact that "Your people will be my people" had nonetheless applied as well to the joining of two families on that day in Germany when we had set aside our sad histories and rejoiced together for what the future held.

The future held a little girl. My only granddaughter was born, to dual citizenship, five years after the day of the marriage, and by then our families had indeed become each other's people. Language remained a barrier, but all of us tried and we learned to laugh at our mistakes. Once, in a *Gasthaus*, my younger son, Ben, was served the sweet local wine and asked for dry instead. "Dry," he requested, pointing at his glass, and the barmaid brought him three more glasses of the sweet (*Eins. Zwei. Drei.* Of course).

The baby was baptized in the local Catholic church, and all the villagers came, as was their custom. Back in the States, I watched the video my son sent of the ceremony. I was looking at the backs of the congregation, and suddenly I could see them turn to each other, murmuring, when my granddaughter began to cry in her mother's arms as they stood at the baptismal font, and Grey reached over and took her to comfort her.

"What were they saying?" I asked Margret, my daughter-in-law, on the phone. "When Grey took the baby from you, there was quite a stir. But I couldn't make out what they were saying."

She laughed and explained. "They were saying: 'Oh look, that's so American.' A German father would never have done that."

Though I acknowledged that I couldn't speak it, I briefly thought that I could understand German. Once, during a visit, I held my eighteen-month-old granddaughter at the window of their home, looking across the road at a field of recumbent cows with their eyes closed. "*Die Kühe schlafen,*" the little girl said to me, and pointed.

"Yes," I replied, "the cows are sleeping." Then I called to my son: "She said it in German, and I understood!"

He chuckled. "It's pretty easy to understand the obvious . . . just the way you understood at dinner, when she dropped her pacifier from the high chair."

"Mein Schnuller ist kaputt!" she had wailed.

It was only a month after she had commented on the sleeping cows that my granddaughter began the refrain that would break all of our hearts. *"Wo ist mein Papa?"* she asked again and again.

Where is my papa?

I flew to Germany two days after it happened, when the wreckage was still visible from the highway. Doomed by a mechanic's error, his plane had crashed fewer than ten miles from his home. Again I sat in a Catholic church and heard ancient words in another language, this time a funeral Mass. I watched his friends and fellow pilots fly the missing man formation, the aerial tribute to a fallen flier. They had come from all over the world to honor him—one from as far as Korea.

My daughter-in-law sat by my side with her parents. Again, all of us had gathered. After the Mass, at the nearby village cemetery, we watched, listening to a bugler play "Taps," as he was laid to rest near Margret's grandparents. The countess stood there, separate from the villagers, anguished and alone with another unspeakable loss. We were fifty yards from the cellar where a little girl had hidden sobbing as the Americans marched into this town, where she had looked up at a black man who reached into his pocket and gave her candy.

> Your people will be my people. Where you die, I will die, and there I will be buried.

Martin is gone, now. So is the countess. And Margret's parents, Johann and Katerina, are in declining health. It has been twenty-seven years since we shared schnapps and stories, and twenty since we buried my son in a German cemetery near the graves of young men killed on the Russian front. I return several times each year to visit my daughter-in-law and my granddaughter, who speaks four languages and is deep in her studies at a German university. I ponder all of it now, wondering why I am still so moved by the Old Testament words of a young widow who chose to stay by the side of her mother-in-law, to follow her to a strange land.

There is no need, now, for such choices. We are all so connected. E-mail was in its infancy when my granddaughter was, but they are both grown up now. Last summer she e-mailed me, and attached photographs, from Costa Rica, where she was doing volunteer work in a school for troubled boys. She—and they—were for a time "each other's people," making a difference in each other's lives.

In my book *The Giver,* the young boy, Jonas, as he begins to realize the truth about his world, says in surprise: "I thought there was only us. I thought there was only now." It was the great untruth that he had been taught—the one that we are still being taught, the one that some of us are still teaching.

But there is no *only us* in this world anymore. We are no longer separate.

Today's Ruth has no need to leave Moab and her own history behind in order to follow Naomi to Bethlehem, to live and die there. Today they are interconnected. One of my daughters married a Greek Orthodox man, another a Turkish Muslim, all of them combining their histories. The Palestinian boy of today may one day watch his daughter marry the son of an Israeli, and perhaps the parents will clink glasses together and recall the time long ago when they had been enemies.

The American GI who once gave candy to a frightened child probably has grandchildren, or even great-grandchildren; one of them may be a judge in Denver, or a doctor in Botswana, or a teacher in the Bronx. They may have heard him tell the story of the day when he marched into a bombed village and opened the door to a cellar. Or perhaps they don't know that he is connected forever to a *Hausfrau* in a small German town, the same town in which my son rests now. It once seemed a foreign place. But now, to me, it is simply a piece of earth where two families are intertwined and will be, like Ruth and Naomi, forever each other's people.

Why Psalms Is My Favorite Biblical Book

The Book of Psalms

Reverend Al Sharpton

There are many things we might say about the Psalms, but at the very least it should be noted that the Psalms represent the best of what religion has to offer the human experience when the bonds of life are frail, and the coming of night is as immediate as it is real. For inasmuch as we know that the Psalms were written by a multiplicity of writers, we also know that this diversity of authorship endows this, the most poetic book of the Bible, to sing across the spectrum of human emotion—without any regard for premodernist claims about the ruse of reason and the bondage of desire as such. Unlike the rest of the Bible, the Book of Psalms is offered to us without the prerogatives of social pretense as each chapter dares to take the reader into the subjective concerns of the writer. So much so that the internal conversations of the heart are laid bare and extended to us as modern readers with all of the sound and fury that encompasses the unfolding of any life. The Book of Psalms is as lyrical as it is poetic. It is as subjective as it is religious. But perhaps most of all, it stands to bear witness to the truth of life's enduring claim, namely, that the project of being human is an incomplete work and always in a state of flux and motion.

But this is the genius of the book. For no matter what stage of life in which the reader may find himself, the Psalms have something to say about the value of that emotional condition—and attempt to offer us a language by which we might express the unutterable trials and triumphs that none of us can avoid. In fact, you might even say that each chapter is a biopsy of the human condition. That is to suggest that, as the book moves from the courts of David's palace to the unforgiving rivers of Babylon, this great collection of religious verse attempts to audit the painted scenes of a man's or woman's life without the need to make it pretty or idealistic. The Psalms are for real people. Living with real problems. Serving a real God, determined to have real victory over the powers of death, dread, disease, and despair.

For in the case of the Psalms, subjectivity is what authenticity is all about. There is nothing objective about the Psalms. You simply cannot read this book, and expect to understand it, as long as you are unwilling to feel something in the process. Every page is saturated with emotion. Every chapter stands to evoke the living memory of an experience that cuts to the bone, and makes the soul sing in the wee hours of the night. And perhaps there are those who would proffer before the world the idea that religion should be a completely cerebral experience, but the Bible does not condone this approach to God, as, time and time again, we read of David (and many others) crying out to God for relief, or in thanksgiving, but never without the passions that invariably come together to make us children of the living God. And it is here that I would suggest to you that the writers of the Psalms offer to us a foray into the full humanity of every believer—for is it not the case that when a man encounters God, he in fact meets himself for the first time?

This is not to suggest that men and women are divine, but rather that whatever relationship we claim to have with the true and living God will always be mediated through the prism of what ultimately isolates and elevates the stature of our humanity. And this is the great witness of the Psalms. The more we cry out, the more we can be heard. The more we reach, the more we find something to grasp. And the more we weep, the more we experience the power of God to wipe tears from our eyes, and give us morning strength in the evening of our years. The Psalms demonstrate for us what the potential range and power of our being could be like, if we would only free ourselves from the need to be something that we are not. The Psalms give us permission to be free. They give us all the room we need to be as deep and as wide as we really are—without apology, and without the need to compromise the best of who we are just to fit into somebody else's life. Reading the Psalms validates the truth of the believer's emotional existence, as they remind us that we are not uniquely rational creatures. The great misnomers of European attempts at theological anthropology were always rooted in the denigration of our emotive capacities in order to validate the dictates of the mind. But the witness of the Psalms is clear. In order to survive the trials and tribulations of everyday living, we must engage in the defiant act of faith with both head and heart. For even as we hear David, Hezekiah, and Solomon pleading in the pages of the Psalms, we are invariably empowered to summon every inch of our vitality into the great work of loving justice, doing mercy, and walking humbly with our God.

Let us never forget that this book was intended to be the great hymnbook of the nation of Israel—to which they turned when the vicissitudes of life took them beyond the limits of grammatical construction, and into that place buried within the embers of the human spirit where no words abide. This is not simply a book of poetry but a collection of strivings, set to music when the heart is at high tide. You simply cannot understand the power of this marvelous book until you confront the truth that it is first and foremost a collection of songs, refrains, and melodies—for did not Shakespeare remind us, long ago, that music is the language of the soul?

Consequently, it is needless to look for the particular historical circumstances of the Psalms, because their words are set to a rhythm so representative of national sorrow that anyone who knows the tones of personal anguish can understand the source of its creation. In almost every case, these are the words of a recorded life—given to us with obvious reference to the plaintive cry of every believer, who dares to push back the cold and often unfeeling hands of opposition. And whether they are extolling the vindication of a life well lived or seeking relief from the heartbreak of personal demise, the Psalms were written in blood. Or to say the same, this is a music bequeathed to us as a way to communicate what we feel when there are no words to express what we are struggling to say. This is the power of music. For when syntax and grammar cannot comport themselves into emotion, the heart will always reach for melody to create a transcript of that perennial experience best described to us as the will to live.

I am reminded here of the role of the blues in the lexicon of African American religious thought. That is to say, inasmuch as it is the case that the sufferings of black people in America have been acute and seemingly compounded at every stage, it is no less the case that our music maintains such a subversive commitment to joy that the lingering effects of systemic suffering are undermined by its stubbornness. This is the music of the cotton fields and the chain gangs. It is the sound of mothers wailing in the night. It is the hope of the slave and the promise of a new day greeted from afar and with eyes ablaze. For we have always been a musical people. Indeed, the secret to our political and cultural success has always been rooted in the relationship we insisted upon having with the tortured rhythms of our unaccomplished deliverance. And what makes the stated lives of black people so dynamic in this country is directly related to the defiant vitality that forms the base content of our music in every stage of our struggle to be free. Even in my own work, I am keenly aware of the fact that every movement depends almost entirely on the success of its music. From Selma, Alabama, to Ferguson, Missouri, the struggle for equal protection under the law has always been accompanied by the need to mitigate the pain of a promise long denied through the act of turning misery into melody. The old African proverb is right. The Spirit don't come without the beat.

And when you consider the fact that almost every word of the Bible was written under one form of subjugation or another (be it Egyptian, Assyrian, Babylonian, Persian, or Roman oppression), it is no wonder that the Psalms were so central to the lives of the Hebrew people. Over and over again, the New Testament recounts how Jesus extensively quoted the Psalms. Even on the cross, we hear the words of David echoing out of the mouth of Jesus as a way to express the horror of that horrific moment, in the absence of friends, and amid the desperate search for a lyric adept enough to allow his suffering to speak. In fact, I would go so far as to say that you cannot understand the spiritual genius of Jesus without an appreciation of the role the Psalms played in the development of his spiritual life. The Gospel of Matthew crystallizes the matter for us, when it is recorded that, before Jesus went out to the garden of Gethsemane, he gathered his disciples and sang a hymn. And although we may not know what he decided to sing that night, we certainly can surmise that whatever he sang was taken out of this, the great hymnbook of the nation of Israel known to us today as the Book of Psalms.

But there is something else I should like us to consider. The Book of Psalms is soul music. You might even say that the Psalms constitute the first attempt in human record to create a form of music that, while rooted in the existential concerns of a people, did not conveniently sublimate the political aspirations of a nation, or pass them off as mere emotional fodder. It is at this stage of the conversation that I should like to posit before the reader the idea that the Psalms, while emotional, and subjective, are the first music of public protest in a long tradition that would later find its culmination in the descendants of slaves.

Take for instance the words of the 137th Psalm:

By the rivers of Babylon,
There we sat down, yea, we wept
When we remembered Zion.
We hung our harps
Upon the willows in the midst of it.

For there those who carried us away captive asked of us a song,
And those who plundered us requested mirth,
Saying, "Sing us one of the songs of Zion!"
How shall we sing the Lord's song
In a foreign land?
If I forget you, O Jerusalem,
Let my right hand forget its skill!
If I do not remember you,
Let my tongue cling to the roof of my mouth—
If I do not exalt Jerusalem
Above my chief joy.
Remember, O Lord, against the sons of Edom
The day of Jerusalem,
Who said, "Raze it, raze it,
To its very foundation!"
O daughter of Babylon, who are to be destroyed,
Happy the one who repays you as you have served us!
Happy the one who takes and dashes
Your little ones against the rock!

Contrary to what some might believe, this psalm is not a lamentation cataloging the vices of Babylonian oppression; it is rather a song of resistance that begins with the determination not to drown in silence (even in the presence of mocking ears) and ends with a vision of the destruction of Israel's enemies. And while modern audiences may not condone the fratricidal murder of children, it should not be missed that the writing of this psalm constitutes an act of blatant resistance. The writer longs for the death of his enemies, but only tangentially, because it will result in the end of his oppression. The real concern of this psalm has nothing to do with murder, but everything to do with freedom, and the restoration of Israel's dignity at a time when all hope was gone—and not a stone lay upon a stone. Let us be clear. I am suggesting here that, amid the threatening dangers and inverted petitions of this oppressed people, there arose among the children of the Red Sea experience the voice of a psalmist who wanted not just the dissolution of the gates of spiritual death—but, more important, an end to the political disenfranchisement of an entire people.

The 137th Psalm is a rich record of the will required of anyone who dares to respond, in public space, to the systemic forces of evil active in any age. The producers of modern compositions would do well to remember that music is as political as it is artistic, because, at its best, art is never neutral, or disinterested in the conspiring circumstances of the artist out of whom it was born. The time has come for our generation to move beyond the sedentary concerns of cosmetic beauty and crude physicality—to take up the great questions of our era. Even in the church, the kind of music we hear today makes no statement against the systemic forces that seek to lock generations of our people into endless cycles of grinding poverty with no relief in sight. But this is not the tradition of the Psalms. The Book of Psalms has something to say about the work of evildoers who mock the humanity of the people of God. The Book of Psalms has something to say to the evil empires of grain that exist to lay waste to the promises of God spoken to us in the whispers of peace and love. Martin King said it best—there comes a time in the unfolding of every life when silence is a betrayal.

Whether we like it or not, we are living at a time in human history when questions of war and peace, reproductive rights, racial justice, democratic policing, and wealth inequality continue to vex, if not jeopardize, the promise of full equality in America—and in the face of all that, our music cannot be objectively silent. We owe it to generations yet to be born to find our voice, and add our song to the great witness of biblical psalmists who used the full measure of their artistic gifts to create a music that would sing beyond its season.

Finally, let me say a personal word about the Book of Psalms. Recently I celebrated my sixtieth birthday amid a host of friends and well-wishers; and, as I stood there taking in the moment, I couldn't help but think of my mother (who has now gone home to be with the Lord) and how she taught me to find strength in those enduring words "weeping may endure for a night, but joy cometh in the morning."

I stood there that night remembering what the Psalms meant to her, and to our family after the winter of our legitimate discontent had finally set in. I realize, now more than ever, that I have become the man I am today in no small measure because of this book's ability to provide a soothing place against which I continue to gauge the advancing cause of my life. Just like the writers of the Psalms, I have had several rendezvous with change. But for me the saving grace has always been the truth that, while I was yet forming in the morning of my years, I found in the fading pages of the Psalms a wisdom that has kept me rooted in the power of a tradition so much greater than myself. Even now, the memories of the time I spent at the Bethany Baptist Church, hearing William Augustus Jones preach from the wisdom of the Psalms, are made sweet by the chasm of the years, which invariably rush back to me whenever I find myself on the front lines fighting for the rights of others. And if there is one thing I know for sure, it is this. Leadership is a lonely road set to consume the traveler unless he has found within the resources of his inner life a voice to lead him through the uncertain hours of the night. And it doesn't matter where I have found myself, be it marching amid the jeers of an angry mob in Howard Beach, or in a Puerto Rican prison protesting the bombing of Vieques Island, or even being wheeled into surgery after having been stabbed for standing up for what I believe, the godly sorrow of the Psalms has been my constant companion through it all.

And now, as I look over the fifty-six years that I have been a preacher of the Gospel of Jesus Christ, it remains clear to me that there has been no abidingness in my life like the constant and comforting words that ring up from the pages of this book like the countenance of an old familiar friend. I, too, sing the Psalms. And have made them the source of my strength in whatever struggles my work may lead me in. It is my prayer that, as emerging generations meet the challenges that are sure to come, they will do so armed with the great spiritual resources that lifted a people out of slavery, and made a black man the president of the United States. I, too, sing the Psalms. And I sing them because I know that the same God that lifted David out of a cave, and put a crown on his head, is still able to lift children out of poverty, and move mountains out of the minds of broken people. I, too, sing the Psalms. And I will sing them until justice rolls down like waters—and righteousness like a mighty stream.

No justice. No peace.

A Reading of the Shepherd's Psalm

Psalm 23

Lydia Davis

Once you have heard the Psalm of David a few times—or, more likely, many times, since this very popular and moving poem, or fragments of it, regularly recurs in movies, TV shows, songs—you tend to remember it, or at least isolated lines from it. Of all the many translations that exist, however, it is the King James Version that is so memorable and so often quoted. The very first verse, with its four strong beats, is the first that remains engraved on our memory:

The Lord is my shepherd; I shall not want.

One source of its power is probably the immediate homely domestic or animal imagery—the introduction of the extended analogy that will follow: the Lord compared to the shepherd and the *I* of the poem compared to a sheep within a flock. Another source of the power of the line is its mostly monosyllabic, Anglo-Saxon vocabulary: *lord, shepherd, want*. Every word, in fact, is Anglo-Saxon, and every word is monosyllabic except for *shepherd*. The meter is initially the dancing amphibrachic (unstressed, stressed, unstressed; the meter of the limerick: "There once was/ a girl from/ Nantucket"; as well as other kinds of poems: "How dear to/ my heart are/ the scenes of/ my childhood"), which then slows to the walking iambic.

Want is a strong word, though with a different meaning from the one we usually give it today, the same meaning as in the sensible alliterative maxim "waste not, want not"—if you are careful with what you have, you will never lack for what you need.

The plainness of the statement is further strengthened by the four-monosyllable negative: *I shall not want*. Contrast this KJV version with the Good News Translation: "The Lord is my shepherd; I have everything I need": the meanings are not quite the same, for one thing, but for another, whereas "I shall not want" suggests a modest sufficiency, "I have everything I need" suggests covetousness, a desire for material things, and (in the repetition of *I*) a preoccupation with self. The emphasis in this version is on *have* and *need, I,* and *I,* as opposed to the KJV double negative meaning not lack.

The extended metaphor of shepherd and flock continues in the second verse:

> He maketh me to lie down in green pastures: he leadeth me beside the still waters.

This verse, too, is pleasingly constructed, almost perfectly symmetrical—in fact, the beginning and end of each of the parts is symmetrical: *He maketh me . . . green pastures: he leadeth me . . . still waters.*

In this verse, I puzzle over a couple of things: the many flocks of sheep I have seen over the years grazing in various pastures, here in upstate New York, or across the road from where my old school friend lives in the Cotswolds outside Bath, England, or as seen from the train in the Scottish countryside, are without a shepherd and seem to decide when they wish to lie down and when they prefer to be up on their feet grazing. However, one of the many dedicated, anonymous commentators on the various websites that invite reactions to this psalm says, many times over, that sheep are stupid and, further, that they need to be made to lie down. (Contrast this with the clear declaration of an online sheepherding manual, which implies at least one kind of intelligence: "Sheep have excellent memories." I have read elsewhere—where and when I no longer remember—that a sheep can recognize the face of another sheep for as long as two years.) Perhaps one of the other translations, the nineteenth-century Young's Literal, employing a gentler or more indirect verb, is closer to reality here: "He causeth me to lie down"—in other words, he brings it about indirectly, by simply providing the pasture.

On the other hand, another of these website commentators offers—whether from personal experience or sound scholarship, or neither—the startling idea that if a lamb strayed too often from a flock, the shepherd might break one of its legs so that it would remain lying down in the pasture. I have not heard of this before, and I can't imagine that the psalmist had this in mind.

Yet another commentator asserts that sheep are afraid of moving water and will drink only from quiet water. A picture I have in my mind, from a farm not far from where I live, is of a small, still pond with a single file of six or eight sheep on the far side of it walking calmly, as though in a dream, along the water's edge toward another field. The water was still—though they did not happen to be drinking from it; they were walking past it of their own accord, not led or driven.

Certainly it is true, however, that green pastures and still waters together create the image of a harmonious, fertile, and safe landscape in which sheep may flourish.

The parallel structure is continued in the next verse, which has two parts, like the preceding verse and the first verse, and each of the two parts opens with *he* and a verb. The second verb, *leadeth,* is in fact the same as the second verb in the preceding verse, and this repetition reinforces for us the idea of the shepherd as guide: first leading the sheep beside the still waters, now leading the sheep in the paths of righteousness. The interaction between *he*—the Lord—and *I*—the sheep—continues, though the sheep-ness of the I is abandoned in the first part—"He restoreth my soul"—and in the second part is sustained only by two words, *leadeth* and the strong and important (in sheep rearing): *paths*.

> He restoreth my soul: he leadeth me in the paths of righteousness for his name's sake.

In this verse, the two parts of the sentence are separated by a colon rather than a period or a semicolon, and this change of punctuation creates a change of relationship between the two parts. Whereas the period and the semicolon signaled that the two parts of the verse were equal, syntactically, the colon signals to us that the second part follows from the first and explains it: evidently, what the author of this psalm *means* by "he restoreth my soul" is that "he leadeth me in the paths of righteousness for his name's sake." The use of a colon in the previous verse, to separate two apparently equal and equivalent statements, is more puzzling.

With the third verse, then, we are moving away from the shepherd-sheep metaphor and into the more explicit message concerning the Lord's spiritual guidance and our salvation.

Now, in the fourth verse, we come to another very famous part of the psalm and also to an interesting shift in person. The psalm up to this point has been narrated in the third and first persons: *The Lord* and *he* interact with *me* and *my*. Now, although the *I* is retained, the *he* is addressed directly and personally as *you*, or, in the KJV, the familiar *thou*.

> Yea, though I walk through the valley of the shadow of death, I will fear no evil: for thou art with me; thy rod and thy staff they comfort me.

This shift could be read as an emotional one: the speaker has been objectively describing a situation, how the Lord interacts with him; now, overcome with the emotion of this relationship, he—if it is a "he"—directly addresses the Lord, in gratitude, perhaps.

The explanation could also be that the two parts of the psalm—the first three verses and the last three verses—were composed by different hands.

This fourth verse is perhaps the emotional heart of the psalm, strong though the first verse is; longer, more dramatic than the other verses, it is certainly climactic both rhetorically and imagistically. It may be this verse that has made the psalm so memorable to so many believers, and nonbelievers, especially in times of fear or crisis, its phrases being so charged with emotion: "the valley of the shadow of death," "fear no evil," "thou art with me," "comfort me."

It is this verse that I think about when I am contemplating the importance of translation and, more generally, the importance of the effect of the beauty of the King James Version in conveying the spiritual messages contained within many of the most eloquent passages of the Bible.

Would this verse have the same emotional effect if it had been known first, or only, in any of the other available translations?

> Even when I walk through a valley of deep darkness;
> even though I walk through the darkest valley;
> even when I go through the darkest valley;
> even when I must walk through the darkest valley;
> even if I shall walk in the valleys of the shadows of death;

And then Young's Literal, which claims to be the closest to the original—though it does not claim to be the most eloquent and is sometimes impossible to understand:

> also—when I walk in a valley of death-shade.

I can't compare any of these to the original Hebrew, although evidently Young's Literal should be reasonably close, but I do prefer the KJV, again.

It is rhetorically, or stylistically, different from the preceding verses: it begins with an exclamation—"yea"—followed by a dependent clause—"though I walk," in contrast to all the other sentences so far, which have employed a plainer, more direct subject-verb construction.

Yea is not the same in meaning as *even,* the favorite choice of the other translations. Although the word, or at least this spelling, often appears incorrectly in student writing when the author really intends *yeah,* or even the cheer *yay,* it actually means, most simply, yes, as in the phrase "yea or nay"—yes or no. But in some contexts, including this one, it means indeed or truly: "Indeed, though I walk in the valley . . ." And since *though,* here, is ambiguous, meaning either although or even when, the verse may be understood to begin "Truly, even when I walk in the valley . . ." And notice the comma after *yea,* an important pause. The translator is writing *indeed* or *truly* and asking us to pause and prepare ourselves for what will follow. And what will follow is highly dramatic: we are very concretely and suddenly walking through a valley—to continue the sheep and sheepherding imagery—and it lies in shadow, and the shadow is cast by death itself.

Now, this is a phrase I have always found very powerful: "in the valley of the shadow of death." Is it awkward, or not? Is it more, or less, effective writing to repeat the *of*? I vote for more effective, for reasons of both imagery and rhythm: in this translation, the verse unfolds part by part to reveal the image, the valley coming first, the shadow second, and death, climactically, last. Any compression, or economy, I think, takes away from this gradually developing image—any compression such as "darkest valley," "valley of deep darkness" (which, besides the compression, contains an awkward alliteration), or even "valley of death's shadow." To my ear, the repetition of the two *of* phrases creates a strong and pleasing rhythm—and an accumulation of menace, *shadow* being followed by *death.*

The image of the valley, with its unfolding darkness and its repeated phrases, is then followed by the very brief and succinct statement, so strong by contrast: "I will fear no evil." This clause, in turn, is followed by a colon, again signaling that what follows will explain or interpret what came before—"I will fear no evil" *because* "thou art with me" and, after the semicolon—indicating an equivalent statement—"thy rod and thy staff they comfort me." Here, we return to the sheepherding imagery, though it is not at first apparent to me why the shepherd's traditional single staff has been doubled by the rod.

Shepherds have traditionally carried what we normally call crooks—they are staffs, or staves, that serve as walking sticks but also have a hooked end useful for catching hold of the neck or leg of a lamb or ewe or ram that has got caught in an inaccessible, perhaps brambly place, or simply for guiding it along into the correct path or direction, or restraining it for any one of many purposes. The crooked end, I learned at one point, is also useful for hurling clods of earth at recalcitrant sheep to get them moving. But perhaps the ancient biblical shepherds, and others, too, carried a rod as well as a staff. In early medieval illustrations, shepherds are depicted carrying only a sort of cudgel. Perhaps the rod referred to in this psalm was a stout stick or club for fending off predators or even disciplining wayward sheep.

In this context, however, since both the rod and the staff "comfort" the sheep, the rod would be for protecting, not disciplining, the sheep and the staff for gently guiding them.

The penultimate verse seems to desert the sheepherding metaphor:

> Thou preparest a table before me in the presence of mine enemies: thou anointest my head with oil; my cup runneth over.

One commentator, however, ingeniously defends the idea that the metaphor has not actually been abandoned, since, he maintains, it was an ancient practice, in at least one sheepherding culture, to lay out feed for the sheep on low stone tables. Similarly, the anointing of the head, he posits, was possibly the administering of a protective medical treatment to the sheep.

Structurally, the elegance of the prose style is maintained with the alliteration of the *pr*'s in the first clause—*preparest* and *presence*; the parallel structure of "Thou preparest" and "thou anointest"; and the harmony of the set of three clauses—three statements—within the one sentence, the clauses becoming progressively shorter.

The colon suggests that the second and third statements, the anointing and the cup overflowing, describe events that take place as part of the dinner.

The last clause returns us from the second-person address ("thou") to the third-person narration ("the Lord"):

> Surely goodness and mercy shall follow me all the days of my life: and I will dwell in the house of the Lord for ever.

Here, the opening *Surely* echoes the earlier opening *Yea*, creating another parallel within the six verses of the psalm—both *Yea* and *Surely* being adverbs of intensification, as opposed to the openings of the first three verses and the fifth, which are subject-verb pairs. Adding to the eloquence of this final stanza, I hear the alliteration in *follow* and *life*, though it is subtle; I hear the alliteration also in *dwell* and *Lord*, and *Surely* and *shall*, and the assonance in *life* and *I*. Quiet though these echoes are, they effectively bind these closing statements together and strengthen their emotional impact.

Besides the positive emphasis of the opening *Surely*, and the alliteration and assonance, this last verse gains further force from its return to a mainly Anglo-Saxon vocabulary, as in the opening line. (Only *surely* and *mercy* are Latinate.)

Here, the colon is ambiguous, because of the *and* that follows it: the colon appears to introduce what follows, as an extension of the statement, but the *and* implies something else—that the second part of the sentence provides new and different material.

As for the extended sheepherding metaphor, though it would seem to have been definitively left behind in this final sentence, the same determined commentator who found a husbandry reference in "preparing a table" made an interpretive reach and chose to see "goodness" and "mercy" as, just possibly . . . two kindly and watchful sheepdogs.

Guilty Feet Have Got No Rhythm

Psalm 139

James Parker

It's the climactic sequence, the beautifully scored fruits-of-chaos crescendo of Martin Scorsese's mobster opera *Goodfellas*. Henry Hill, played by Ray Liotta, is at the wheel of his car, in the sweatiest spiral of a cocaine binge, driving with desperate, spurious urgency from drug deal to gun deal to hospital to his own kitchen, where—at eleven in the morning—sauce is already being simmered and stirred and meatballs braised for the evening meal. He's a wreck. Daylight is hurting him: snoring pores, sore-looking eyes. He keeps leaning over the wheel and squinting up at the sky—there's a helicopter up there, dangling in the clear blue. Police? Is it following him? Ahead of him? Is he under surveillance? Weaving in and out of the soundtrack, meanwhile, between dislocated surges of George Harrison, the Who, and the Rolling Stones—Scorsese's nervous jukebox—is Harry Nilsson's looping, clanky-funky "Jump into the Fire": "You can climb a mountain, you can swim the sea/ You can jump into the fire, but you'll never be free." The bass line bulges like a dragon's egg, the chorus is a wordless gyre: "Ah-aah-aah-ah-aaaah . . ." Henry Hill, with livid eyes, keeps checking the sky.

If I ascend up into heaven, thou art there: if I make my bed in hell, behold, thou art there. Psalm 139 is the psalm of no escape. It is the psalm of being known, seen, scanned, X-rayed, understood—of jumping into the fire and still not being free. Henry Hill gets busted, of course. Night falls on his day of frenzy, the evening meal is served and consumed, and pulling (again) out of his driveway he hears *"Freeze!"* Cops are all over the street. Zero-degree pulses of blue light. He has made, you might say, a metaphysical error. He thought that justice was transcendent—the chopper in the sky—but it turned out to be immanent: the gun behind his left ear. *Yea, the darkness hideth not from thee; but the night shineth as the day: the darkness and the light are both alike to thee.*

Twenty years ago, when I was a young man living in London, the notion of being understood by God would never have entered my head. Not that I was particularly worldly or secular, or even rational; in fact I had a strong interest in the superreality of universal love as it had been revealed to me, in clubs and warehouses and fields full of laser beams, by the drug Ecstasy. We were all doing it, all drugging and dancing, wobbling through the disco smoke with weird fraternal ardor, sharing numinous moments and shivery musicopharmacological expansions of the spirit, chastely embracing one another and then floating homeward in the dawn, innocent, wrecked, pale, babbling, on the top decks of red buses. But I wasn't religious. Certainly not. The Catholicism into which I was born, and in which I had to some extent been educated, had fallen off quite naturally and noiselessly in my teens—a cultural accident, a mere excrescence of my upbringing—and nothing had replaced it. (Amazing to me now, the ease with which that happened.) So I loomed across the dance floor, prickling and raving and reveling, praising creation in my marrow and telling strangers that I loved them—and meaning it, too—without once relating these uncontrollably glad intuitions to the possibility of a divine source. The night shone as the day, and God was nowhere in it. We did other drugs, too—acid, speed—but ecstasy was the sacrament. A miracle cure for Englishness: for repression, class division, cold hearts and nondancing. "Guilty feet have got no rhythm," George Michael once sang. Just in time, I'd chemically fixed my guilty feet.

And then, to use that most trenchant phrase, I lost the plot. I cracked up, I went down. Two days after a minor drug-based scrape with the police, riding the Underground on my way home from having dinner with my parents, I stared at the man in the seat opposite mine and saw his face distend horribly, demonically, the eyes converging and the jaw shifting until he resembled an enormous and somewhat sickened ferret. A ferret with vertigo, perhaps. Ten minutes later, on the street, on the surface, I was conscious of a sort of catastrophic removal or abandonment: I seemed to travel a short but interstellar distance, dropping out of the ether that—I realized only in the instant of leaving it—had been sustaining me my whole life, and into a new and unfamiliar element. Henceforward the things of the world would be in a continual state of departure, telescoping away from me. Something was wrong with my eyes. Something was wrong with my brain. My relation to the universe had been altered—broken, as I felt. Like Humpty Dumpty, like the baby in the treetop, like Lucifer, son of the morning, I had fallen.

Is a panic attack a religious experience? In the sense that it orients us—abruptly, radically, and terrifyingly—to the abyss of existence and the mystery of our origins, I think it is. I didn't think so at the time, mind you. At the time I just thought I was going insane. Public transport had become a special nightmare. On another Tube train, a crowded one, I observed with horrid clairvoyance the bulbed and separated consciousness of every single passenger, each sealed mental world swaying balloon-like on its brain stem, the membrane transparent but impermeable, gently bumping against its neighbor. Poor humans! What a condition, what isolation! The train howled and sagged in its tunnel; I howled and sagged in mine. On a bus one night I felt myself overwhelmed by an inner river of psychic blackness—of glittering, slowly surging Jungian sludge. It had a physical presence, this stuff; it nearly sludged me off my seat. Lovely everyday life, moving busily and horizontally through time, was lost to me: I lived in a kind of frozen verticality, exposed at all times to the up, the down, the Ultimate. I was Henry Hill, in a way, peering green-faced through broken panes of perspiration, fearing the distant rage of the police chopper. These were panic attacks, and I classified them as such: neurological events, mere cerebral misfires—symptoms of my disorder, whatever it was, depression or too many drugs or . . . I wasn't a mystic; I'd just fried out my serotonin.

I tell this story, I suppose, in an effort to establish my credentials. Not with you, patient reader—too late for that—but with the psalmist. With the author, whoever he is (and I've done just enough reading to satisfy myself that nobody has a clue), of this terrifying and consoling poem-encephalogram: Psalm 139. Because as I stumble out of my life to meet him on the ground of this ancient text, as I read these words that spike and plunge with his personal Bronze Age brain jags, I want him to know that I've been there. I must have been there, mustn't I, or somewhere round there—why else would he be speaking to me? His voice is harsh, his voice is other; but so is mine to him. I never raised my heavy metal harp to God in the desert; but he never lost his mind on the London Underground.

O lord, thou hast searched me, and known me. Thou knowest my down-sitting and mine uprising, thou understandest my thought afar off. Thou compassest my path and my lying down, and art acquainted with all my ways. "It is a joy to be hidden," wrote the psychologist D. W. Winnicott, "but a disaster not to be found." Life searches us, searches us out thoroughly—probes and tests and sounds us. We can rely on life to do that. But God *knows* us. Isn't this the true sting of mortification in our most secret shames, in our best-hidden private places—the feeling that there, especially there, we cannot be alone? That shame, that shrinking, that disappearance of light: the soul has its back to God. Could it only turn around . . . But this is pious imagery. I'm beginning to sermonize. I mustn't do that. The psalmist doesn't sermonize. The psalmist makes his report.

Whither shall I go from thy spirit? or whither shall I flee from thy presence? If I ascend up into heaven, thou art there: if I make my bed in hell, behold, thou art there. If I take the wings of the morning, and dwell in the uttermost parts of the sea; Even there shall thy hand lead me, and thy right hand shall hold me. Anxiety is bottomless. If there was a bottom to it, it would be something else: a hypothesis, perhaps. So anxiety has no floor. Down and down it goes, like the Great Glass Elevator in reverse, cabled with individual daily dreads that finally open out into the last incurable dread, which is existence itself. And at that point, little ego, you're screwed. At that point, you turn to God. Not for help, necessarily, but out of a clear apprehension, a simple recognition—as you twizzle and twirl in the gulf of Being with Harry Nilsson singing his vertiginous chorus: "Ah-aah-aah-ah-aaaah . . ."—that this is just too much, too much, for you, for anyone, beyond human capacity. The too-muchness, in other words, points you right into the Absolute. The heart of light. Where, paradoxically, you come to rest. This is not theology, I should say, or philosophy, because I'm quite sure I have no aptitude for either. This is my experience.

You'll notice that I'm ignoring utterly the beauty of the biblical language here, the flower of Jacobean England, et cetera, et cetera. It's because I must listen to what the psalmist has to say. I must attend to this extraordinary terrifying/consoling vision of cosmic intimacy that he is laying out. *For thou hast possessed my reins: thou hast covered me in my mother's womb. I will praise thee; for I am fearfully and wonderfully made: marvellous are thy works; and that my soul knoweth right well. My substance was not hid from thee, when I was made in secret, and curiously wrought in the lowest parts of the earth.* "Possessed my reins"—I see strings of umbilical cartilage when I read that. Taut, twanging cords, uterine tethers, organic tension. "God has me on a pretty short leash," a wise and gentle monk once told me. "You, he lets you run around a bit." But not that much. It's consoling because we are held and cherished; we are attached, we are loved, impossible as that is to believe. It is terrifying, stifling, nausea-inducing, because we are surrounded. We are prevented, in the Latinate sense that Eliot uses the word in "East Coker": "the absolute paternal care/ That will not leave us, but prevents us everywhere." It goes before us; it has seen us coming. Thwop-thwop-thwop, says the police chopper overhead. *Thou understandest my thought afar off.* The psalmist, unlike me, never fears for his sanity; he hurls himself to the limits of his consciousness, and then he picks up his heavy metal harp and sings a song of praise.

Or vituperation. Because in the almost-last lines of Psalm 139, out of nowhere, the psalmist lets rip with one of his disfiguring blasts of spleen: *Surely thou wilt slay the wicked, O God: depart from me therefore, ye bloody men. For they speak against thee wickedly, and thine enemies take thy name in vain. Do not I hate them, O Lord, that hate thee? and am not I grieved with those that rise up against thee? I hate them with perfect hatred: I count them mine enemies.* What just happened? The *Ipsum Esse* has become a common or garden-variety avenging deity. How did we go from cosmic obstetrics to this petty wrath and fist shaking? Mood swings like this occur throughout the Book of Psalms: I will adore you, O Lord, and all your works, and then I will call in a divine air strike upon my neighbor. Bereave him, Lord, madden him, kill his dog and burn his tongue to a stump. Such sudden changes in tone are supposedly troubling to us moderns, although in reality I think we understand them very well. "I hate them with perfect hatred"—that's hard-core, that's our language. A scouring, visionary, instantaneous hatred. Loyal always to the crude current of his feeling, the psalmist has abruptly remembered that the world is full of trolls—of snipers and hecklers and hackers and stalkers and phishers and profaners and idolaters. And so like Kurt Cobain he stamps on his distortion pedal, makes a bipolar quiet-to-loud shift, and lets us feel it, too.

Search me, O God, and know my heart: try me, and know my thoughts: And see if there be any wicked way in me, and lead me in the way everlasting. We return, for the conclusion, to our theme. "Prayer really is the lowest form of literature," writes the poet Don Paterson, in disgust. "Desire and flattery are nowhere sung so nakedly." He might be right, inasmuch as the impulse to pray is essentially preliterary. It's a blurt, a gawp; it's Caedmon looking at his cows in Northumbria and feeling a strange syllable of praise swell within him. And the nakedness is not in doubt; the psalmist is stripped bare before God and before his own emotions. But I don't hear flattery. The dedicatee of Psalm 139 is not flattered: the God who takes possession, the God of the panic attack. Henry Hill, at the end of *Goodfellas,* goes into the Witness Protection Program: a half-life, a little purgatory. My own small crackup, plot-losing, gift of descent was a long time ago. I've been around since then, and I've seen some things. Monks and homeless men keep the same hours, did you know that? Up at dawn, muttering, smoking, praying, looking for coffee; limbering up, squaring up again to him—to the God who, every day, with open arms, backs them into a corner.

The Song of Songs

The Song of Solomon

Pico Iyer

Father Cyprian was serving me and two other friends a simple dinner in his cell. The sun had been burning on the ocean down below, and the slopes of pampas grass across the eight-hundred-acre property turned gold when the last light caught them. Now we were under a canopy of stars—the winking lights of planes tracing patterns between them—as he tossed a glistening salad in a bowl and served us sweet apple juice, given by a friend of the monastery, in tumblers.

"So, Pico, what are you up to?" he asked, my friend for almost all the twenty-three years I'd been coming to the place, though only recently made prior. Cyprian is a lover of India and travel, a professional musician and a burning mystic, direct and undistracted as an arrow on fire.

"Well," I said, a bit embarrassed to be saying this to a priest—I'm not even a member of the Judeo-Christian tradition—"I'm working on, well, actually, on the Song of Songs."

"Right on!" cried the father, his whole face lighting up. Without another word, he jumped up from his chair and went across to put on a CD; chords began rising up around us. "If I had to listen to just one piece of music in the world," he said, returning to sit on the floor around our small table, "it would be this. Look! I have my Bible open to the lyrics."

It was a piece of music composed by Palestrina, voices going up and up as the song cries, "Rise up." It used to be said, my old friend explained, that the sixteenth-century Italian had written the piece at a time when the Church wanted to ban harmonies, because they blurred the meaning of holy words. Palestrina had found a way to deploy overlapping lines so the voices could come in on top of one another, chiming, even as the meaning of every word was crystalline.

It seemed—even if this was no longer believed—a perfect accompaniment to a song that is itself a kind of chorus, a harmony of intertwining voices, all coming together to sing of love and sometime loss.

"The Song of Songs was the most written-about book in the Bible, by the ancient Christian Fathers," Father Cyprian went on, still visibly aflame. "For the rabbis, it was not just the Song of Songs, but the Holy of Holies. Because it told the story of Israel, and the marriage of God and Jerusalem. And then, for many Christians, of course, it sang about the courtship of Christ and the Church. But later, for the mystics, it sang about God and the individual soul. Bernard of Clairvaux wrote eighty-six sermons about the Song of Songs."

Cyprian looked across at me, and I caught a little fire by contagion. "Sorry for the deluge," he said. "You really put a nickel in my jukebox."

It comes like a thunderbolt, streaming light. No one knows who wrote it, or when; it exists without a context, its date placed, not very helpfully, sometime between the tenth century before Christ and the second. The other books of the Bible are all called Books; this is the only Song, whether it's referred to as the Song of Songs or the Song of Solomon (who's mentioned briefly in its third canticle). The New Testament, of course, is alight with Gospels and Letters; but this is a sudden cry in the middle of a crowded temple, at the time of harvesting, summoning us outdoors.

> "Rise up, my love, my fair one, and come away. For, lo, the winter is past, the rain is over and gone."

It falls, in my Bible, between the wise verses of Ecclesiastes and the prophecies of Isaiah, like an interlude. It's one of the shortest books in the Bible—only four pages long in my edition, with just eight canticles. There is no story to it, or history, no reference to God; it is unique in the Old Testament for not even mentioning the law, or offering genealogy or explicit parable.

Nobody knows whether it came from one hand or from many, whether it's a single narrative or an anthology. Sometimes it feels like a wall on which someone has inscribed his love, his prayer (there may not be a difference); and someone else, inspired by that, has added his own. Soon there is a mounting firestorm of songs of praise and hallelujahs—though, to the late-arriving newcomer, all of them exist in a kind of vacuum.

> Behold, he cometh leaping upon the mountains, skipping upon the hills.

All we do know, the minute it begins, is that it comes to us as urgently, as without frame or introduction, as a taste of wine, a lover's touch, as April sun. Through enumerating the features of creation, it might almost be teaching us to love it, and to love it, as we love everything, in part for what we cannot understand. It might even, in truth, be teaching us—with its locked gates and inner gardens—how to read the world symbolically; in the midst of a holy book telling the history of humanity and the commandments of God, suddenly there comes an incitation to see all the world as gateway and charged code.

The first real line of the poem announces, "Let him kiss me with the kisses of his mouth"; it's as impatient as your beloved when she throws open the door. And very quickly we're in a landscape of silver and gold, rich with doves and roes, with myrrh and frankincense, with lilies. The scenes and visions that proceed have something of the illumination we might associate with Revelation—"pillars of smoke" and a "tower of ivory"—but always one feels that the spirit that is being reached for is affirmation.

One thing that so stirs me about the Song is that it seems to travel in and out of the day-to-day, as if its singer were going back and forth between her stern admonitions to the "daughters of Zion" and another world, as close as sunlight, that is eternal. You take it in as you might a piece of music, as much for its atmosphere, its cadences—now *allegro*, now *andante*—as for its words. It sings the constant dance of rest and invigoration, inner chamber and outer. The mystery of its composition has the effect of making it feel like a world seen in the round—a wide-angle, Whitman's eye brought to all creation, yet delivered with such intimacy that it really does feel like being in love with the universe (the earthly lover's blessing).

The fact that it keeps switching voices makes it seem a roundelay, a choir of presences that ensures we're never locked within a single heart; and yet the language is as particular as any lover anatomizing the features of his beloved, one by one, as if running his memory down her body. As every reader notices, the Song is as cluttered with proper names—Lebanon, Mount Gilead, the tower of David—as with fig trees and apple trees and cedars and firs.

This all gives it the feeling of reality, not romance or fantasy. And part of its power, for me, is that it never sidesteps the pain or desolation that hide within earthly kinds of love. Returning to the poem one buoyant spring morning recently—the first plum blossoms showing on the bare black branches around me in Japan, against skies of palest blue—I noticed how the singer is "sick of love" (in the King James Version) at the beginning of the poem, replete, with her lover beside her; and "sick of love" toward the end, because she is without her love. Again and again she warns the "daughters of Jerusalem" not to stir up her love before the time is right, to handle such a charge with care.

Belief is a relationship, it might be saying, as intense and palpable as the one we know with someone we can see and touch. In the Beatitudes, those who "do hunger and thirst after righteousness" are among the blessed (and the word *righteous*, I've read one scholar claim, comes from a Greek term referring to a yearning for oneness with God). Revisiting the poem, I think of how lovers, in many a wedding ceremony (one of which sits at the heart of the Song), say, "With my body, I thee worship"—and how Jesus's first miracle would come at a wedding. The Song might be a B-side to the Book of Job, telling us to love creation not because we must, but because we can.

Critics inform us that the narrative moves between the worlds of dream and wakefulness; that sometimes the sense of absence is imagined, as every monk in his cell feels God at moments lost from him. But this speaks to that deeper logic Proust knew, which is that a beloved is never so present to us, never felt and remembered with such vividness and intensity, as when he or she is gone from us. It's only when we lose something, too often, that we realize how we treasure it.

It's not hard to see how the poem sings the tale that many who have given themselves up to God have lived. "Ah! How sweet was that first kiss of Jesus!" wrote Thérèse of Lisieux, upon receiving her first Communion. "It was a kiss of love; I felt that I was loved, and I said: 'I love You, and I give myself to You forever.'" After she surrendered herself to a lifetime of worship, she wrote, "I know, O my God! that the more You want to give, the more You make us desire. I feel in my heart immense desires and it is with confidence I ask You to come and take possession of my soul."

An angel thrust and thrust a golden spear into Teresa of Avila's heart; and when he drew it out, he left her "all on fire with a great love of God. The pain was so great that it made me moan; and yet so surpassing was the sweetness of this excessive pain that I could not wish to be rid of it." She might have been singing, with the Song, "I rose up to open to my beloved."

But every parent knows that the object of one's devotion—what can seem one's life itself—must at some point leave; every lover of God is aware that light cannot be constant, and the sign of true love is that it continues through the dark. I'm often struck by how repeatedly this strain sounds through the New Testament, in the Parable of the Lost Sheep or of the Prodigal Son, in the Parable of the Lost Coin. Seeking is how we keep honest and fresh adoration it would be heresy to take for granted. John of the Cross, in his dark night of the soul, thought of the second verse of the third canticle of the Song.

I love all this because there is almost no human, alive or dead, who does not know the taste of "honey and milk," the transport of losing yourself in something beyond your control, and then, perhaps, of being at a loss through sorrow, the feeling you have lost that which sustains you most. The Song of Songs is the most universal book in the Bible. It lends itself, with its cryptic, suggestive nature, to any number of interpretations, but on its surface it could not be more explicit. One breathes it as much as reads it. And at its end, unusually for the Bible, it leaves a space open for the reader to make complete and real.

When I read it, therefore, I'm back in the domain that Leonard Cohen has made his own, down on his knees, exhaling love songs to a "you" that could be a goddess or his G-d (or, most likely, one grasped through the other). I'm with the Sixth Dalai Lama on the wrong side of the Potala Palace, haunting the taverns of Lhasa and hymning its pretty girls; to this day, Tibetans cherish his poems because they see the sensual, worldly songs as a call to higher devotion. The only way we can begin to approach the love that exists out of time is through the love that doesn't.

Of course—and this, too, is part of the point of the Song—to elide or confuse the two is to play with fire. I recall how Thomas Merton, when first released from the main monastery in Gethsemani to a private hermitage, so he could be alone with God, could not stop scribbling down, from the Book of Wisdom, "When I enter my house, I shall find rest with her, for nothing is bitter in her company; when life is shared with her there is no pain, nothing but pleasure and joy." A little later, he was writing, "I had decided to marry the silence of the forest. The sweet dark warmth of the whole world will have to be my wife." Yet only a year after that, he was writing with even more fervent (though anguished) passion to a twenty-year-old student nurse he'd met while in St. Joseph's Hospital in Louisville for back surgery, and trying to persuade himself (and her) that their love on earth was a reflection of, a gift from, some higher love.

"Love is stern as death," warns the Song of Songs, near its end. "Jealousy is cruel as the grave; the coals thereof are coals of fire, which hath a most vehement flame." Those who most profoundly revere the Song believe that to misread it, to turn it into a literal rhapsody, is to commit a kind of blasphemy and lose your place in Paradise.

Or look at how the great twelfth-century Persian poet Attar (who shares his name with a perfume) writes of a soldier on watch all night, assisted by his sleepless love. "True lovers who wish to surrender themselves to the intoxication of love go apart together. He who has spiritual love holds in his hand the keys of the two worlds. If one is a woman one becomes a man; and if one is a man one becomes a deep ocean."

D. H. Lawrence, Emily Dickinson, Rumi would have known what he was talking about.

The Song of Songs will always be talked about, puzzled over, cherished precisely because it does not give away its secrets; its power lies in its rare mix of sensual immediacy and mystical symbolism. It presents us with the taste of love, unfootnoted—and asks us to unlock the door according to our purity.

In his radiant, charged book on the Sabbath, the great Jewish theologian Abraham Joshua Heschel describes how the seventh day comes as a beautiful bride who graces us with her presence for a few hours. Candles are lit, a meal is prepared, we take care of all our earthly duties, so as to have them behind us. Then the hour "arrives like a guide, and raises our minds above accustomed thoughts." We step outside the calendar, you could say, and into a back street of Eternity. It is, as he points out, "a moment of resurrection of the dormant spirit in our souls."

And at this moment of expectancy and celebration, when we are brought to a peak, of closeness and elevation, some people "chant the greatest of all songs: The Song of Songs." It is, for Heschel, "a chant of love for God, a song of passion, nostalgia and tender apology." The day becomes a time of flame and water. For the early-second-century Rabbi Akiba, it was something even more. "All of time is not as worthy," he wrote, "as the day on which the Song of Songs was given to Israel, for all the songs are holy, but the Song of Songs is the holiest of holies." Just as Cyprian told me: it's how the light gets in.

One spring afternoon, not long ago, I went into a small cinema in Los Angeles and saw Terrence Malick's film *To the Wonder*, named after the haunting image, out of time, that features at the very beginning of the movie, Mont-Saint-Michel, rising from an island in the middle of worldly France like a reminder of something higher. It's an exasperating film, elliptical and private and not very grounded, sparing with plot and character and dialogue. But at some point, as I watched light through the trees and the sun burning on the water, as I saw faces golden in the magic hour so they looked like Botticelli angels and somehow felt—this the director's art—something of the transport one feels when one's in love, and everything seems hallowed, I realized that the film was more or less a faithful director's Song of Songs.

There was plenty of room for doubt in his work, too, for a priest who's lost his God, for disfigurement and betrayal and loneliness. The movie Malick made immediately before, *The Tree of Life*, was an all but explicit modern reenactment of the Book of Job. This might have been his latest visit to an Old Testament landscape (his great work, *Days of Heaven*, replays the story of Sarah and Abraham and the Pharaoh, and even includes a reading from an ancient book for a wedding ceremony). But it is also a richly sensual, rapt, wide-awake celebration of creation.

The Song of Songs is the one book in the Bible that all of us enact, if we're lucky. We may put it in the terms of the Bible or not, but we have tasted what it is to be in the Garden, for a moment, or exiled from it, so raised up by our love that we feel ourselves transfigured and moved to cry, "Rise up."

There are no coincidences when one is in love; everything, it seems, was meant to be. The beloved has just picked up the book that you have just finished reading; the letters in her name turn out to be an anagram of yours. Everything makes sense. It's as if, in that temporarily enhanced, even enchanted state, suddenly one sees the world from on high, and can make out its secret harmonies, the way everything fits together. We see and become the people we always hoped to be.

The sensation seldom lasts, but the moments are important; they show us where we could be the rest of the time. They give us an intimation of some higher home, the way someone may show us a postcard of a cathedral and that card alone becomes the first step toward our going there. The loves that die give us a taste of what it would be to have a love that never dies, encircled forever by something harmonious and singing.

The beauty of the Song of Songs is that it's set in everybody's home, otherwise known as the heart. It's uniquely intimate. The first time I came to the monastery over which Cyprian presides, I realized that all the monks there were at some level lovers. Of course they are all celibate; their lives are as full of drudgery and routine and boredom (of doubt, and self-doubt, I'm sure) as any workers' might be. They're not in the throes of romance but caught up in the hard labor of marriage, a lifelong commitment sealed by solemn vows.

But when they talk to me, they tell me how God won't let them go; he was hunting them from the time they were young boys. Or how they felt this gravitational pull, which they couldn't explain or resist, even if they were going in an opposite direction. One man in his mid-eighties told me he'd simply seen a picture in *Time* magazine, in 1958, and he had come to stay in the hermitage in its first year there—he didn't know how or why the place summoned him so instantly—fifty-five years ago.

We read the other books of the Bible to learn the laws of conduct for believers, to be shown parables of good and evil, to be caught up in whirlwinds that remind us—as in Job—how little stands to human reason. The power of many of them is forbidding, dark, and it gains its force from alienness, the fact we can't understand very much.

The power of the Song of Songs is that everyone can understand it, at some instinctual level, even if every interpretation differs. It is the book that makes life itself—or joy, or even God—embraceable.

The Valley of Dry Bones

Ezekiel 37

Samuel G. Freedman

One Saturday afternoon in 1978, my father asked me to drive him from our home in New Jersey to Kennedy Airport in Queens, from which he was flying abroad on a business trip. I dropped him off at the TWA terminal and got on the Belt Parkway to head back. Almost immediately, though, I rolled to a halt at the tail end of a traffic jam that stretched ahead as far as I could see. I didn't know this part of the city other than its expressways, so while idling in the unmoving mass, I pulled a map out of the glove compartment and looked for alternate routes. It seemed like all I had to do was take the next exit onto Conduit Boulevard and then veer onto Linden Boulevard, which would carry me across Brooklyn toward the Verrazano Narrows Bridge and ultimately back to my evening plans with friends from my newspaper job in Jersey.

Relieved to be rid of the traffic jam, I lead-footed the accelerator and raced along Conduit and onto Linden. Maybe fifty feet ahead of me, I could see a panel van moving at about the same speed, nothing to worry about. Just then, the rear doors were flung open and I saw a pair of arms shove out a woman. For a split second, I registered the scene and the gruesome insight it afforded: a human being could bounce off pavement something like a basketball. Jolted back into the moment, I swerved hard to avoid hitting the woman and nearly ran off the road.

By the time I had righted my car, with my heart and lungs pumping like pistons, I was too far down Linden Boulevard to stop and give help. So I drove up and down the side streets, searching for a cop. There wasn't one to be found.

I did not realize it at the time, but I had just made the acquaintance of the East New York section of Brooklyn. I would not return for more than a decade, until the morning in October 1989 when I rode the subway from Manhattan until I was the last white person aboard and made my tentative, wary way on foot a dozen blocks to Saint Paul Community Baptist Church.

At that point, I was in the very early stages of working on a book about an African American church—so very early, in fact, that I was still trying to choose the right one. I had not come to this topic for particularly religious reasons. I was the secular son of a family of proud, fervent atheists. My parents, though, had been die-hard liberals, devoted to the civil rights movement, and I was fascinated to find out how the black church, as the central institution of that crusade, had adapted to the challenges of the 1980s: white flight, the crack and AIDS epidemics, deindustrialization, Reagan trickle-down economics.

In those maladies, as I soon learned, East New York abounded. The neighborhood's police precinct had tallied nearly a hundred murders that year, and its officers wore T-shirts emblazoned, in grim bravado, THE KILLING FIELDS. East New York had almost always been a neighborhood of the working class and the working poor, but in just a few years of the mid-1960s, aggravated by property crime and alarmed by block-busting real-estate agents, its longtime population of Italians and Jews fled. In their place came blacks, some of them educated and aspirational, some of them welfare cases dumped by city policy into distant neighborhoods. Another city policy of the time went by the deceptively tepid name of "planned shrinkage." It meant, in practical terms, that mayoral administrations believed that nothing could save East New York and the adjacent slum of Brownsville, that any money spent on public services there would be wasted. The cost-effective solution was for East New York and Brownsville to die off and start over from scratch. When Boston's then-mayor Kevin White visited Brownsville in 1968 and beheld its landscape of abandoned buildings, its fields of waist-high weeds and broken bricks, he said that he had seen "the beginning of the end of our civilization." He could just as justifiably have read the first verses from the thirty-seventh chapter of the Book of Ezekiel:

> The hand of the Lord came upon me. He took me out by the spirit of the Lord and set me down in the valley. It was full of bones. He led me all around them; there were very many of them spread over the valley, and they were very dry. He said to me, "O mortal, can these bones live again?" I replied, "O Lord God, only You know." [Jewish Publication Society translation]

I did not know then about the prophet Ezekiel and his vision of the Valley of Dry Bones. Worse, I didn't know that I didn't know. Nothing in my upbringing had imbued me with any familiarity or comfort with Judaism. During Passover when I was probably ten or eleven, my mother took me to visit an elderly relative who happened to be observant. She pointed to her stovetop, covered in aluminum foil. Clearly meaning to toss a precocious child a softball question so she could then pretend to be impressed, the relative asked, "Sammy, do you know why the stove is that way?" I stumbled, completely oblivious to the tradition and requirement of ridding a house of *chametz*, of leavened products, during Passover. "Because it's easier to clean up?" I finally stammered. Taking pity, the old woman gave me a candy anyway. During Hanukkah, we lit our menorah on a Ping-Pong table in the basement, a direct contradiction of the religious injunction that the candles and the miracle they represent be made visible to the outside world. My brief, yearning dalliance with religious practice, when I sought to become a bar mitzvah, ended with the rabbi trying to shake down my father for a bribe. We located another rabbi to perform the ceremony, but the damage had been done. My parents' critique had been ratified. Religion really was, as they always put it, "sectarian and materialistic."

So during high school or college, when an aunt of mine bought me a subscription to *The Jerusalem Post*'s international edition, I had no clue whatsoever why its comic strip was called "Dry Bones." In my early thirties, just a few months before my first visit to Saint Paul, I went to the Broadway opening of August Wilson's masterwork, *Joe Turner's Come and Gone.* The play follows a freed slave named Herald Loomis, who has been captured by a bounty hunter and pressed back into bondage—events, by the way, with historical parallels. Finally liberated, Loomis travels from Tennessee to Pittsburgh in search of the wife from whom he was sundered. In one of the play's most wrenching moments, Loomis falls to the ground, unable to get back to his feet, haunted by a vision of "bones walking on top of the water," then sinking to the bottom of the sea, then being tossed by a great wave onto the land. There is a conjurer named Bynum living in the same boardinghouse as Loomis, and he completes the image: "Everybody's standing and walking toward the road . . . They shaking hands and saying goodbye to each other . . . They walking around here now. Mens. Just like you and me. Come right up out of the water." I understood in that moment that I had witnessed theater at its most transfixing and transformative. I had no idea whatsoever, though, that I had heard August Wilson channeling Ezekiel 37 through the Middle Passage and four centuries of slavery. But August Wilson, who had grown up in church, surely knew these verses:

> And He said to me, "Prophesy over these bones and say to them: O dry bones, hear the word of the Lord! Thus said the Lord God to these bones: I will cause breath to enter you and you shall live again. I will lay sinews upon you, and cover you with flesh, and form skin over you. And I will put breath into you, and you shall live again. And you shall know that I am the Lord!"
>
> I prophesied as I had been commanded. And while I was proph-

> esying, suddenly there was a sound of rattling, and the bones came together, bone to matching bone. I looked, and there were sinews on them, and flesh had grown, and skin had formed over them; but there was no breath in them. Then He said to me, "Prophesy to the breath, prophesy, O mortal!" . . . I prophesied as He commanded me. The breath entered them, and they came to life and stood up on their feet, a vast multitude.

Soon enough, though, I would start to learn.

My first glimpse of Saint Paul shattered my expectations. I had envisioned a black church as a storefront operation straight out of the pages of *Go Tell It on the Mountain*. Saint Paul, to the contrary, had a handsome building of tinted glass and tan bricks, with a sanctuary of soaring cedar beams. The offices had a linked system of desktop computers, a very high-tech arrangement for 1989. The annual budget of nearly $3 million came entirely from the contributions of members. Saint Paul ran everything from a twelve-step program for recovering substance abusers to a rites-of-passage program for teenagers to its own elementary school and credit union. And the revelation for me was that Saint Paul undertook all of these efforts not as forms of public policy or NGO initiative but as acts of doing God's work. There was no border for its people between secular and sacred.

Reverend Doctor Johnny Ray Youngblood, Saint Paul's pastor, had taken its pulpit in 1974, when he was twenty-six and fresh out of divinity school and the congregation had dwindled to eighty-two members in a decrepit building in Brownsville. One of Reverend Youngblood's mentors in ministry had warned him, "You're going to God's Alcatraz." Defying those words, Reverend Youngblood proceeded to build the membership up to five thousand and moved the congregation from Brownsville to a fifteen-year-old former synagogue in East New York.

As I read into the history and theology of the African American church, I came to understand that there were three central biblical texts. One was the Jesus narrative, with Christ interpreted as a radical liberator, a champion of the oppressed. The other two arose from the Hebrew Bible: the Exodus saga, for its obvious parallels to black slavery and emancipation in America, and the social justice prophets, for their fierce critique of the powerful.

For a black minister, Reverend Youngblood was very much a New Testament man. His most penetrating sermons drew upon the Jesus saga. In one that he titled "Christmas in the Raw," he presented baby Jesus as the child of a teenage mother who can't explain how she got pregnant—an eloquent way of having Christianity speak to, rather than reject, all the single mothers in a place like East New York. On Easter morning, Reverend Youngblood preached "Lazarus and the Black Man," in which the resurrection that Jesus performs on Lazarus serves as the metaphor for Christianity uplifting the black men of East New York and Brownsville, so many of them survivors of drug addiction or prison, so many with pasts that made them feel unworthy of church, undeserving of grace.

Yet the prophets also informed Reverend Youngblood's sensibility. He called Luke 4:18 his mission statement, with its admonition "to preach good news to the poor . . . proclaim freedom for the prisoners and recovery of sight for the blind . . . release the oppressed" [NIV]. That verse was an almost verbatim restatement of Isaiah 61:1–2. Several years before my arrival at Saint Paul, Reverend Youngblood had begun working with community organizers from the Industrial Areas Foundation on a plan to build new housing in East New York and Brownsville, to erect tidy, affordable, owner-occupied row houses on the wrecked terrain of "planned shrinkage." The program needed a name, and Reverend Youngblood supplied it. These row houses would be called the Nehemiah Homes, a reference to the prophet who urged the ancient Jews, returning from Babylonian exile, to rebuild the shattered walls of Jerusalem.

If Reverend Youngblood ever preached on Ezekiel 37, I do not recall it. But the Book of Ezekiel makes reference to the disgrace and reproach of Jerusalem's fallen walls, for Ezekiel was also a product of that national calamity. The son of a priestly family, possibly descended from Joshua, Ezekiel was about twenty-five years old when the Babylonians led by Nebuchadnezzar conquered the kingdom of Judah in 597 B.C.E. During the fifth year of exile, Ezekiel received his vision, to be a "watchman for the house of Israel," and he issued prophecies over the next twenty-two years.

To be a prophet in the Old Testament/Hebrew Bible was to be, by definition, a dissident, an outsider, a provocateur, a public scold. It was to castigate society during times of security and prosperity and to blame the victims for their iniquity during times of tragedy. The prophets, as Abraham Joshua Heschel put it, were "some of the most disturbing people who have ever lived." And even by their standards, Ezekiel stuck out as especially eccentric, tilting between periods of illness and paralysis and waves of hallucinatory ecstasy. Drawing on modern psychiatric studies, E. C. Broome diagnosed Ezekiel's behavior as being "consistent with paranoid schizophrenia."

Deluded or not, deranged or not, Ezekiel in his vision of dry bones paints an indelible picture of the Jewish people defeated and exiled, their temple in ruins, their national institutions desolated. These are people, God says through Ezekiel, who cry, "Our bones are dried up, our hope is gone; we are doomed" [JPS 37:11]. Uprooted and oppressed, disoriented and powerless, they might as well be skeletons. Yet even though Ezekiel died in 570, thirty-one years before Babylon fell to the Persians and Cyrus allowed the Jews to return, the prophet foresaw redemption, redemption in the form of resurrection. Through Ezekiel's mouth, God promises, "I am going to open your graves and lift you out of the graves, O my people, and bring you to the land of Israel" [JPS 37:12].

Centuries later, during another Babylonian exile, this one caused by the Roman conquest of Judea and the destruction of the Second Temple, the rabbis of the Talmud debated whether Ezekiel's vision of the resurrection should be taken as literal or symbolic. On the one hand,

Hebrew scripture contains several other direct or implied references to resurrection—by Elijah and Elisha, in the Book of Daniel. On the other hand, by time of the Talmudic era, Christianity had emerged as a distinct religion, and its central, supernatural episode was the resurrection of Jesus. The belief in actual resurrection in real time, not at the End of Days, drew a line between Judaism and Christianity. Over time, Catholic churches came to link Ezekiel 37 to Easter, particularly using it in relation to baptisms conducted on the holy day's eve. Modern Jews, in contrast, clung to the metaphorical power of the vision. Israel's national anthem, "Hatikvah," alludes to Ezekiel 37:11, while inserting one dispositive addition, with its assertion, "Our hope is *not yet* lost" [emphasis mine].

There is, though, a third way to parse Ezekiel. In the Talmud's tractate Sanhedrin, as the sages argue reality versus symbol regarding Ezekiel's vision, Rabbi Judah says, "It was truth; it was a parable." And I found the truth in his seeming oxymoron at Saint Paul Community Baptist Church.

Long before I got there, long before Reverend Youngblood was born, the exiled Africans of the slavery era had begun appropriating the white-supremacist version of Christianity taught by their masters and transmuting it into what we would now call liberation theology. As the minister and scholar Allen Dwight Callahan has written, "The Bible became the medium through which Africans in North America held on to the precious vestiges of otherwise lost cultural patrimony that survived the protracted slaughter of the Middle Passage."

For black Americans, there could be no physical return to an intact physical homeland such as the Jews returning from Babylon enjoyed. Despite the founding of Liberia by freed slaves, Marcus Garvey's back-to-Africa campaign, and the Afrocentricity movement of recent decades, relatively few black Americans have tried to repatriate the way millions of modern Jews have made aliyah to Israel. I vividly remember traveling to Ghana with Reverend Youngblood in late 1990. On our first morning in the capital, Accra, we each had to complete a visitor's form for a government agency. On the line for nationality, Reverend Youngblood wrote, "African-American." The clerk ostentatiously crossed out "African."

Ezekiel's vision of rebirth, restoration, and resurrection, however, mapped itself exactly onto the African American experience, from the Middle Passage to the Cotton Empire, from the Jim Crow South to the northern 'hood. Ezekiel explained why black people felt like no other Americans, more alienated from the nation's ideals, or perhaps more attuned to its hypocrisy, than even the most recent planeload of immigrants by choice. Ezekiel also solaced black Americans with the assurance, in Callahan's phrase, that "the catastrophe of exile did not end Israel's story."

This "canonical narrative," as Henry Louis Gates calls Ezekiel 37, recurs in the spiritual "Dry Bones," in James Weldon Johnson's collection of sermonic poems *God's Trombones*, in Paul Robeson's role as a preacher in Oscar Micheaux's film *Body and Soul*, and, of course, in August Wilson's play *Joe Turner's Come and Gone*. No expression of Ezekiel in the black idiom may be more resonant than the sermon "Dry Bones in the Valley" by the renowned Reverend C. L. Franklin (who is also known as Aretha's father). This version, recorded in Detroit in the mid-1950s, conveys the sense of righteous grievance that would explode in that city barely a decade later with the 1967 riot:

> You see, a city may be one thing to one people, or a country may mean one thing to one people and altogether another thing to another people. When the white Europeans came to this country, embarked upon these shores, America to them was a land of promise, was a mountaintop of possibilities, was a mountaintop of adventure. But to the Negro, when he embarked upon these shores, America to him was a valley: a valley of slave huts, a valley of slavery and oppression, a valley of sorrows.

It was truth; it was a parable. I saw the truth and the parable when that woman got thrown out of the van and there were no police in sight. I saw the truth and the parable during my time at Saint Paul when two students were shot in the hallways of the neighborhood high school. I saw the truth and the parable when the financial manager of Saint Paul, a supremely dignified man named Rochester Blanks, known to the church's children as Uncle Rocky, needed to carry a gun for the block-long walk to a bank branch to deposit Sunday's tithes and offerings.

But all of that served as counterpoint, too, just as C. L. Franklin preached that, even for those in the valley of sorrow, "One of these days the chariot of God will swing low."

On Easter morning in 1990, the day when Reverend Youngblood delivered his sermon "Lazarus and the Black Man," the first of three services began at 6:00 A.M. As I drove toward church in the ashen darkness, I caught sight of the high-rise housing project nearby. So many lights were on, so many lights. I had seen those same yellow pinpricks on other early mornings, weekdays, school days, working days. They gave the evidence of people waking up, showering, getting dressed, eating breakfast, and, to put it another way, rising from the grave.

By now, nearly a quarter century has passed since my first trip to Saint Paul. I still visit at least once a year. That is not as often as I'd like, but it is often enough to take note of each new batch of Nehemiah Homes. East New York has its first full-service supermarket in decades, largely through the efforts of the Industrial Areas Foundation. The church operates a charter school. It helps to recruit black applicants for the New York Police Department. The Seventy-Fifth Precinct recorded 18 murders in 2013, compared to 109 in 1990. Personally, I've become an observant Jew over the years, and when people ask me how it happened, what's the secret, I say that I learned how to be a Jew at a black church.

As for Reverend Youngblood, the closest thing to a prophet I'm ever likely to know, he retired from the Saint Paul pulpit in 2009. Back when I first met him, when he was in his early forties, Reverend Youngblood had promised to step down at age sixty, imagining sixty as pretty darn old. Once he got there, though, he didn't feel so ready for the retirement home he'd bought in Houston. And there was a small, struggling congregation at Mount Pisgah Baptist in Bedford-Stuyvesant that wanted him to become its full-time pastor. So, early in his sixty-first year, he reported to another one of God's Alcatrazes, which is just another way of saying the Valley of Dry Bones, called once more to prophesy.

The Book of Jonah: A Postmodern Exegesis

The Book of Jonah

Daniel Menaker

The first knowledge that ever came unto me of the prophet Jonah, son of Amittai, who be-ith also a prophet in the faith of Islam, btw, was at the camp of boys of my uncle Peter, son of Solomon and Fanny. In the Mountains *called* Berkshireth—I mean Berkshires—where many of camps were of a political hue of pink, yea, even unto red. Peter wath the middle son of Seven, which hath naught to do *with* this. Except that even with the seven fruits of the loins of Solomon and Fanny, they were never lawfully married under the sight of God or even a Justice of the Peace, because lo, they hath believed that marriage wath an oppression of the bourgeois state (yea, IMO not the most foolish *position* about the matter). They also did not know or worship any god, except maybe Karl Marx.

How be-ith it, then, that knowledge of this Famous Book of the Bible, Jonah, hath come upon me at the Camp of Peter? Because I shall tell thee: lo, there were many campfires and group sing-alongs in the lodge, whereat songs *were* sung, loudly and without quiet, as loudly as yea unto the growling of the lion and the bleating of the sheep, but not *as* loudly as quite a few other loud things. And were they not camp songs? Yeth, they were. One of these songs hath remained rooted in my brain as the times tables are also rooted therein, and *with* similar tedium. And lo, yea, and behold, it resideth here:

Who Did Swallow Jonah?

Written by: Unknown

Who did, who did,
Who did, who did
Who did swallow
Jo, Jo, Jo, Jo

Who did, who did,
Who did, who did
Who did swallow
Jo, Jo, Jo, Jo

Who did, who did,
Who did, who did
Who did swallow
Jo, Jo, Jo, Jo

Who did swallow Jonah,
Who did swallow Jonah
Who did swallow Jonah down?

Whale did, whale did,
Whale did, whale did
Whale did swallow
Jo, Jo, Jo, Jo

Whale did, whale did,
Whale did, whale did
Whale did swallow
Jo, Jo, Jo, Jo

Whale did, whale did,
Whale did, whale did
Whale did swallow
Jo, Jo, Jo, Jo

Whale did swallow Jonah,
Whale did swallow Jonah
Whale did swallow Jonah down.

The song proceedeth to exhort Gabriel to blow his trum, trum, trumpet; to celebrate unto Heaven Daniel in the li, li, lion's den; and to observe Noah in the Arky Arky. But as a mere child, I wath sore afraid for Jonah in the belly of the whale. As I am of a family who doth not have a large portion of truck with religion, it wath only later did I learn *that* the whale yanked Jonah safe and sound even if disgusting onto the shore, and he was OK, more or less, given the floods and famines and plagues that beset the people from one day unto the next, and right and, yea, even unto left. This jolly little song left him therein, in a darkness as dark as black as the night when the moon hideth his face from the eyes of man, to be mulched around with the juices of digestion of the whale. Yucketh, is what I hath thought.

In truth I was much relieved later to learn that Jonah hath not gone, yea, all the way through the whale, if you knoweth what I mean, but was cast *up* upon the land. And yea yet again, much later, as my studies brought forth upon me the requirement to read and study the Bible, I waxed fascinated with the Book of Jonah, and waned not. The first three chapters tell a tale that is as clear as the day: God requireth Jonah to convert the Ninevites but Jonah duckethed his responsibilities by fleeing on a ship to Tarshish. Seeing Jonah's truancy, God, who Himself waxed, but in this case wroth, caused a "mighty tempest upon the sea, so that the ship was like to be broken." In order to placate God, Jonah hath himself—or hath had himself—thrown into the sea, which wath calmed as quickly as the silence returneth after the storm's last thundering. God then gives again unto Jonah his orders to convert the sinful Ninevites, and by Heaven, he doth it.

Now cometh the hard part, Chapter Four, which I set down here—preceded by the last verse of the third chapter—as full as . . . well, the moon on the night of the full moon:

> [10] And God saw their works, that they turned from their evil way; and God repented of the evil, that he had said that he would do unto them; and he did it not.

Jonah.4

[1] But it displeased Jonah exceedingly, and he was very angry.

[2] And he prayed unto the LORD, and said, I pray thee, O LORD, was not this my saying, when I was yet in my country? Therefore I fled before unto Tarshish: for I knew that thou art a gracious God, and merciful, slow to anger, and of great kindness, and repentest thee of the evil.

[3] Therefore now, O LORD, take, I beseech thee, my life from me; for it is better for me to die than to live.

[4] Then said the LORD, Doest thou well to be angry?

[5] So Jonah went out of the city, and sat on the east side of the city, and there made him a booth, and sat under it in the shadow, till he might see what would become of the city.

[6] And the LORD God prepared a gourd, and made it to come up over Jonah, that it might be a shadow over his head, to deliver him from his grief. So Jonah was exceeding glad of the gourd.

[7] But God prepared a worm when the morning rose the next day, and it smote the gourd that it withered.

[8] And it came to pass, when the sun did arise, that God prepared a vehement east wind; and the sun beat upon the head of Jonah, that he fainted, and wished in himself to die, and said, It is better for me to die than to live.

[9] And God said to Jonah, Doest thou well to be angry for the gourd? And he said, I do well to be angry, even unto death.

[10] Then said the LORD, Thou hast had pity on the gourd, for the which thou hast not laboured, neither madest it grow; which came up in a night, and perished in a night:

[11] And should not I spare Nineveh, that great city, wherein are more than sixscore thousand persons that cannot discern between their right hand and their left hand; and also much cattle?

WTF? Why wath Jonah angered? I guesseth because God had mercy upon the Ninevites. But wath that not the whole point? But yea, evidently not for Jonah, who went to the east side of the city and sulkethed in a booth that he himself hath built. A Sulking Booth. Perhaps this *wath* a custom of the day, wherein disgruntled prophets always went to the east side of the mighty cities they hath just somewhat reluctantly converted and therein sulked. Who knoweth?

There followeth more strange doings in and around the Sulking Booth of Noah, with a veritable parade of vines, gourds, and a worm. A worm? you may ask. Yea, verily I say unto ye, a worm. What goeth on here? I beseech thee to read the last six or seven verses numerous times and explain to me God's and Noah's *behavior.* For I understand it not, except as a bickering between God and man, in which the Lord attempteth to teach a lesson about repentance and forgiveness and what all.

Nor do the exegetes of the Holy Book appear to understand this conclusion, in their commentaries on Jonah. Take this, from "Free Bible Commentary," as an example:

Verses 9–11 Jonah still did not understand how wrong he was. God has no pleasure in seeing evil people die. He told Jonah that he was wrong not to pity the people of Nineveh. God knew that they were like children. They needed God to be like a good father to them.

> God cares for everything that he has made. He cares for every person and he cares for every animal (Psalm 145:9). He is very patient. He will go to great trouble to try to persuade every person in every nation to trust in him and to follow him.

Really? I say unto ye, Doth that cleareth things up? I thinketh not. Then there is this, a slight modification of "Exegetical Exposition of Jonah 4," by Brian LePort, a paper presented to Dr. David Eckman in partial fulfillment of the requirements for the Course OTS 510S, Hebrew Exegesis: Acquiring Interpretive Skills:

> The structure of Jonah 4 provides an imperfect, yet noticeable, chiasm:
>
> A. Jonah displeased with YHWH's actions (v. 1)
> B. Jonah addresses YHWH's compassion for Nineveh (v. 2)
> C. Jonah requests death (v. 3)
> D. YHWH questions Jonah's anger (v. 4)
> E. Jonah under a shelter and watches the city (v. 5)
> F. God provides a plant (v. 6)
> F'. God removes the plant (v. 7)
> E'. Jonah without a shelter and wishes for death (v. 8)
> D'. YHWH questions Jonah's anger (v. 9a)
> C'. Jonah wishes for death (v. 9b)
> B'. YHWH addresses Jonah's compassion for a simple plant (v. 10)
> A'. YHWH justifies His actions (v. 11)

And yet again: Really? If thou lookest at the word *imperfect* and then items F and F', thee will find there, as surely as the kine findeth her cud, the oddness and arbitrariness of these goings-on.

But I say unto ye, yea, for all the bewilderment it hath given me, the Book of Jonah, in especial its final chapter, is nevertheless a very successful "meta" (as they sayeth in these modern days) text. Its ending is not unlike in its way the ending of the ultimate episode of *The Sopranos*. The family sitteth there, under the menace and threatened vengeance *of*

Tony's enemies. Jonah sitteth there, his Sulking Booth blown away by God's wind, baking, being shaded, asking for death, watching a worm devour the gourd, or whatever, and we Just Don't Know What to Maketh of It All.

Is this not a lesson taught by the Good Book about life and our actions in general? That things goeth back and forth, that we shirketh and then shirketh not, that our Sulking Booths may be blown away by God, and that a worm may eateth our gourd? We knoweth not and we sitteth here, yea, like unto the frog on a lily pad, or a large person occupying half of our seat on the flying machine, not fully knowing what the meaning is of what we and God hath done, or what will hapenneth next.

Bible, King James Version

Jonah

Jonah.1

[1] Now the word of the LORD came unto Jonah the son of Amittai, saying,

[2] Arise, go to Nineveh, that great city, and cry against it; for their wickedness is come up before me.

[3] But Jonah rose up to flee unto Tarshish from the presence of the LORD, and went down to Joppa; and he found a ship going to Tarshish: so he paid the fare thereof, and went down into it, to go with them unto Tarshish from the presence of the LORD.

[4] But the LORD sent out a great wind into the sea, and there was a mighty tempest in the sea, so that the ship was like to be broken.

[5] Then the mariners were afraid, and cried every man unto his god, and cast forth the wares that were in the ship into the sea, to

lighten it of them. But Jonah was gone down into the sides of the ship; and he lay, and was fast asleep.

[6] So the shipmaster came to him, and said unto him, What meanest thou, O sleeper? arise, call upon thy God, if so be that God will think upon us, that we perish not.

[7] And they said every one to his fellow, Come, and let us cast lots, that we may know for whose cause this evil is upon us. So they cast lots, and the lot fell upon Jonah.

[8] Then said they unto him, Tell us, we pray thee, for whose cause this evil is upon us; What is thine occupation? and whence comest thou? what is thy country? and of what people art thou?

[9] And he said unto them, I am an Hebrew; and I fear the LORD, the God of heaven, which hath made the sea and the dry land.

[10] Then were the men exceedingly afraid, and said unto him, Why hast thou done this? For the men knew that he fled from the presence of the LORD, because he had told them.

[11] Then said they unto him, What shall we do unto thee, that the sea may be calm unto us? for the sea wrought, and was tempestuous.

[12] And he said unto them, Take me up, and cast me forth into the sea; so shall the sea be calm unto you: for I know that for my sake this great tempest is upon you.

[13] Nevertheless the men rowed hard to bring it to the land; but they could not: for the sea wrought, and was tempestuous against them.

[14] Wherefore they cried unto the LORD, and said, We beseech thee, O LORD, we beseech thee, let us not perish for this man's life, and lay not upon us innocent blood: for thou, O LORD, hast done as it pleased thee.

[15] So they took up Jonah, and cast him forth into the sea: and the sea ceased from her raging.

[16] Then the men feared the LORD exceedingly, and offered a sacrifice unto the LORD, and made vows.

[17] Now the LORD had prepared a great fish to swallow up Jonah. And Jonah was in the belly of the fish three days and three nights.

Jonah.2

[1] Then Jonah prayed unto the LORD his God out of the fish's belly,

[2] And said, I cried by reason of mine affliction unto the LORD, and he heard me; out of the belly of hell cried I, and thou heardest my voice.

[3] For thou hadst cast me into the deep, in the midst of the seas; and the floods compassed me about: all thy billows and thy waves passed over me.

[4] Then I said, I am cast out of thy sight; yet I will look again toward thy holy temple.

[5] The waters compassed me about, even to the soul: the depth closed me round about, the weeds were wrapped about my head.

[6] I went down to the bottoms of the mountains; the earth with her bars was about me for ever: yet hast thou brought up my life from corruption, O LORD my God.

[7] When my soul fainted within me I remembered the LORD: and my prayer came in unto thee, into thine holy temple.

[8] They that observe lying vanities forsake their own mercy.

[9] But I will sacrifice unto thee with the voice of thanksgiving; I will pay that that I have vowed. Salvation is of the LORD.

[10] And the LORD spake unto the fish, and it vomited out Jonah upon the dry land.

Jonah.3

[1] And the word of the LORD came unto Jonah the second time, saying,

[2] Arise, go unto Nineveh, that great city, and preach unto it the preaching that I bid thee.

[3] So Jonah arose, and went unto Nineveh, according to the word of the LORD. Now Nineveh was an exceeding great city of three days' journey.

[4] And Jonah began to enter into the city a day's journey, and he cried, and said, Yet forty days, and Nineveh shall be overthrown.

[5] So the people of Nineveh believed God, and proclaimed a fast, and put on sackcloth, from the greatest of them even to the least of them.

[6] For word came unto the king of Nineveh, and he arose from his throne, and he laid his robe from him, and covered him with sackcloth, and sat in ashes.

[7] And he caused it to be proclaimed and published through Nineveh by the decree of the king and his nobles, saying, Let neither man nor beast, herd nor flock, taste any thing: let them not feed, nor drink water:

[8] But let man and beast be covered with sackcloth, and cry mightily unto God: yea, let them turn every one from his evil way, and from the violence that is in their hands.

[9] Who can tell if God will turn and repent, and turn away from his fierce anger, that we perish not?

[10] And God saw their works, that they turned from their evil way; and God repented of the evil, that he had said that he would do unto them; and he did it not.

Jonah.4

[1] But it displeased Jonah exceedingly, and he was very angry.

[2] And he prayed unto the LORD, and said, I pray thee, O LORD, was not this my saying, when I was yet in my country? Therefore I fled before unto Tarshish: for I knew that thou art a

gracious God, and merciful, slow to anger, and of great kindness, and repentest thee of the evil.

[3] Therefore now, O LORD, take, I beseech thee, my life from me; for it is better for me to die than to live.

[4] Then said the LORD, Doest thou well to be angry?

[5] So Jonah went out of the city, and sat on the east side of the city, and there made him a booth, and sat under it in the shadow, till he might see what would become of the city.

[6] And the LORD God prepared a gourd, and made it to come up over Jonah, that it might be a shadow over his head, to deliver him from his grief. So Jonah was exceeding glad of the gourd.

[7] But God prepared a worm when the morning rose the next day, and it smote the gourd that it withered.

[8] And it came to pass, when the sun did arise, that God prepared a vehement east wind; and the sun beat upon the head of Jonah, that he fainted, and wished in himself to die, and said, It is better for me to die than to live.

[9] And God said to Jonah, Doest thou well to be angry for the gourd? And he said, I do well to be angry, even unto death.

[10] Then said the LORD, Thou hast had pity on the gourd, for the which thou hast not laboured, neither madest it grow; which came up in a night, and perished in a night:

[11] And should not I spare Nineveh, that great city, wherein are more than sixscore thousand persons that cannot discern between their right hand and their left hand; and also much cattle?

New Moon Haftorah

Robert Pinsky

I hate your new moons, your appointed holidays,
God says. A boy pipes the memorized syllables,
Koh aumar! Adonai, hashawmayim keesee.

God hates your empty rituals and sacrifices.
He says it's like watching you cut a dog's throat
Machey-eesh ohveyach hazeh aureyf keleb.

In the high-pitched voice of the boy chanting
Uncomprehending the mighty sounds, God says:
Behold, the faithful city has become a whore.

By fire and by the sword will the Lord plead
With all flesh, that sanctify themselves and hide in
Gardens to eat impure flesh of swine and of mice.

Mere gestures of worship disgust the Lord. The boy
Faithfully sings the disintegrating words,
Losheh kay-awkh, like one whom his mother comforteth.

He will make, between one new moon and another,
The child's fresh voice promises in the old words,
Ahl-akhat, ehrkhat: new heavens and a new earth.

THE NEW TESTAMENT

The Good Thief

The Gospel of Luke

Ian Caldwell

There was a time in my life when competitive swimming was religion. By high school I was in the pool up to nine times a week and ten thousand yards a day. My coach had recently sent an athlete to Olympic Trials, so his regimen was proven. The only thing that remained to be seen was the commitment of his swimmers.

Much of swimming is a battle for air. In freestyle and butterfly, raising the head wastes motion and costs time, so at an early age swimmers begin "hypoxic" training. An eight-year-old can finish a one-lap race without breathing. Young teenagers can swim two laps this way. At their peak, some swimmers can hold off the blackout point long enough to finish three laps. This is central to the culture of the sport. A competitor who loses a close race because he breathed too often, or came up for air too soon after a turn, is viewed as undisciplined. Young swimmers learn that surrendering to the painful, fundamental urge for oxygen is shortsighted and destructive. Self-denial is essential to success.

My specialty was the marathon of high school swimming, the five-hundred-yard freestyle. The 500 free is a race so long—twenty laps—that athletes aren't expected to keep track of their own progress. Teammates mark the lap count for them by dunking numerical boards into the water as they approach the wall for a turn. Training for the 500 is miserable. In the years before I had entered the sport, the orthodoxy of distance swimming had changed. On the theory that athletes could profit from technique training as much as from brute yardage, coaches had underprepared a generation of American distance swimmers, who proved unable to dig as deep or suffer as much. Now the coaches were repenting. Our workouts were ever more grueling.

Today I ask myself why I did it. Why, for the last two years of high school, I came home in the evening from swim practice, bolted my dinner, and hurried to finish my homework by half past ten, knowing that I was unable to survive on fewer than five and a half hours of sleep, and that I would miss my swimming carpool if I woke later than 4:00 A.M. Why, on Friday nights, after our high school team had competed in a weekly meet, and the upperclassmen had gone out together to celebrate, I allowed my pleasure to be fringed with dread of the next morning, when we distance swimmers would be sequestered in our own lane with our own workout for the longest and most hated practice of the week.

One reason I did it is that swimming had changed me. I'd begun the sport as an asthmatic eight-year-old, surviving allergy season on a careful program of Choledyl syrup, albuterol inhalers, and weekly injections. I was not allowed outside for recess in the spring, and I wore a breathing mask at the bus stop when the pollen count was high. Yet by the time I entered high school, the yearly breathing tests with the allergist revealed an almost miraculous change. My lung strength and capacity were far above average. I could hold my breath easily for two minutes. In addition, swimming had stretched me. I was almost six foot two, with an arm span nearly triple the waist measurement of my racing suit. My competition times were in free fall, and the messianic possibility that crosses every athlete's mind at least once had finally settled over mine: Could I be the one?

The other reason I swam was Tom Dolan, who led the distance lane on Saturday mornings. Tom was six foot six and cadaverously thin. Shambling across the pool deck in his hooded swimming parka, he was a vision of death. We couldn't have imagined this at the time, but in the

500 free he would go on to win three national championships in college and set an American record. Later he would win gold at the Atlanta Olympics, repeat this at Sydney, and become famous not just as the world record holder in one of our most grueling events but as the severe asthmatic who had done so with only 20 percent of his lung capacity.

On Saturday mornings, Tom was our lead dog. In the distance lane, we drafted off him. There are two standard pool lengths in competitive swimming—twenty-five-yard short course and Olympic fifty-meter long course—and when the movable bulkhead of the Saturday pool was dragged back to convert it from one to the other, the laps suddenly felt endless. The distance between walls made the water flat, dead, because currents dissipated rather than reflected, so that my body would feel becalmed. Yet Tom could force a wedge even through an Olympic-size pool. The water simply parted for him. After a few months of training in his lane, I felt myself on the cusp of finding out what I was capable of.

Early the following spring, I qualified to swim the 500 free in the finals of the high school state championships. For the first time, in that heat, I would compete side by side against Tom. Since I was a junior and he was a senior, this would be my only chance to see how we measured up before he graduated. My strategy was simple. I had learned to use his draft better than any other competitor. I would stay with him until the final burst. Then we would see what I was made of.

That night, Tom taught all of us a lesson. On his way to shattering the meet record, he finished twenty lengths of the pool before the rest of us could finish eighteen. In the language of swimming, Tom lapped us. The only part of it I remember clearly is that Tom was still in the water, waiting to shake our hands, when the rest of us finished. As I swam toward that final wall, the ghostly cross of his body came into focus, legs dangling in exhaustion, arms stretched out along the gutter to support them. He was going places the rest of us couldn't follow, but one final time, he waited for us.

* * *

I lasted two or three months on my college team before the lesson took full root: I was not the one. I stayed on the varsity squad just long enough to attend one particular team meeting, overseen by the head coach in one of the training rooms by the pool, that turned out to be a proselytizing session by a campus Christian group, Athletes in Action. At the end of it, we were asked to sign up for Bible study. We freshmen, in the spirit of compliance, agreed.

I had arrived at Princeton a confident atheist. Now, twice a week, I was visited by a former college wrestler named Brian, who came to my dorm room with Bible in hand to discuss scripture in an Evangelical framework, teasing the sense from passages in Paul and then recommending books by C. S. Lewis that would help me understand the general thrust. All of this was odious in a way I couldn't quite put my finger on. To be mistaken for a person who would commit so deeply to something so dubious, on the basis of conversations so superficial, seemed patronizing, except that it was obviously the honest mistake of someone who happened to be such a person himself. Out of fellowship and charity, Brian was offering to me what had meant so much to him. He was capable of looking at me and seeing a younger version of himself.

This was my first taste of the loss. My demotion from student-athlete to mere student came with a great sense of abandonment. So many years, so much struggle and sacrifice: How could it now be invisible? What I had done in the swimming pool, year after year, was surely one of the most important testaments I had written about myself, and, even if it had ended, it remained a guidepost to more invisible, more abiding qualities in me. I felt angry and afraid that a fellow athlete—who must have understood what it meant to be relentless and striving, never satisfied, intent on the hard way—could think I would be persuaded by a hasty reading of a few haphazard Bible verses. I felt compelled to show him his mistake.

The great discovery of my early college career, and the one that ultimately absorbed the shock waves of the loss of swimming, was that I could redirect all those hours from the pool to the library, with better results and more pleasure. In the first week of term, one of my courses assigned the *Iliad*, the *Odyssey*, and assorted poems by Sappho. It sent a ripple of disbelief and terror through most of the class to be assigned one thousand pages of reading in seven days. It was then that I discovered some of my fellow freshmen felt otherwise. They had spent high school learning Latin and even Greek. One was finishing his translation of the *Aeneid*. These students, far from being panicked by the reading list, proceeded to bring little green Loeb editions to our seminars in order to discuss points of translation. Here was something new and wonderful: not just the experience of classical literature, and of reading critically, but of finding myself grossly behind at something I was quickly deciding I loved. Within a few weeks, that same class turned its sights toward the Bible.

The first and only gospel I read with Brian was the Gospel of Matthew. It soon became clear that we were reading it for the fifth chapter, the Sermon on the Mount, which contains the quintessence of Jesus's moral teaching. Brian must have thought even the most heartless atheist couldn't object to that. By now, though, I had an agenda of my own.

The Gospel of Matthew is a thorny book. Whoever wrote it—most scholars today would say it can't have been the disciple Matthew, for whom it is named—was influenced by a private trauma: the author seems to have lived during a tumultuous period of the early Church when the Christian movement had reached a crisis point. Jews were not converting in great numbers, and, instead, the movement was being expelled from the synagogues it had formerly called home. Jews who believed in Jesus—including the gospel's author—were being forced to acknowledge their separateness, their homelessness, and their countrymen's refusal to join them. A close comparison of the Gospels reveals that Matthew repeatedly compares Jesus to the Jewish hero Moses: no other gospel claims that, when Jesus was an infant, a king tried to kill him by ordering the extermination of all young children in the vicinity. (This echoes the story of Moses's birth.) No other gospel rearranges the order of Jesus's miracles so that ten of them can occur in a row. (This echoes the story of Moses and the ten plagues.) It seems the gospel was written for an audience of Jewish Christians, to reassure them of Jesus's triumphant place in the Jewish tradition embodied in Moses.

But this background also gives Matthew its dark side. A deep vein of bitterness and frustration runs through the gospel, as if its author was wounded by other Jews' refusal to consider Jesus the Messiah. Thus only in Matthew's gospel does Jesus compare himself to a stone that is rejected by builders, even though it later proves to be the cornerstone. In no other gospel does Jesus say that the Jewish Pharisees who reject his ministry are a "brood of vipers" who cannot "flee from the judgment of hell." The closer Jesus comes to his death in the story, the more the author's feelings rise to the surface. Finally, at 27:25, Matthew delivers the most chilling line in any gospel. The Jewish crowd, condemning Jesus to death, cries out, "His blood be upon us and upon our children."

Here, beneath Jesus's message of love, was a private record of injury and anger, the ugly reality of human nature. Not even an evangelist, the best of Christians, could turn the other cheek to his experience of abandonment and failure. I recoiled. Perhaps I detected the reflection of my own experience, my own injury. If so, the resemblance only disgusted me. This was the last part of the Bible I read with Brian. After our discussion that day, I called off our meetings. Not for many years would I so much as pretend to read any part of the Good Book with an open heart.

Ten years later, almost to the day, my wife and I were married. The ceremony took place on a beach rather than in a church. I hadn't swum a lap since quitting the college team, but something about the ocean beckoned. The old religion. But no other: not a verse of scripture was read.

Our son was born nine months later. The night we brought him home, I nervously placed him in my lap and began reading aloud from the *Odyssey*. A father-son story, and the beginning of a promise: to share with him the touchstones of my life. I could no longer fathom how I'd once devoured all of Homer in a week; now it took a month of nightly reading for us to bring Odysseus home to Ithaca. In the year that followed we read seven plays by Shakespeare and two novels by Dickens. By then I had discovered how deeply this promise mattered to me. How doggedly I would honor it even as other good intentions gradually slipped out of keep.

It was my wife who decided the time had come for swimming lessons. The class at the rec center was for parents to stand in the shallow end and raise and lower their infants into the water. This was silly, but I agreed. In parenting a baby, as in training for a distance race, the sets and intervals are really just illusions. They create a tolerable reality out of what is really a long, undifferentiated test of will. Swimming classes are not for the drowning child. They are for the drowning parent.

We dressed him in a wet suit, not wanting him to catch a chill, and because the suit had flotation pads around the chest, his proportions were those of a real swimmer: spindly legs and outsize torso and shoulders. His head, like the heads of all children, was too big, so that when I page through pictures of him at that age, I find myself staring at a caricature of the boy I had created: half swimmer, half reader. I am also staring at the father *he* created. My son, the only power under heaven that could drag his father back into the pool.

By now, we had arrived at a crisis in our reading. There is only so far down the canon one can go before even an atheist becomes self-conscious about overlooking the Bible. I thought back sometimes to Matthew's story, found in no other gospel, of the wise men who bring gifts to the newborn Jesus. This captured something essential about my experience of parenthood. The impulse to give, and then give more. The compulsion to leave behind the place I had called home before, just to be at his side. This was a gloss I would have been ashamed to offer in college, a simple, subjective, dead-end one. I had been trained to read as a surgeon operates—dissect, find weakness, diagnose—and my atheism went hand in hand with this approach. It was the height of laziness to see nothing more in a text than a reflection of myself. Fatherhood, it seemed, had made me soft.

And so, at Christmas, I reopened the Bible. There are only two gospels, Matthew and Luke, that tell a birth story about Jesus. Since their accounts are almost irreconcilable, and since both of them depend on historical events that almost certainly never happened, reading them side by side was a reflex test, a stab at self-diagnosis, to see whether I had surrendered to contradiction and illogic. Whether my atheism was beginning to slip.

I read the first two chapters of Matthew, then the first two of Luke. If I had noticed the difference before, it had never made an impression until now. All the Gospels except Luke's begin in the same voice: the omniscient third person, the sound of God talking. But Luke opens with a prologue in the first person. He acknowledges that he has written this gospel himself, that he isn't the first to have done so, and that he wasn't an eyewitness to the events of Jesus's life. But he promises that he has taken pains to "investigat[e] everything accurately" so that he can "write it down in an orderly sequence." It is hard not to be charmed by this scrupulous, almost self-effacing beginning. It piqued my interest. I read the gospel to its end.

Matthew and Luke are believed to have been written around the same time, and both by the same process: weaving together the earlier Gospel of Mark with a second document that recorded Jesus's teachings. Considering this, the differences between them seemed stark. Matthew had placed so much stress on comparing Jesus to Moses; Luke placed very little. Luke's audience must have been Gentile, since, in addition to this lack of emphasis on Moses, Luke simplifies or has to explain his "Jewish" material, as if his readers are not familiar with it. Perhaps for this same reason, Matthew's bitterness and frustration—the gall of abandonment felt by a Jewish Christian toward fellow Jews who refused Jesus—is much harder to find in Luke.

Instead, Luke radiates love. His theme, more than that of any other gospel, is the innate goodness of people, a subject he is able to find everywhere. Eleven of Jesus's parables exist in no other gospel but Luke, including two of the most famous: the Good Samaritan, about the unexpected mercy of our presumed enemies; and the Prodigal Son, about a wayward young man who returns home in shame, having wasted his inheritance, only to find that his father's love and forgiveness are bottomless. This optimism and generosity are pervasive in Luke. It is hard not to feel that, in this author, Jesus has found the ideal messenger, a man able to see past misfortunes in order to keep heartfelt faith in a radical, transformative love.

The contrast between Matthew and Luke hits hardest at the end, where Matthew's love of Jesus, and anger at Jesus's death, leads him to those words seemingly bereft of redemption or forgiveness: "His blood be upon us and upon our children." Matthew does not even change the devastating final words of Jesus on the cross, as reported by the Gospel of Mark: "My God, my God, why have you forsaken me?" Rather, it is Luke who changes them. And it is in Luke's improbable version of the crucifixion that I see Jesus most vividly: as the hero of mercy and embodiment of love; as the man intent on seeing the goodness in us even when we give him no reason.

I see, also, Luke himself: his own mercy and love, his capacity to overlook the horror Matthew could not. As Jesus dies on the cross, crucified with two thieves, Luke adds a final story found in no other gospel:

> Now one of the criminals hanging there reviled Jesus, saying, "Are you not the Messiah? Save yourself and us." The other, however, rebuking him, said in reply, "Have you no fear of God, for you are subject to the same condemnation? And indeed, we have been condemned justly, for the sentence we received corresponds to our crimes, but this man has done nothing criminal." Then he said, "Jesus, remember me when you come into your kingdom." Jesus replied to him, "Amen, I say to you, today you will be with me in Paradise."

Today I have three sons. The oldest are nine and seven. They are competitive swimmers.

At one of their practices, I recently discovered a group of adults training in the adjacent lane. So I bought a new suit and joined them. For the first time in two decades, I have a practice group.

These days I swim side by side with my boys, separated only by a lane rope. When the old feeling returns, that the pool is infinite and the laps endless, I peer through the murk of the next lane and I wait for a glimpse of them.

How hard they work for every yard. How desperately they want air but force themselves not to breathe. Every once in a while, they catch me watching. And when they do, they try to keep up. Their arms spin faster, their kicks start to beat the water white. Unconsciously, as if they have inherited this instinct, they veer over toward the lane rope between us. They draft off me.

The final words of Jesus on the cross, according to the Gospel of Luke, are: "Father, into your hands I commit my spirit." I push forward. Stroke on stroke, I try to part the water.

The Womb and the Cistern Cell

John the Baptist

Brooks Hansen

> Now when John in prison heard about the deeds of Christ, he sent word by his disciples and said to him, "Are you the one who is to come, or shall we look for another?"
>
> *Matthew 11:2–4*

As vivid a character as he may be—with his ragged camel-skin cloak, his diet of locusts and honey, and his howling sermon-diatribes—there is legitimate cause to doubt the portrayal of John the Baptist in the Gospels, especially once one understands that John is a required element of Jesus's narrative.

Remember, the evangelists lived in the grip of a highly prophetic mind-set. There was nothing the prophets had not seen, nothing that had not been foretold—or nothing of significance to the children of Abraham anyway. If one wanted one's words or actions to be taken seriously as part of that legacy, they had on some level to be seen as a fulfillment of the word of the prophets. And the prophets had been fairly clear about the coming of the Messiah. Malachi had spoken of how the Lord would send a messenger "to prepare the way."* Isaiah had

* Malachi 3:1 ESV (English Standard Version).

described an Elijah-like figure, a voice calling in the wilderness who likewise would come to "make straight in the desert a highway for our God."* Even Jesus's disciples—hardly a learned bunch—understood this. Immediately after recognizing that Jesus might actually be the savior, they asked him: "But why do the scribes say that first Elijah must come?" Jesus replied that Elijah *had* come, and they all apparently knew he was talking about John.†

All of which is to say—or admit—that if there hadn't been a John the Baptist, the evangelists would have had to come up with one.

But they didn't because there was. The Jewish historian Josephus tells us that there was a good man around whom the people of Judea massed, one who "urged the Jews to be more virtuous . . . and having done so to join together in washing."‡ Josephus calls him the Dipper. The fact that the Dipper made no mention of Jesus or any Messiah—in Josephine's account, that is—may give pause to the devout heart, but is certainly explainable. Not all perspectives on a given historic figure are going to be the same, particularly the more contemporaneous ones, but that just points up the inherent diceyness of the proposition at question—of taking the story of one charismatic spiritual leader and using it, after the fact, to substantiate the messianic claim of another probably-less-popular-at-the-time successor.§ Again, one doesn't have to be too cynical to suspect that such an effort might lend itself to moments of invention here and there, or might even—absent a good editor—descend to the level of a fairy tale, with angels and magical doves and voices from heaven and things like that.

However, to chide the evangelists for their use of poetic license—if they did use it—is to be guilty of another kind of provincialism, of

---

* Isaiah 40:3–5 ESV.

† Mark 9:11–13 ESV.

‡ Josephus, *Antiquities* 18.5.2 116–119.

§ The testimony of Josephus suggests this, as does the fact that when Jesus's disciples went out after his death to places like Antioch to spread the word, the people there already knew about John but not Jesus. Jesus was often mistaken for John, in fact. So far as we know, John was never mistaken for Jesus.

assuming that such men should be bound by the same rules as David McCullough, say, or of assuming that they shared our contemporary western assumption that what is "literal" or "factual" somehow has a greater claim upon truth than what we call figurative or metaphorical. Given the profound skepticism with which the religious mind has always treated the world of appearances—that tacky realm where *facts* have purchase—it is doubtful that the gospel authors would have thought twice about taking liberties with the stories they received from it. They were attempting to convey eternal—and eternally pertinent—truths, after all, not temporal or temporary ones. They were drawing a map of the soul. In that context, John's story—and the project of weaving it into Jesus's—may be seen as presenting an opportunity through which both the spiritual *and* the literary intelligence of its several authors could shine. And does.

Consider first the fact that John is almost certainly the best *drawn* character in the Gospels. We are told how he dressed, groomed, what he liked to eat, the sorts of things he said, and the manner in which he said them.* John is, moreover, the only character—other than Jesus—whose birth and infancy are presented in any detail; and while he is not the only character whose *death* is mentioned,† John's is remarkable in the fact that it has no immediate bearing on Jesus's mission. Rather, it seems to have been presented for the same reason that informs all the other moments and episodes in John's story: to reinforce the idea of his worthiness as Jesus's first, most emphatic, and long-foretold witness.

But among these various moments in John's life, there are two in particular—the bookends—that taken together testify most eloquently and powerfully to the quality of mind behind the assembly of this very intricate braid.

---

* Mark 1: 4–8;Luke 3:3–18; Matthew 3:1–12. Though I'm not familiar with any such scholarship, I'm willing to bet that John is a crucial figure in the history of the exclamation point.

† See Jesus again, Lazarus, and the son of the widow at Nain.

As mentioned, we learn from Luke a great deal about the circumstances surrounding John's birth. There was an older couple named Zechariah and Elizabeth, who prayed and prayed and prayed for a child until those prayers were answered, first by angelic visitation and then by a son.* Readers conversant with sacred literature will recognize that this story comes from a fairly old playbook. It recalls the struggles of Abraham and Sarah,† as well as Hannah and her husband, Elkanah,‡ as well as Anna and Joachim.§ We furthermore learn that John's mother, Elizabeth, was apparently "kin" to Jesus's mother, Mary, which again is certainly possible—it was a smaller world back then—but could just as well be one of those poetic inventions, an attempt to convey the spiritual kinship between Jesus and John by asserting . . . actual kinship.

Either way, it's the family connection that sets the stage for an undeniably affecting moment, often called "the quickening." Perhaps to conceal her pregnancy from prying eyes, Mary goes to visit Zechariah and Elizabeth in the hill country. Once again it is Luke who tells us that "when Elizabeth heard the greeting of Mary, the baby leaped in her womb."¶

A simple sentence recounting a common occurrence, yet it summons to mind one of the more beautiful and unexpected images in all the Bible: of the unborn John, adrift in the dark, soothing shadow of his mother's womb, awakened from his slumber not so much by a voice—it's Elizabeth who heard the greeting—but by the awareness of another silent presence nearby, a being still less formed than he but apparently so radiant and delightful that John is inspired to kick. To dance.

That alluded detail is our first real signal—far superior to the more explicit angelic pronouncements and benedictions that come before and after—that John has been chosen, and well chosen, for the eventual

---

* Luke 1: 5–24.
† Genesis 18:9–15.
‡ 1Samuel 1:1–20.
§ The Protevangelium of James, chs 1–5.
¶ Luke 1:41 ESV.

task of recognizing the light of the Holy Spirit. (In fact, this is precisely how his mission is phrased in the Gospel of John the Evangelist, that John was sent by God "to bear witness about the light.")*

The "cousins" then part ways. Regarding John, all we know—from the Gospels at least—is that he lived in the wilderness and there "became strong in spirit."† When next we meet him, his mission is in full swing. Crowds are coming to the banks of the Jordan to receive his baptism and to be warned that he is just a harbinger. There is one coming after him, he says, who will "baptize you with the Holy spirit," who will "gather his wheat into the barn, but the chaff he will burn with unquenchable fire."‡

Enter Jesus, the spiritual adept from Galilee. No further mention is made of any kinship—that metaphor, if it is one, seems to have served its purpose—but John instantly recognizes Jesus's authority. "Should you not baptize me?" he asks. Jesus, ever mindful of the need to stick to the plan, says no. "Let it be so for now, as it is right for us to fulfill all righteousness."§ The baptism goes forward, with God's very vocal blessing.℄

John's disciples, however, are not so quick to glean the significance of the moment, or of this visitor. And this you don't hear as much about on Sunday, when more emphasis is placed on John's willingness to point and step aside, but the gospel is fairly clear that, with the exception of the Pharisees and Sadducees (to whom, let's face it, Jesus gave as good as he got), no one is more hostile to Jesus than the followers of John. Which makes sense. If one has devoted one's life to this master here, it can't be easy to hear him say, "Now follow that one there." They resist. When they see that Jesus does not fast or pray, they challenge him;** and

---

* For alternate histories, the reader might be interested to look at selections for the Mandaean John-book, a.k.a. *Gnostic John the Baptizer*.

† Luke 1:80.

‡ Matthew 3:11–12 ESV.

§ Matthew 3:14–15.

℄ Matthew 3:17.

** According to Matthew at least—9:14.

later on at Aenon, when it is discovered that Jesus is performing baptisms just up the river, they object.* This interloper is not just stealing their rabboni's act, he is debasing it by letting his *disciples* perform the rite, which is apparently something John did not do.

John is not bothered. In fact, he takes the opportunity to express more clearly than ever the subservience of his role. Jesus is the bridegroom, John a mere guest at the wedding; Jesus is from heaven while John is from earth; Jesus must therefore "increase," while he, John, must "decrease."†

His disciples still aren't having it. They have more questions, more seeds of doubt to sow, and it is their final effort in this regard that provides what is the other most surprising and troubling moment in John's story:

Not long after the incident at Aenon, John is arrested, ostensibly for insulting the royal marriage. He is taken to the fortress of Machaerus, down along the eastern coast of the Dead Sea, and held in a cell that lore‡ has come to imagine as a cracked and emptied cistern.

It's there, in his presumably weakened state, that John is finally infected by the lingering suspicions of his disciples. He is told about Jesus's "deeds" in Galilee. We don't know which deeds exactly, but Jesus was performing many of his healing miracles during this time, the most concerning of which would have been the raising of the dead,§ an act that—to most noses, at least—carries the taint of sorcery. Whatever the cause, John was apparently disturbed enough by what he heard to send his disciples back to Jesus to ask him: "Are you the one who is to come, or shall we look for another?"☾

That's an astonishing moment, especially because these will turn out to be the last words we hear from John, and they are an unvarnished

---

* John 3:22-26.

† John 3:30.

‡ See Flaubert's *Herodias*.

§ Luke 7:12–15.

☾ Matthew 11:2; Luke 7:19.

expression of doubt. They are an arrow fired at the heart of the entire Christian mission . . . *from* the heart of the Christian mission.

The disciples oblige. They go and find Jesus and ask him John's question to his face, and he replies at length with one of his more vexingly oblique and brilliant passages, but his answer to the question itself is fairly succinct. "Go and tell John what you hear and see," he says. "The blind receive their sight and the lame walk, lepers are cleansed and the deaf hear, and the dead are raised up, and the poor have good news preached to them. And blessed is the one who is not offended by me."*

Notable here is how the phrasing manages to upend the priority that literal meaning usually enjoys over the metaphorical, and suggests what Jesus *really* wants John to hear: that the deeds in question are symbolic of a far deeper transformation in which John should take great comfort. The people are seeing now, and hearing, being purified and reborn.

Readers can decide for themselves whether this reply satisfies them. Presumably that's what John's disciples did. The question for this discussion is whether the response satisfied *John*. And did he even hear it?

The answer, remarkably, is that we don't know. The next we hear about John, it's the night of Herod's banquet when—famously—Herod's stepdaughter, in return for having just entertained all the guests with a dance, requests that the Baptist's head be brought to her on a platter.† It's a stunning and chillingly capricious end to the prophet's life, and almost surreal enough to distract us from the issue at hand: what was John's state of mind just prior to the ax's fall? Did he still doubt Jesus, or was he reconciled?

There are, in fact, two morsels of information from which we may be able to draw some conclusion, and once again it is an unsettling one.

We know from Mark that while in prison John apparently spoke to Herod, that Herod "was greatly perplexed" by the things John said,

* Matthew 11:4-6 ESV.
† Mark 6:21–26.

but that "he kept him safe" and "heard him gladly,"* all of which paints a frankly entertaining picture: of the king who *really* only arrested the prophet in order to hear him speak, to sit outside his cell and hang on every terrifying word. But did those words pertain to Jesus, the one who came from heaven? The one whose sandal John had previously suggested he was not fit to tie?

It wouldn't seem so, since we also know that sometime later, *after* John's beheading, Herod was told of the deeds that Jesus was performing in his territory. Herod's reply? "This is John the Baptist; he has risen from the dead, and that is why miraculous powers are at work in him."†

Hardly the response of a man who has been warned of a new Messiah. No, this is the response of a man who feared and revered *John*, and was regretting the role he'd played in John's death. And kudos to the evangelists for their willingness to muddy these waters, because again the inference is clear: that in his conversations with Herod—the last he is known to have engaged in—John seems to have abnegated his role as witness to Jesus. He was *not* consoled—at least not at that point—a conclusion that requires our pause if only to consider the depth of the anguish it represents. John was not just in prison, not just facing the likelihood that he would never get out alive, but also—and far worse—confronting the possibility that he had conferred his mission and following on a fraud, a man who he had reason to believe might corrupt and pervert the cause to which he had devoted his life, which was to prepare the people for the coming of the Lord.

Hard to imagine a darker dungeon than that.

Now, readers of faith are of course still free to hope—for John's sake—that, at some point between his last conversation with Herod and the arrival of his executioner these doubts were answered, and that he was visited by some intuition or some presence, sent to reassure him

* Mark 6:20.
† Matthew 14:1.

that in the fullness of time (or perhaps the next six months) his efforts would be gloriously vindicated.

But if one does imagine such a moment, some glimmer of light entering John's literal and figurative darkness, one is bound to recognize that this scene is in fact a *reprise*, and by that token to acknowledge the striking (and deliciously disturbing) resemblance between the implied setting that opens John's story—which was the warmth and comfort of his mother's womb—and the setting that closes it—which is the dank, dark cold of the cistern at Machaerus. These two shadows are, in fact, the *alpha* and *omega* moments of John's story, and it is the exquisitely implied entrance of light into the first—shed by the near presence of his cousin Jesus—that encourages us to think that maybe a similar light pierced his prison cell; to imagine, in other words, that the very same hope that awakened him to this world should have been the one that finally allowed him to leave it in peace.

But even this—the extraordinary imagery and literary stagecraft used to convey the intercession of grace in John's life—does not answer the question why? Why, posed the task of recounting John's role in promoting the cause of Jesus—which is the only reason John is mentioned in the gospel in the first place—did the evangelists see fit to include such stark expressions of doubt in both word and symbol?

The answer may be chalked up to a lack of editorial vigilance, sure, a failure to nip every Derridean bud that might undermine the evangelists' clearly stated purpose. But perhaps the decision was more deliberate than that, evidence of a collective intuition that lifts the gospel enterprise above mere history or biography, and obviates the question of whether certain of its details are "true" or "false," seeing as they are True:

Light is born of darkness. Darkness is the necessary precondition of light.

Belief, likewise, is born of doubt, which is its necessary precondition. Doubt is the soil from which faith grows.

Therefore, if one is determined to imagine John the Baptist as the first and most authoritative voice to recognize Jesus as savior—the first, in other words, to *believe*—then John must, by that token, have been the first to doubt. That, too, is Law. And if ever we encounter any teaching, or feel ourselves succumbing to any creed or system of belief, that does not admit this, and does not struggle intimately and often—in the cistern of its soul—with the fear that it is mistaken, misdirected, falsely premised, or corrupt at its heart—we should take heed:

That is not faith.

That, in fact, is a fairy tale.

Sermon on the Mount

Matthew 5–7

Jay Parini

My heart lies with the language of the King James Version, with its tender poetic effects. But it's often refreshing to turn to some other translation, such as the Jerusalem Bible (1966), best read in the 1973 revision, as it clarifies many things and adds further scholarship in the annotations. I've been rereading my favorite biblical passage lately, the Sermon on the Mount, which is neatly folded into Matthew 5–7. These chapters contain the Beatitudes, the Antitheses, the Lord's Prayer, the Golden Rule, and several key sayings of Jesus. All of the essential teachings of Jesus, in succinct form, lie in this section of the gospel.

It's such a neat compilation of wisdom, laid out with such care, that many scholars believe it must have been used as a textbook in some early version of a Christian seminary, perhaps in Antioch. In any case, it reminds us that Jesus was, among his disciples and followers in ancient Palestine, first and foremost a teacher. It's also worth recalling that when Mary Magdalene, one of his closest followers, visits him in the tomb on Easter morning—the first person to encounter Jesus after the crucifixion—she doesn't recognize him until he speaks her name, "Mary." She replies, in Aramaic: "Rabboni!" He was her teacher, which is what that term means. He is our teacher, too.

The Beatitudes consist of nine definitive statements. Each has a simple formula, "Blessed are *x*," for they shall be rewarded in kind. For example, the "poor in spirit" will inherit the kingdom of heaven. The gentle (or meek, as KJV prefers) shall inherit the earth. Those who mourn shall find comfort. Those who hunger for righteousness will be filled, presumably with righteousness. Those who show mercy to others will receive the mercy of God. The pure in heart shall see God, so they are blessed. The peacemakers are blessed, for God recognizes them as his true children. Finally, those who are persecuted for the sake of righteous behavior will inherit the kingdom.

The word for blessed, in Greek, is *makários*, which also means delighted or happy. Jesus, in effect, provides a recipe for happiness here, and it's deeply connected to the idea of karma, a concept that is central to Eastern religions and probably flowed into Palestine along the Silk Road, a branch of which passed through Capernaum, a fishing village along the northern shore of the Sea of Galilee, where Jesus headquartered his ministry. *Karma* defies easy definition, though it is often associated with the notion of rebirth in Hinduism and Buddhism. But its most straightforward meaning involves reciprocity. If you are merciful, mercy will be yours. You will reap what you sow. It's a common theme in the teachings of Jesus, but in Matthew it's stated in the most direct way. And it shows that Jesus, born into a time of immense political and religious turbulence, was able to garner the best ideas afloat in the world and reformulate them in fresh ways.

Jesus knew his audience. He taught mostly in Galilee, a rural area, quite removed from the bustle of Jerusalem. He and his disciples apparently skirted even the cities within easy reach, such as Sepphoris, an urban center only a short walk from Nazareth during Jesus's childhood. (It's very possible that he worked in that city during the years before he felt called to teach. If his father was, indeed, some kind of carpenter or laborer, it's likely that he worked there, and Jesus may have assisted him: but this is all speculation.) It was mainly an audience of farmers and fishermen who came to hear Jesus preach, the poorest of the poor.

So Jesus, as a good rabbi, reached for images and metaphors from the field, from the fishing village for his parables and examples.

In the Beatitudes, Jesus acknowledges the poor from the outset. They are the poor in goods and the poor "in spirit." The latter were those humble folk who didn't move through the world with ostentation, demanding attention, commanding others. This is of a piece with "Blessed are the gentle," those who don't force their will on others, who walk in amity with those around them. These are also "the peacemakers." Jesus was adamant about this in the Sermon on the Mount. It makes no sense to read Jesus in any other way than as a proponent of peace. The peacemakers are the true "children of God," those who have already found themselves in accord with eternal truths, with the spirit. And he follows up on this mightily in the Antitheses, a series of six revisions of the Hebrew law, put forward by God through Moses in the commandments as recorded in Exodus 20:2–17.

Jesus suggests that living in accordance with these ideas will create a kind of heaven on earth, what he often calls "the kingdom." It's an arresting concept, one that has preoccupied theologians for millennia, although it seems difficult to define or comprehend. One recalls that Jesus is asked by someone where this kingdom lies, and he says: "The kingdom of God is within you" (Luke 17:21). Or "in your midst." I tend to prefer the former: "within you." Jesus certainly does not mean that it's a physical place, or a heaven-on-earth where all political and religious enemies are vanquished and the righteous live in accord forever. I like to think of this as a space that exists out of linear time, an Eternal Now, although I often imagine a gradually realizing kingdom, an awareness of God that comes slowly, that keeps coming, that is perhaps never quite resolved but always drawing into clear focus.

After the Beatitudes we get an important discussion by Jesus of how he regards his new covenant, therefore replacing (without erasing) the old covenant between the Jews and God. Of course Jesus did not remotely think he was not a Jew, and a very good Jew. "Do not imagine that I have come to abolish the Law or the Prophets," he says in 5:17.

He has come, he says, to "fulfill" the law. And by the law he means the commandments and the teachings of the great prophets who came before him. He doesn't say that you can forget about the old prophets and only look to him. But he does regard himself as adding something essential. The core of his fresh claim lies in the six Antitheses, which complete the fifth chapter.

Each of these follows a formula: "It used to be said that *x*, but now I say *y*." The first one takes up a famous dictum: *Thou shalt not kill.* But Jesus goes further here. He says: "Anyone who is angry with a brother will answer for it before the court." That is quite a revolutionary thing to say. It's not enough not to murder someone. Don't even get mad at them. In a sense, the follow-up to this comes in the fifth and six antitheses, which seem to me the core of Jesus's teachings. In the fifth, he says: "You have heard how it was said: *Eye for eye and tooth for tooth.* But I say this to you: offer no resistance to the wicked." He tells his audience to turn the other cheek when struck. In the sixth antithesis, he goes even further: "You have heard how it was said, *You will love your neighbor and hate your enemy.* But I say this to you, love your enemies and pray for those who persecute you." Does any Christian take this seriously?

G. K. Chesterton once said that Christianity would be an interesting and effective religion if anybody bothered to try it. He meant that one should think about taking seriously the key ideas in the Sermon on the Mount: turning the other cheek when struck, even loving your enemies. One can't imagine any serious political leader taking on such a course of action without public outcry. Imagine if, after 9/11, George W. Bush had said, "I'm a Christian, so I will not strike back at those who crashed planes into our towers." What would have been the reaction among his followers in his (very Christian) home state of Texas? Yet a serious question arises. Must one resist evil in a nonviolent way? Should the Jews in the thirties and forties have turned the other cheek when Hitler rounded them up? Should the United States have said after Pearl Harbor: "Oh well, too bad," and turned the other cheek to the Japanese imperial forces?

These are hard teachings of Jesus. They are radical teachings, and they seem almost impossible to put into effect in the public sphere, although it may well be possible that he was correct, and that even in the cases I have cited the best approach would have been to turn the other cheek, to seek to love those who did wrong to one group or another. We will never know. But the doctrine of passive resistance to evil has inspired a fair number of important figures, including Henry David Thoreau, Leo Tolstoy, Mahatma Gandhi, Martin Luther King, and Nelson Mandela. The last three public figures put into practice the theory of nonviolent resistance in ways that produced social and political changes.

The complications of the idea of nonviolent resistance certainly bedeviled Thoreau, who wrote in support of John Brown, a white abolitionist who answered the violence of slavery with a violence of his own in the 1859 raid at Harpers Ferry, Virginia. Brown's idea was one of "interference," believing he stood between the slave owners and the slaves, thus breaking the evil circuit, as it were. The morality of a given situation very often depends on the context, of course; the right to self-defense cannot be denied, and I'm sure that many will argue that having a violent response to the violence of 9/11 was justifiable. And perhaps they are right, in theory. (I suspect few will deny that Bush, in attacking Iraq, made the mistake of attacking the wrong people, therefore complicating the argument in ways that stretch human reason.)

In any case, Jesus put a teaching before his audience in the Sermon on the Mount that must have severely tested them. In doing so, he made huge claims for himself, putting forward radical ideas and creating a new covenant. For a start, he is speaking from a mount, not unlike Moses on Mount Sinai. In doing so, he becomes the new Moses, implicitly. On the one hand, he asks his listeners to pay attention to the Jewish law, but he also rings changes, modifying the commandments in sharp ways, even overturning them at certain junctures. There can be no doubt that he resists the idea of "an eye for an eye, a tooth for a tooth." That is the old covenant. The new covenant disallows such primitive thinking.

Having revised the law, Jesus explains to his followers how they should live and worship. He makes a case for the practice of private religion, for modesty, arguing that one should *not* be seen to be generous, giving alms to the poor in a showy way. "Be careful not to parade your uprightness in public," he says in 6:1. In the next passage, he recommends that people should pray alone. "Go to your private room," he says. That is where you will find God, not in the synagogue or on the street corner. One must suppose that he dealt with a lot of hypocritical people who liked to be seen to be holy. There is, in fact, a constant war through the Gospels with that movement in Judaism known as the Pharisees, an influential group who tried to live their religion with a special intensity. But this group probably attracted many hypocrites, and it's those who win the scorn of Jesus. "Do not imitate the hypocrites," he says in 6:5.

Now he gives his followers a kind of rubric for prayer. It's the Lord's Prayer, still the most repeated prayer in the world, a beautiful expression of humility before God. It begins with praise: "May your name be held holy." It moves toward submission to the will of God: "Your will be done." The request for "daily bread" gives way to repentance, which lies at the heart of the prayer: "And forgive us our debts, as we forgive those who are in debt to us." Finally, there is the wish to be kept out of the line of fire: "And do not put us to the test, but save us from the Evil One."

Let me suggest that the Evil One lives inside each of us. It's like the parable of the weeds and the good grain, which comes in 13:24–30. In this complex parable, the field is sown with good seed and bad. The Evil One has mingled them. Should one just mow the whole field, getting rid of everything? No, says Jesus. Wait till harvest arrives, and let the weeds be sorted out and burned at that moment. This is a beautiful teaching, and one that relates back to the ending of the Lord's Prayer. That is, in each of us there is the good and bad, and it's not going to solve anything to wipe us away. In the end there must be some sorting. We have an adversarial nature within us. Indeed, the word *Satan* comes from the Hebrew *ha'satan*, which means the Adversary. It's not that there is good and evil on either side of some great divide. They intermingle. And it's important to let time tell us what we really need to know about what is good and what isn't.

Through the sixth chapter of Matthew, Jesus puts forward a plan for a life that is connected to God in proper ways, telling his listeners not to store up treasures on earth but to think about spiritual treasures, which cannot be counted. "You cannot be the slave both of God and money," he declares in 6:24. This doesn't mean you can't be wealthy. It means you can't spend your time worrying about your bank account, which is indeed the main problem for most of us in the western world in the twenty-first century, where money means power, safety, and countless other things. But Jesus is asking for emotional separation between money and self-esteem. In this, he seems very like the Buddha, who didn't disparage wealth but suggested that it should be used only to attain practical ends. He preached (in the *Anguttara Nikaya*) the idea of "right livelihood," meaning that one acquired material goods, food, housing, and so forth, by applying one's energies in ethical ways. And he talked about the true joy that comes from sharing your wealth with those in need.

The sixth chapter closes with the injunction to trust in God and whatever happens, not unlike what Wallace Stevens meant when he wrote: "Let be be finale of seem." It's the passage that, in the KJV, so charmingly 6:28 begins: "Consider the lilies of the field, how they grow; they toil not, neither do they spin." Jesus tells the people below him, many of whom must have perched on the very edge of existence, not to worry about food or drink or clothing or shelter. Forget material needs. If God takes care to put grass on the fields, clothing them with greenery, he will take care of you. "Set your hearts on his kingdom first," he says in 6:33–34. "So do not worry about tomorrow: tomorrow will take care of itself." This is a liberating thought. We have nothing to worry about if we trust in God, in providence, in the beneficent universe that lifts us every day.

Jesus begins the seventh chapter with "Do not judge, and you will be not judged." It's another crucial teaching, and it's a difficult one. Those who follow the Way of Jesus must not condemn the actions of others. We live in a thoroughly judgmental society now, where any crime is attended by a thousand shaming voices. Even worse, perhaps, we judge ourselves harshly. Jesus suggests that God can do the judging himself. Leave it to him. If we condemn others, or ourselves, we consign ourselves to judgment in a way that will please no one.

The end of the Sermon on the Mount moves toward measures of deep reassurance: "Ask, and it will be given you. Search, and you will find; knock, and the door will be opened to you." These words in 7:7–8 must have put his listeners at ease, suggesting that prayer is valid, that God is listening. Indeed, we get a blizzard of sayings now, moving toward the Golden Rule in 7:12, the ethic of reciprocity: treat other people in the ways you would wish to be treated. In truth, Jesus didn't invent this idea: it has a long history, going back to the Code of Hammurabi, dating from the eighteenth century B.C.E. A version of the Golden Rule was also put forward by Rabbi Hillel, a major Jewish teacher and contemporary of Jesus. Hardly any religion doesn't have some version of this precept, which has proven a sturdy rule of thumb for ethical behavior: do nothing to someone if you wouldn't want them to do the same thing to you.

The Sermon on the Mount ends with the parable of the house built on solid rock. That is a good house, and it won't easily be dislodged. A house built on sand is less stable, subject to the prevailing winds and rains. We read in 7:24: "Therefore, everyone who listens to these words of mine and acts on them will be like a sensible man who built his house on rock." A solid foundation for behavior has been laid in these three chapters, where Jesus puts forward in succinct form his basic teachings. We're told by Matthew in a kind of coda: "Jesus had now finished what he wanted to say, and his teaching made a deep impression on the people because he taught them with authority, unlike their own scribes."

Who were these "scribes" who didn't teach with authority, by the way? Matthew perhaps meant the Pharisees, once again: those who sought precedents for everything they said in Hebrew scriptures. Jesus, in fact, taught "with authority." That authority set him apart, and it's why his disciples felt in awe of him, and were willing to drop everything to assist him as he moved through Palestine as a rabbi, gathering his wisdom into words, teaching in ways that for millennia people would remember. It's an authority that derives from deep in the self, where that spark of the kingdom could be found.

Ralph Waldo Emerson put the matter succinctly in his "Divinity School Address" in 1838, at Harvard, and it seems to me utterly relevant to my reading of the Sermon on the Mount:

> Jesus Christ belonged to the true race of the prophets. He saw with open eye the mystery of the soul. Drawn by its severe harmony, ravished with its beauty, he lived in it, and had his being there. Alone in all history, he estimated the greatness of man. One man was true to what is in you and me. He saw that God incarnates himself in man, and evermore goes forth anew to take possession of his World. He said, in this jubilee of sublime emotion, "I am divine. Through me, God acts; through me, speaks. Would you see God, see me."

This Saying

Matthew 15 & Mark 7

Ian Frazier

The Gospels of Matthew and Mark begin the New Testament with a grainy immediacy. Their recountings of Christ's life and ministry, written toward the end of the first century, are like the words of eyewitnesses who have not yet completely processed what they've seen. If these two Gospels were regular news reports, they'd be the kind that appear among a newspaper's back pages, in a lower corner, remembered only later, when their scoops have completely taken over page one.

Most of what is in Matthew is also in Mark. A brief incident—that is, two versions of the same event—appears in both, and nowhere else in the Bible. Commentators refer to it as the story of the Canaanite woman (Matthew) or the story of the Syrophoenician woman (Mark). In both versions the essential details are the same. The story takes up eight verses in the first gospel and seven verses in the second, and passes by without further notice.

Syrophoenicia was a section of Syria that had been known as Phoenicia, the name Greeks gave to Canaan. Phoenicians were more commonly called Canaanites; as wide-ranging traders, they brought their culture to most of the early Mediterranean world. The Syrophoenician woman would have been Greek-speaking. Most important for the meaning of the story, the Syrophoenician woman (as I'll call her, for simplicity, and because I like how the word *Syrophoenician* sounds) was not a Jew. The short interaction between this Gentile woman and Jesus at the beginning of the Gospels is a signpost that shows where the entire New Testament is going.

Here is the story in Matthew (15:21–28):

> And Jesus went away from there and withdrew to the district of Tyre and Sidon. And behold, a Canaanite woman from that region came out and cried, "Have mercy on me, O Lord, Son of David; my daughter is severely possessed by a demon." But he did not answer her a word. And his disciples came and begged him, saying, "Send her away, for she is crying after us." He said, "I was sent only to the lost sheep of the house of Israel." But she came and knelt before him, saying, "Lord, help me." And he answered, "It is not fair to take the children's bread and throw it to the dogs." She said, "Yes, Lord, yet even the dogs eat the crumbs that fall from their masters' table." Then Jesus answered her, "O woman, great is your faith! Be it done for you as you desire." And her daughter was healed instantly.

Here is Mark (7:24–30):

> And from there he arose and went away to the region of Tyre and Sidon. And he entered a house, and would not have any one know it; yet he could not be hid. But immediately a woman, whose little daughter was possessed by an unclean spirit, heard of him, and came and fell down at his feet. Now the woman was a Greek, a Syrophoenician by birth. And she begged him to cast the demon out of her daughter. And he said to her, "Let the children first be fed, for it is not right to take the children's bread and throw it to the dogs." But she answered him, "Yes, Lord; yet even the dogs under the table eat the children's crumbs." And he said to her, "For this saying you may go your way; the demon has left your daughter." And she went home, and found the child lying in bed, and the demon gone.

I grew up in a small Ohio town where there were almost no Jews. It had a tradition of Protestant devoutness that was now fading (local stores had begun to be open on Sundays), but we still did study the Bible. Because of that, partly, I felt a familiarity when I left Ohio and moved to New York and became a writer and finally did meet a lot of Jewish people. They seemed to talk more and faster and more wittily than most of the people I grew up with—not to say that I hadn't known a lot of funny people in Ohio, but our humor had a different style. To my ear, New Yorkers in general talked sort of like Jesus's disciples. They disputed, answered back, asked difficult questions, had a certain tone (I'm avoiding the word *attitude*). An example: in Mark there's a moment when Jesus is walking in a crowd and a woman who wants to be healed touches his robe without his seeing her. He feels the healing power leap to her, and he asks his disciples, "Who touched my garments?" With some exasperation, they reply, "You see the crowd pressing around you, and yet you say, 'Who touched me?'" This exchange, minus its miraculous elements, could have been reset on a New York City street with no updating required.

In those years, hanging out with fast and funny people was the greatest sport I could imagine. The thrill of coming up with the comment that got the biggest laugh, as happened even to me every once in a while, kept me sped-up and eager for more. People topping each other, and then some brilliant person from out of left field topping everybody, made a kind of mythology out of what could also be construed as just sitting around and talking. For a few years in my early twenties, you could say that was the basic thing I did with my life.

What I love about the Syrophoenician woman is that she tops Jesus. Nowhere else in the Bible does anyone come close to matching her amazing accomplishment. She tops him, and Jesus knows she has topped him, and he acknowledges the fact: "*For this saying* you may go your way; the demon has left your daughter."

"For this saying . . ."

If I was hanging out with someone who got off a deathlessly good remark, I sometimes went back later and tried to reconstruct how it had happened. In the passages from Matthew and Mark, I regard the Syrophoenician woman in the same way: How did she do it? She is crying, desperate, almost beyond shame. The annoyance, perhaps even contempt, with which the disciples have treated her can be inferred. Jesus puts her off, important-man style: in Matthew he says, essentially, she's not his department, and in Mark he says he has to take care of his own first. She persists; she is at his feet. Then he tosses off a comment that not many parents could bear. Never again, not even when he is prophesying damnation to the Pharisees, will he be so cold and hard. That he compares the woman to a dog is bad enough. Saying that her sick daughter's life is of no more consequence than a dog's—that her daughter is not a child as the sons and daughters of the house of Israel are children—tears the last strand of human connection.

So how does the Syrophoenician woman respond to this crushing dismissal? She is at a point where despair and faith and hope and fear are interpenetrating each other and swapping back and forth at cosmic speeds—if you've ever feared for a sick child you may recognize this moment—and the energy driving the reaction, her love for her child, creates a glorious flash. The woman is inspired. Jesus often speaks in parables that even the disciples need to have explained; at once this suffering mother understands his metaphorical speech, accepts it, and takes a role in the metaphor. She says (in effect), Okay, yes, I am a Gentile and a dog. But we dogs are in your family: as I am here at your feet in my helpless pleading, we dogs are under your dinner table. Can't we poor dogs eat your children's crumbs?

Throughout his ministry Jesus is in motion. He is gathering disciples, traveling, crossing from one side of the Sea of Galilee to the other, preaching, healing, confronting religious authorities, confounding the Pharisees when they challenge him. He corrects people who speak to him—"Why do you call me 'good'?" he says to the man who addresses him as "Good Rabbi"—and he knows what others are going to say before they say it. The encounter with the Syrophoenician woman is one of the few times in Jesus's ministry when he comes to a complete stop. What she says takes him by surprise. He hears it and he observes her for the first time as an actual woman and not as a faceless member of a tribe to whom (as he supposes) he has not been sent. For that instant, the course of his ministry has left his hands.

In my youth the visual images we had of Jesus combined the qualities of the generic Hollywood leading man. Our 1950s Jesus had blond hair, blue eyes, a ginger-colored beard, and a strong Canadian Mountie–type jaw. Later I would learn about the art museums' Jesus, with his haggard, suffering face and upturned eyes (we Protestants had no crucifixes of our own). Whatever Jesus actually looked like, trying to adjust him to any physical image is misleading, because he was both God and man. This concept is so powerful, yet so challenging, to hold in the mind that whole huge heresies have thrown in the towel and simply picked one side or the other. I try to think of Jesus as being a sort of oscillation between the two. A similar idea in physics is the uncertainty principle, which says you cannot know both the position and the speed of a particle at the same time. Jesus was God and man oscillating back and forth—either and both, both or either, simultaneously.

Usually Jesus's oscillation hummed back and forth so fast as to seem at rest, but sometimes one aspect or the other unbalanced it and briefly won out. Just before he meets the Syrophoenician woman, the oscillation has seized up. At that moment, Jesus is just a man. He is tired, he wants to get away and rest, and he identifies by his human membership in the tribe of Israel. What the Syrophoenician woman says to him breaks the freeze-up and restores him to his true nature. He gets her deeper message as fast as she picked up his metaphor. In many encounters, Jesus tells people what God the Father wants them to understand. Here, for the only time in the Bible, God is addressing the Son through another human being.

* * *

The question of whom Jesus was sent to gets clearer as the New Testament goes along. In his commission to his disciples early in Matthew, he tells them they are to minister to the Jews, not the Gentiles. What the encounter with the Syrophoenician woman demonstrates is that he won't be able to do the former while leaving out the latter. In Mark the forget-the-Gentiles rule is repeated, but by the Book of Luke it is loosening. In Luke, we are given the Good Samaritan, the parable that ends all such distinctions forever.

He tells it in order to answer a question. A man asks what one should do to lead a good life, and Jesus says that the essence of the law is to love your God with all your strength and all your heart and all your mind, and to love your neighbor as yourself. Following up, the man asks, "But who then is my neighbor?" After telling of the robbed and beaten traveler by the side of the road who is helped not by his fellow Jews who come upon him but by a passing Samaritan, Jesus answers the man's question with a question: "Which one of these was his neighbor?" To the answer "The one who showed him kindness," Jesus does not simply say, "Correct." What he says instead is far more subtle and demanding: "Go thou and do likewise." The neighbor is indeed the one who shows kindness to the helpless man, but the real point is that the neighbor is you. And therefore you are neighbor to everybody: "Go *thou* and do likewise."

It figures that the characters in this parable are travelers and the setting is the road, because the larger plot of the New Testament is the bringing of the gospel to the Gentiles. By the fifth book, the Acts of the Apostles, with its stories of the many journeys of Paul, the New Testament has become a travel narrative. To get a sense of Paul's letters, which follow Acts, you need an atlas to keep all the destinations straight. From the perspective of faith, the Christian Bible exists to solve a practical problem: there is one God, the God of Israel; how, then, to bring the one true God to the rest of the world? The life of Jesus effects that almost unimaginable, gigantically world-changing crossover.

By refusing to be excluded from Jesus's mission, and by inserting herself imaginatively in his parable, the Syrophoenician woman opens his mission out. If Jesus is the one true, living God, then he must be God for everybody. At the jump of the spark from the Syrophoenician woman to Jesus and from him instantly back to her, the New Testament's motion has begun.

For this saying . . .

A few years ago I went to a display of the Dead Sea Scrolls at an exhibition hall in Times Square. Because of the amber, low-impact light I had to lean in very close to see. The carefulness of the scrolls' lettering, the obvious fluency of the writing motion, the simple, practiced regularity of each stroke, like perfect stitching—all contributed to an almost mystical beauty. My admiration of these objects caused me to wonder why Jesus had been so down on the scribes. His preaching against hypocritical Pharisees I could understand, but why did he throw the scribes in with them? "Woe unto you, scribes and Pharisees!" What did the scribes ever do, besides have good handwriting?

Wall labels said that the scrolls date to the second century before Christ, that they are among the most important artifacts of ancient civilization, and that the Jews were and are known as the People of the Book. One label noted that not only did Israel revere the holy scriptures but its people were, in a sense, the scriptures' product; the people produced the scriptures, but the scriptures also sustained the people, directed them, molded them, carried them into their future. These artifacts, like all of the Jewish Bible, were multimillennial survival—in a sense, a living thing.

Throughout Jesus's teachings he commented on scripture and on the laws set down in it. He knew its every word; quotations from it amplified and reverberated in everything he said. As the aliveness of scripture bumped up against him, he bumped back. The laws against Sabbath breaking, for example, often came up when people criticized him. Among his answers was the hard-to-argue-with observation "The sabbath was made for man, not man for the sabbath." His ministry consisted of healing and other miracles, but mostly it occurred in words. Miracles existed within a framework of space and time: you had to be there. But his words, like the Jews' holy scriptures, endured. Jesus's abrupt return to himself when he hears the Syrophoenician woman's faith-powered improvisation shows how he lived in words. At that moment it's almost as if the hood is lifted from the word-engine that drives him. When he replies, "For this saying," he is acknowledging the literary and conceptual way in which his work on earth will be accomplished. Compelled by fierce love, uplifted by faith, gifted by God with witty, brilliant words, the Syrophoenician woman enters, in an instant, into scripture.

Faith is an oscillation between certainty and doubt, just as Jesus is an oscillation between God and man. Doubt gives faith its tenor, its resistance, its meter. When you need faith the most is exactly at the point when it seems to be the most unwarranted. As I read the Bible my faith sometimes goes far over onto the doubt side of the scale. Some of the gospel miracles, certain "hard teachings" about marriage and adultery, the pronouncements of Paul about how slaves should obey their masters, and many other passages slide me toward doubt. Yet somehow the doubt never completely takes over.

I think every word in the Bible was meant to be pushed against so that we can see how it pushes back. The Syrophoenician woman, who approaches Jesus in suffering and fear, interacts with him at first against his will. By her pushing, she comes maybe as close to comprehending God as a human being can get. For me, the oscillation between faith and doubt surges strongly toward faith when I consider the Syrophoenician woman. I believe an actual woman who once lived on the earth said what she is reported to have said, I believe an actual man answered her as Matthew and Mark say Jesus answered her, and I believe that actual, living man was God.

Miracles

Mark 2:1–12

Thomas Lynch

Our tribe did not read the Bible. We got it in doses, daily or weekly, from a priest bound by the lectionary to give us bits and pieces in collects, Epistles, Gospels, and graduals, which, along with the Confiteor and Kyrie, formed the front-loaded, word-rich portion of the Tridentine Mass. These were followed by sacred table work and common feed, to wit laving and consecration, communion, thanksgiving, and benediction. On Sundays, it'd all be seasoned with some lackluster homiletics—linked haphazardly to the scriptures on the day. These liturgies were labor-intensive, heavy on metaphor and stagecraft, holy theater. Possibly this is why few priests put much time into preaching, preferring, as the writing workshops say, "to show rather than to tell."

Still, we knew the stories: Eden and the apple, the murderous brother, the prodigal son, floods and leviathans, mangers and magi, scribes and Pharisees and repentant thieves. I remember my excitement, the first time I heard about the woman washing the savior's feet with her tears, and wiping them with her long hair and anointing them with perfume. My father, a local undertaker, was especially fond of Joseph of Arimathea and his sidekick, Nicodemus, who'd bargained with Pilate for the corpse of Christ and tended to the burial of same, in Joseph's own tomb, newly hewn from rock, the body wrapped in linen with spices "in keeping with the customs of the Jews." My father claimed this "a corporal work of mercy." This he'd been told by the parish priest, who furthermore gave him what my father called "a standing dispensation" from attendance at Mass whenever he was called, as he fairly often was, to tend to the dead and the bereaved on Sundays and Holy Days of Obligation.

The biblical narratives were told and retold through our formative years at school, by nuns who had done their little bit of editing and elaboration, the better to fit the predicaments of our station. And though we had a Bible at home—an old Counter-Reformation, Douay-Rheims translation from the Latin Vulgate of St. Jerome's fourth-century text—we never read the thing. It was a holy knickknack, like the statue of the Blessed Mother, the picture of the Sacred Heart, the tabletop manger scene that came out for Christmas, the crucifix over each of our bedroom doors, the holy water font at the front door—all designed to suit our daily devotional lives. We prayed the family rosary in May and October, kept the fasts and abstinences of Lent and Advent along with whatever novena was in fashion and most likely to inure to our spiritual betterments. We abstained from meat on Friday, confessed our sins on Saturday, kept holy the Sabbath, such as we knew it, and basked in the assurance that ours was the one true faith. Ours was a Holy, Roman, Irish-American, postwar-baby-booming, suburban family—sacramental, liturgical, replete with none-too-subtle guilt and shaming, the big magic of transubstantiation, binding and loosing, the true presence, cardinal sins, contrary virtues, states of grace, and the hope for salvation. Litanies and chaplets stood in for scriptures and hermeneutics. That was a thing the "other crowd" did, godhelpthem, bound to their idolatries about the Good Book, lost, we reckoned, in the error of their ways.

I memorized, through the weekly instructions of Father Thomas Kenny, the responses to the priests' incantations at Mass, attracted as I was to the stately cadences of Latin and the mystery of a secret language. I took up my service as an altar boy at age seven, sharing duties for the 6:20 A.M. Mass with my brothers, Dan and Pat, a year older and younger, respectively, three weeks out of every four, at our parish church, St. Columban's. Then we'd hustle off to Holy Name School across town, where the day's tutelage began with a students' Mass at 8:15 read by the saintly, white-maned Monsignor Paddock, beneath a huge mosaic on the general theme, the good sisters told us, of the Eucharist.

Old Melchizedek was on one side and Abraham and Isaac on the other, prefiguring the Risen Christ on his cross occupying the mosaic space between them—each a different version of priesthood, sacrifice, and Eucharist. This was the image I stared at all through the mornings of my boyhood, never knowing the chapters or verses I might have read for a more fulsome understanding of it all, how Abraham's willingness to sacrifice his son prefigured the death of Jesus on the cross; how the bloody business of worship and communion became the loaf and cup of the Last Supper and the priesthood of Melchizedek became the holy orders of churchmen down the centuries. Priesthood was something I understood in the cassocked and collared, biretta-topped celibates, the parish priests and curates, Jesuits and Franciscans in their habits who'd heard the voice of God—their vocation—and answered the call.

By twenty I was happily apostate, having come into my disbelief some few years after puberty, when a fellow pilgrim showed me all that she could on the mystery of life. If the nuns had been wrong about sex, and they surely had been, it followed, I reasoned, they were wrong on other things.

"Why do you reason about these things in your hearts?" Jesus asks the naysaying elders in Capernaum, in Mark's telling of the healing of a paralytic. They are trying to catch his blaspheming out, in the way we are always conniving against our spiritual betters.

I'd been named for a dead priest—my father's late uncle Tom—and for the famously skeptical apostle, whose finger and dubiety still hover over the wounds of Christ, waiting, in the words of that great evangelist Ronald Reagan, to "trust but verify." True to which code, I questioned everything.

The deaths of children, the random little disasters that swept young mothers to their dooms in childbirth, their infants to their sudden crib deaths, young lovers to their demises in cars, perfect strangers to their hapless ends, seemed more evidence than anyone should need that whoever is in charge of these matters had a hit-and-miss record on humanity.

My work—I eventually got about my father's business—put me in earshot, albeit over corpses, of some of the best preaching on theodicy available. The Book of Job, however god-awful and comfortless it is, remained for me a testament of faith: "blessed be the name of the Lord." Nonetheless, I remained devoutly lapsed in my confession and praxis.

So I was fairly shocked when years later, having achieved the rank of former husband and custodial father, small-town undertaker and internationally ignored poet, I got a call from one of my fellow Rotarians to say they were looking for "a good Catholic to join their Bible study."

"Let me know if you find one" is what I answered, and we both laughed a little, but he persisted. "No, really, you'll like it. We're going to meet at the Big Boy on Tuesday mornings at half past six. We'll be done by eight so everyone can get to work." Before I had time to construct a proper excuse he said, "See you then!" and hung up the phone.

What harm? I thought. It'll never last. A god-awful hour and crummy eatery, not a great book, if a "good" one—like cocker spaniels, serviceable but ineluctably dull.

That was going thirty years ago. Our little study has outlived the restaurant, the Rotary, a few of our roughly dozen charter members, our denominations and divided politics, and still we meet—at my funeral home now—every early Tuesday morning, every season, every weather, to read and discuss various books of the Bible. We've done everything from Genesis to Revelation, all of the Gospels, some extracanonical texts, the letters of Paul. Job we've done three times, James maybe twice. We'll likely never do the Apocalypse again.

I only go to church now for baptisms, funerals, or weddings. The mysteries of birth and death and sex are regular enough that I remain familiar with the liturgies and language of worship. But dogma and dicta defy sound reason, and the management class of the Church is uniquely wrongheaded and feckless. What's more, my own views on same-sex marriage, the ordination of women, priestly celibacy, and redemptive suffering would put me so sufficiently at odds with them as to render me, no doubt, an ex-communicant.

Oddly enough, the less observant I became, in belief or devotion, the better the "good" book seemed to me. I didn't need the religious epic so much as a good story, something to share, a party piece.

I can't remember not knowing about the healing of the paralytic, whether I heard it at Mass or from one of the nuns or Christian Brothers who were in charge of my education, or read it as part of our Bible study. There it is, in three Gospels out of four, the details more or less the same. It is one of the three dozen or so miracle stories that punctuate the New Testament, including Jesus changing water into wine at Cana, calming the storm and filling the fishnets, healing lepers and the blind and lame, and raising the dead, himself included. There are endless demons and devils cast out, sins forgiven, apparitions after his death. A poem in a book published a few years back brought it newly to life for me.

The last time I heard Seamus Heaney read was in the Glenn Memorial Chapel at Emory University. It was and remains a Methodist church, which doubles as an auditorium for gatherings of a certain size. It was the second of March, 2013, and I was occupying the McDonald Family Chair, a cushy sinecure with the Candler School of Theology at Emory, teaching a course with the great preacher and theologian Thomas Long called the Poetics of the Sermon. Dr. Long and I were just putting the final touches on a book we'd coauthored titled *The Good Funeral,* due out later that year and written for clergy, mere mortals, and mortuary sorts. And I was learning words like *exegesis* and *hermeneutics* and studying the dynamics of fiction, which Dr. Long regarded as a workable template for homiletics. We examined narrative arc and point of view, plot and character and setting. We read poems and short fictions and published sermons.

I was delighted that Heaney would be coming to town. His had been the most amplified and ever-present voice of my generation of poets. His work, since I first encountered it forty-five years ago, reading by the fire in the ancestral home in County Clare I would later inherit, had never failed to return a rich trove of the word horde and metaphorical treasures. Because so much of his poetry came out of a Catholic upbringing in rural Ireland, he became for me a useful guide for the parish of language and imagination.

Possibly because I first encountered prayer as poetry, or at least as language cast in rhyme and meter, addressed to the heavens as a sort of raised speech, poetry had always seemed sacerdotal, proper for addressing the mysteries of happenstance and creation. That Heaney held the natural world and human work—the chore and toil of the mundane, earthbound and near to hand—in awe and reverence seemed more attuned to the holy than the politicized religiosity of the culture. Still, the Latin I'd learned as an altar boy in the 1950s, the sacraments, devotions, and sensibilities I'd been raised with echoed in the early poems of the Irish master, even if my own life's experience and further examinations of scripture and secular texts had left me apostate. Though freighted with doubts and wonders and religiously adrift, I treasured the language of faith as an outright gift—the hymns of Charles Wesley, the angel-wrestling contemplations of John Calvin, the exile and anchoritic adventures of Columcille, and the rubrics of holy women and men—I retained some level of religious literacy given me by nuns and Christian Brothers, but rejected the magisterium of the church.

By the time I'd arrived at Emory in the late winter of 2013, I was deeply devoted to a church of latter-day poets, skeptics, and noncompliant but kindly sorts. The irony of such a backslidden fellow as myself teaching at a school of theology named for the Methodist bishop and first chancellor of Emory, whose brother was the owner of our national sugar water, Coca-Cola, was not lost on me. Though I had been schooled in my apostasy by H. L. Mencken, Robert Ingersoll, Christopher Hitchens, and Richard Dawkins, and by the malfeasance of bishops and abusive priests, I had also witnessed, over four decades in funeral service, the charity of pastors, priests, rabbis, and imams. These were men and women of faith who showed up whenever there was trouble. Their best preaching was done when the chips were down, in extremis, at deathbeds, in the hospitals and nursing homes and family homes and funeral homes. They pitch in and do their part even though they cannot fix the terrible things that happen. They are present, they pray, they keep open the possibility of hope. And I'd been schooled by my semester among the Methodists and seminarians at Emory, and by my friendship with the Reverend Thomas Long, whose scholarship and work in words has re-formed me in a way I thought impossible.

Thus, Heaney's reading from the raised sanctuary of Glenn Memorial Chapel seemed a "keeping holy" of a Sabbath, and his poems, portions of a sacred text. And when he said, deep into what would be one of his last public readings, that he'd like to read some poems from his "last book," and then corrected himself to say, "my most recent collection," I thought the insertion of the shadow of death was a deft touch by a seasoned performer of his work. It is also true that his "most recent collection," *Human Chain*, seemed so haunted a book, dogged by death and impendency and the urgency of last things.

On that day he read one of my favorites of his poems. "Miracle" proposes a shift of focus in the scriptural story of Jesus healing the paralytic, my favorite rendition of which occurs in Mark 2:1–12. Jesus is preaching in Capernaum, and the crowd is so great, filling the room and spilling out the door into the street, that four men bringing the paralytic to be healed have to hoist him up to the roof, remove the roof tiles, or dig through the sod, and lower him down on his bed by ropes, whereupon Jesus, impressed by their faith, tells the poor cripple his sins are forgiven. Of course, the begrudgers among them—and there are always begrudgers—begin to mumble among themselves about blasphemy, because "Who can forgive sins but God, alone?" Jesus questions them, saying, Which is easier—by which he means the lesser miracle—"to say, 'your sins are forgiven' or to say, 'Arise, take up your bed and walk'?" It is, of course, a trick question.

Because forgiveness seems impossible, whether to give it or to receive it, and impossible to see. It would always take a miracle. Nor is God the only one capable of forgiving. Do we not pray to be forgiven our trespasses "as we forgive those who trespass against us"? Who among us is not withered and weighed down by the accrual of actual or imagined slights, betrayals, resentments, estrangements, and wrongdoings done unto us most often by someone we've loved. And in ways I needn't number, we're all paralyzed, hobbled by our grievances and heartbreaks, by the press of sin, the failure of vision, by fear, by worry, by anxieties about the end.

Whereas the scripture directs our attention to the paralytic, and to the quibbles between Jesus and the scribes, Heaney's poem bids us be mindful of the less learned toil and utterly miraculous decency of "the ones who have known [us] all along," who lift us up, bear us in our brokenness, and get us where we need to go. On any given day it seems miracle enough.

The everyday and deeply human miracle, void of heavenly hosts or interventions, has especial meaning for Heaney, who, in August of 2006, woke up in a guesthouse in Donegal paralyzed by a stroke. He had attended the birthday party for Anne Friel, wife of the playwright and Heaney's schoolmate and lifelong friend, Brian Friel. After the night's festivities the Heaneys were spending the night with other friends and fellow poets in the local B and B. He awakened to paralysis on the left side of his body. So it was his wife, Marie, and Des and Mary Kavanagh, Peter and Jean Fallon, and Tom Kilroy—ones who had known him all along—who helped strap him onto the gurney and get him down the steep stairs, out of the building and into the waiting ambulance to ride with his wife to Letterkenny Hospital. In the poem, which took shape in the weeks of what he called "rest cure," in the Royal Hospital, Donnybrook, in Dublin, the narrative power proceeds "Not

[to] the one who takes up his bed and walks," rather to "the ones who have known him all along/and carry him in—" who do the heavy lifting of his care and transport. They are the agents of rescue and restoration, their faithful friendship miraculous and salvific. Their hefting and lifting and large muscle work is the stuff and substance of salvation. Here is the short poem.

MIRACLE

Not the one who takes up his bed and walks
But the ones who have known him all along
And carry him in—
Their shoulders numb, the ache and stoop deeplocked
In their backs, the stretcher handles
Slippery with sweat. And no let-up
Until he's strapped on tight, made tiltable
And raised to the tiled roof, then lowered for healing.
Be mindful of them as they stand and wait
For the burn of the paid-out ropes to cool,
Their slight lightheadedness and incredulity
To pass, those ones who had known him all along.

Hearing its maker read "Miracle" from the pulpit at Emory put me in mind of my conversation with him at the funeral of our friend Dennis O'Driscoll, who had died less than three months before, on Christmas Eve, 2012, and was buried near his home in Naas, County Kildare.

Seamus had been Dennis's principal eulogist on the day, just as Dennis had been Heaney's most insightful interlocutor. His book of interviews with Heaney, *Stepping Stones,* is the nearest thing to an autobiography we will ever have of the Nobel laureate and more thoroughly than ever examines the life of the man in relation to the work.

Following O'Driscoll's funeral liturgy, I walked with Heaney and his wife in the sad cortege from the church to the cemetery, half a mile or so, following the coffin and the other mourners. We chatted about our dead friend and the sadness we all shared. Maybe his stroke six years before, and my open-heart surgery the year before, eventuated in our bringing up the rear of the entourage. We were taking our time, huffing and puffing some at the steeper bits, as we made our slow but steady way up the town, out the road, to the grave behind the hearse. In Ireland the dead are shouldered to the opened ground and lowered in with ropes by the pallbearers. After the priest has had his say, the grave is filled in by family and friends. The miracle of life and the mystery of death are unambiguously tethered by a funiculus of grave ropes and public grieving, religiously bound by the exercise of large-muscle duties—shoulder and shovel work and the heart's indentures, each a linkage in the ongoing, unbroken human chain. And the strain of pallbearers at O'Driscoll's open grave, as they lowered his coffined body into the opened ground with slowly paying out the ropes, seemed like the faithful and existential labor of the paralytic's friends, lowering his bed through the opened roof in Capernaum to the foot of his healer for a cure.

The witness of these things drew a catch in my breath that New Year's Eve morning when we buried Dennis O'Driscoll, in the new row of St. Corban's Cemetery. Watching his pallbearers lower him into the vacancy of the grave, these mundane mortuary chores replicating the miraculous narrative of the Gospels where the paralytic's pals lower him into the place of his healing, the "slight lightheadedness and incredulity" perfectly articulated in Heaney's poem, remains caught in my chest, not yet exhaled, and, like the scribes in Capernaum, that day in Naas, though I'd seen such things all my workaday life, I'd "never seen anything like this before."

And yet I saw it all again, months later, in the late summer, when Heaney's death stunned us all on Friday morning, the thirtieth of August 2013. I woke to texts and e-mails from Dublin. "Seamus is dead" is what they read. "Ah, hell . . ." I wrote back. Ah, hell, indeed.

I called David Fanagan, the Dublin undertaker, and asked if I might ride in the hearse. Someone who knew the poems and the poet should ride along.

I flew to Shannon and stayed at my digs in Clare that night and drove up to Dublin on Sunday morning, stopping in Naas to visit Dennis's grave. At Fanagans in Aungier Street, Heaney was laid out in Chapel 3, the corpse, horizontal and still, "silent beyond silence listened for." Marie greeted me and thanked me for making the long journey and was a little shocked to hear that I'd had my ticket in hand for more than a month, long before Seamus had any notion of dying. She told me she thought he must have had a heart attack on Wednesday, complaining of a pain in his jaw, then tripped leaving a restaurant on Thursday, which got him to the hospital, where they discovered a tear in his aorta. The only thing more risky than operating, she was told, was doing nothing. He was in extremis. A team was assembled to do the procedure at half past seven on Friday morning, just minutes before which he texted her, calm and grateful for the long years of love, and told her not to be afraid. "Noli timere," he wrote at the end, the ancient language englished: *be not afraid*. He was dead before the operation began.

All the way up there people lined the way, on the overpasses, and in the halted cars at intersections whose inhabitants got out to applaud the cortege of the great poet. Women were weeping or wiping tears from their faces. Men held the palms of their hands to their hearts, caps doffed, thumbs up, everyone at their best attention.

"How did you get to be the one?" I asked the man at the wheel of the new Mercedes-Benz hearse, no doubt hustled into service for the TV cameras. "I drew the short straw," he told me. "We used to get extra to drive in the North, what with the Troubles and fanatics. Now it's just a long haul and a long day."

We picked up forty or fifty cars as we made our way, the roughly three-hour drive north from Dublin, then west around Belfast making for Derry, crossing the river that connects Lough Beg to Lough Neagh at Toomebridge, the crowds getting bigger the nearer we got. Police on motorcycles had picked us up at the border, just outside of Newry, and escorted our makeshift motorcade all the way to the cemetery as we went down the boreen off the main road and drove by the family farm and onward to Bellaghy, where a piper met us at the entrance to town and piped us through the village, where the crowd spilled out of shops and pubs and houses and into the road, every man woman and child out applauding, crossing themselves, giving out with bits of "Danny Boy" and holding their hearts in signals of respect. The sadness on their faces and the tribute to the level man behind me in the box was like nothing I'd ever seen, and when we got to the grave, led there by a cadre of churchmen in white albs and copes and cowls, I took the family spray up to the grave through the cordons of paparazzi clicking photos of everything. I walked with Marie and her family behind the coffin as we went to the grave, where against my hopes that Seamus would pop out and proclaim it all a big mistake, his sons and his brothers and her brothers bent to the black ropes and lowered him into the ground, the paid-out ropes and the burn in their arms and hands and the hush of the gathered multitude notwithstanding.

Leaves rustled in the overarching sycamores. The clergy struck up a verse of "Salve Regina" to reinsinuate their imprimatur on it all. We hung around in that sad and self-congratulatory way mourners do, after the heavy lifting is done. The limo had a slow leak in the right front tire that had to be tended to. Des Kavanagh and his wife, Mary, came and spoke to me, wondering if I'd be in Galway anytime soon. Brian Friel's car pulled away, he nodded. Michael, Seamus's son, came over to thank me for going in the hearse with his dad, and I was glad of that. And grateful. I stayed until the sod was back on him, and the flowers sorted on top of that, and then we drove back the road, arriving in Dublin right around dark. Anthony MacDonald, his short-straw, long day nearing its end, dropped me at the corner of Georges Street and Stephen Street Lower. I gave him fifty euros and told him to get something at the off-license with my thanks for taking me up and back on the day, for getting Seamus where he needed to go, and getting me where I needed to be. "No bother," he said. "Not a bit." Nothing out of the utterly ordinary, utterly pedestrian, a miracle.

Possibly these are the miracles we fail to see, on the lookout as we are for signs and wonders: for seas that part for us to pass through, skies that open to a glimpse of heaven, the paralytic who stands and walks, the blind who begin to see, the shortfall that becomes a sudden abundance. Maybe what we miss are the ordinary miracles, the ones who have known us all along—the family and friends, the fellow pilgrims who show up, pitch in, and do their parts to get us where we need to go, within earshot and arm's reach of our healing, the earthbound, everyday miracle of forbearance and forgiveness, the help in dark times to light the way, the ones who show up when there is trouble to save us from our hobbled, heart-wrecked selves.

Never Quite As Simple

Luke 2:19

Owen King

On Christmas Eves my family kept a simple, orderly tradition: first, after we sat ourselves around the tree, my father read aloud Luke 2:1–19, which told the story of Augustus's decree, the appearance of the angels to the shepherds, and, centrally, the birth of Christ in the manger in Bethlehem; then, we all took turns reading from *How the Grinch Stole Christmas* by Dr. Seuss. This was followed by the clear highlight of the evening: my brother and sister and I were each permitted to open up a present that wasn't one of the important ones. Last, we kids laid out some cookies and milk for Santa, and went upstairs to try and sleep.

(Once or twice we left a beer for Santa instead of milk. This seemed hilarious in the way that getting babies to hold cigarettes also seemed hilarious. Later, my dad—i.e., one half of the family Santa—ended up in rehab. Turns out the joke was on us elves.)

I recall dreading the Bible passage. For me as a kid, hours seemed to elapse while my father read those nineteen verses. (I reread them now in less than five minutes.) The story had no context in our secular life. My family didn't go to Mass, not on Christmas, not ever. Church was a free-time-gobbling chore forced on my unluckiest neighborhood friends, spotted from our windows trudging out of their houses in neckties and sour faces on beautiful Sunday mornings. For me, listening to those nineteen verses on our holiday evening was akin to listening to a stewardess's preflight demonstration of how to latch and tighten your safety belt, and where to find the emergency exits. Luke 2:1–19 pertained to subjects—God, Jesus, the Middle East—that, like air safety, I never thought about unless the occasion demanded.

And the story of Jesus's birth struck me as lackluster. It was about parents, parents who had to register for something; a deadly pairing. If there was anything more boring than the doings of parents, it was the act of registering—for anything. There were also angels, shepherds, a foreign setting, a barn, and a baby. Exciting stuff was supposed to happen in stories, but you can't start a fire with damp kindling. If I'd had to file the story of Jesus's birth, I would have tucked it in alongside the fairy tales for little kids—the stories of Goldilocks, Sleeping Beauty, et cetera—and as far down that row as possible, because not even an illustrated version of the story, featuring images of soaring angels, men in turbans, and a baby in a bed of straw could have provided much distraction. If such an illustrated version included a foreshadowing image of the crucifixion, I suppose the ghoulishness of that scenario might have held me for a moment—but only a moment. The adult Jesus was so unreal. (Visual representations of Christ seem to have diversified over the years, but, like most kids of my generation, based on the evidence set before me, I accepted that this gentleman of Middle Eastern descent was a Caucasian who resembled a taller Geddy Lee.) And then, this is what it all led to, his hideous death? I just didn't get anything to do with the Bible. You certainly could not begin to compare something like Luke to *How the Grinch Stole Christmas*.

Which is why it came as a surprise to me when a bit of the passage did, suddenly, catch my attention. I was eight or nine, and I'd been zoning out of Luke for years. But one line tripped me, woke me up. It was 2:19, which follows on the shepherds' revelation to Mary and Joseph that the baby is the Messiah: "But Mary kept all these things in her heart and pondered them."*

I was sitting on the couch, a pudgy arm's reach from the tree, and there was that dusty-sticky smell of pine in the air, and, when my father closed the little white-covered book, it made that particular floppy thwap that only floppy Bibles make.

And I thought, Wait. She pondered . . . she pondered . . . she pondered . . . What?

What was there to ponder?

How could Mary not be thrilled about the news that the shepherds had brought her? On the surface it was perverse. Her son was God! What more could you want? Why wasn't she running around and telling everyone? Mary's reticence was unfathomable.

I kept thinking about it, though, and gradually came to observe that there was, perhaps, a fair amount for Mary to chew over. From the standpoint of my future career as a writer of fiction, whose most important task is the creation of compelling characters, it was a key discovery.

Mary's subdued reaction reveals misgivings that are exceptionally sympathetic and entirely reasonable. Why should she accept the shepherds' incredible tale? They are strangers and she is in a strange place. And if Mary does choose to trust them, then what does it mean to be the mother of the Messiah? Contemplate how transformative parenthood is under normal circumstances. Who could blame Mary for deliberating on such a colossal weight? See her, a new mother huddled with her baby in a manger, approached by men who insist they have heard from angels. I worry about the Mary of Luke 2:19. I'm scared for her. Can she glimpse, even dimly, the personal loss that the shepherds' tidings presage? When I stir around in the passage, what bobs up is the portrait of a person who behaves as a person, doubtful and fearful and

---

* In the Bible I have here, Luke 2:19 is written as "But Mary treasured all these words and pondered them in her heart," producing an entirely different impression.

confused. I don't believe that Jesus Christ was divine, but in Luke 2:19 I believe in Mary as a woman who once lived.

In the second debate of the 2004 presidential campaign, there was a memorable back-and-forth about abortion and whether or not federal money should ever pay for the procedure.*

President Bush had dinged Senator Kerry for making a circuitous response to the question wherein he stated that he was personally opposed to abortion because of his own faith but did not want to "legislate [faith]." Implicit in what Senator Kerry was saying was that it would be legislating faith to outlaw the use of federal money to pay for abortion in all cases. The president was, by contrast, perfectly explicit. He stated, "We're not going to spend federal taxpayers' money on abortion"; he further seized the opportunity to voice his opposition to partial-birth abortion and his support for parental notification laws. It was a direct and authoritative response. Even if this wasn't what you wanted to hear, you were attracted to the way President Bush said it, because he was unfaltering. It's soothing to be told how it will be, to have resolution.

But then the senator did something startling: he added a zest of reality to the discussion. Kerry raised the example of a badly injured mother: Shouldn't a partial-birth abortion be allowed to save the mother's life? And what about a teenage girl who has been raped by her father? Should she be required to notify her rapist if she wants an abortion?

"It's never quite as simple as the president wants you to believe," concluded Senator Kerry, and, boy, was that ever the fucking truth.

Now, was this also, essentially, a talking point? Yes, it was. Senator Kerry was speaking to his base, and so was President Bush, each hitting

---

* A transcript of the debate can be found here: www.debates.org/index.php?page=october-8-2004-debate-transcript.

the expected notes while listening to the sound of change pouring into donation buckets. It has to be said that these two men, white and male like every president and vice president who preceded them, were hugely wealthy. As much as I agreed—and still do agree—with Senator Kerry, and as much as I do consider him an essentially well-meaning man, it must be conceded that he is a mouthpiece, a mouthpiece for affluent liberals like myself.

Which leads us to another valuable aspect of Luke 2:19: it not only gives complexity to a character but grants that complexity to a poor woman, something that is all too uncommon in literature, past and present. There are very few human beings with the pharaonic resources of a John Kerry or a George Bush. There are a lot more people out there that are like Mary.

She's an impoverished mother. She's the one facing the awesome responsibility of caring for a child. For Mary it isn't theory, it's her life, and that life is difficult. Mary is everywhere and she is all colors. She is the mother who worries about what will become of her child in a situation that is not ideal.

An aide to President Bush famously discounted "the reality-based community." I can sympathize with the sentiment. Reality is nerve-racking. It would be nice if Santa Claus was real, but it's Mom and Dad who put the presents under the tree, who eat the cookies and drink the milk, and, whether you like it or not, they walked a long, long corridor before they ever arrived at you. There were lovers and friends and regrets and miseries and confusions, and most of it you'll never catch so much as a whiff of. There was everything that happened while you were dreaming of sugarplums.

Perhaps a truly persuasive narrative cannot, in a sense, help making a political statement, because a truly persuasive narrative expresses that life is complex and people are complex and resolution is difficult to achieve. There is always so much to ponder.

"She was good." "He was bad." "She was lazy and weak." "He was smart and strong." "The child was a perfect saint." No, no, no, no, and especially no. I don't believe it. A story can't tell us everything about a character, but it needs to tell us more than that if it wants to tell us anything.

Limits of scope do apply, obviously. Not every facet of a character can be explored, and not every character can be explored. Take *How the Grinch Stole Christmas*'s Cindy-Lou Who. She is, as far as we know, bland sweetness personified. I have a suspicion that there's more to her and to all the Whos. It's not her story or their story, though. Seuss's portrait of the Grinch—brittle, jealous, isolated, conflicted, curious, keeper of a piteous dog—on the other hand, is indelible. You can't doubt his essential humanity, Grinchy as it is. His too-small heart must be full of secrets.

"Who am I to judge?" Pope Francis, head of the Roman Catholic Church, has remarked, on the subject of gay marriage.

"Abortion compounds the grief of many women who now carry with them deep physical and spiritual wounds after succumbing to the pressures of a secular culture which devalues God's gift of sexuality and the right to life of the unborn," Pope Francis said on another occasion, but then again, who is he to judge? Really, who is he? There is a gulf between these two statements, and in that space is a man named Jorge Mario Bergoglio, who nearly eighty years ago was a wrinkled pink infant swaddled in his mother's arms in Buenos Aires. What about Jorge's mother? When she gazed down upon her beautiful new boy, did she feel only love and joy? I bet it wasn't that simple. It's never that simple, is it? Jorge's mother must have been at least a little afraid, if only on the minutest subconscious level, in that deep place inside that never loses sight of the fact that every man and woman and child does eventually come to dust. All our love and all our joy can't make our babies immortal. This darkness lives inside us from the instant of our child's birth.

Mary felt it. She kept it in her heart and she pondered.

Long Road Home: Thoughts on the Prodigal Son

Luke 15:11–32

Tobias Wolff

When I was in the first years of grade school my mother used to leave me with a farmer's wife on weekends while she worked at the local Dairy Queen. This was in Florida, in the early fifties. I didn't like going to the farm. The farmer was brusque, and I sensed that he resented having me underfoot and useless. His wife was friendly enough but busy with her own children, a girl my age and a boy a little older. They looked at me from a distance, these two, amused by my citified speech and my fastidiousness when served milk still warm from the cow, or when forced to handle a slippery, spiny, whiskered catfish from the pond, or when their father killed a chicken.

The one thing I did like about those weekends was going to revival meetings. These were held in great tents with trucks parked all around, dogs barking from the cabs as we walked past, the farmer in a dark suit, the farmer's wife carrying a tray of food to add to those on the tables outside the tent. It was hot and close under the canvas. Women fanned themselves; men did not, their sun-reddened faces growing even redder. Little kids ran in and out. The folding chairs had no cushions, and got harder and stickier as the hours—and I mean *hours*—went by. There was always a baby crying, over here, over there, like popcorn going off.

None of this distracted me. I loved the music, often led by beautiful twin sisters standing before big radio microphones, broadcasting for a local gospel program. (I still sing some of those songs to myself: "The Old Rugged Cross," "There Is a Balm in Gilead," "I Come to the Garden Alone." Our Catholic hymnal has nothing to compare.) And the preaching! No dry bromides droned from a pulpit; this was theater. The preacher paced the stage, brandishing his big black Bible. He acted out the stories and parables, speaking in the voices of Moses, of Job and his comforters, Martha, the Good Samaritan, the woman at the well, Pilate, the Lord God Himself. I saw Abraham raise the knife over his son, heard the demons shriek as the Gadarene swine carried them over the cliff.

My mother had a Bible, but it stayed on the shelf, and as a divorced Catholic she didn't attend Mass or insist that I go until a few years later. So the stories told by the preacher were mostly new to me. Some of them troubled me, and went on troubling me. Why would God let Satan do such terrible things to Job? Yes, okay, God replaced the wife and sons and sheep, but what about the original wife and sons? Job's happy ending was no happy ending for them. And poor young Isaac, hauled up a mountain to be killed by his father, just so God could make a point about who, or Who, came first. So he got spared at the last minute; it still wasn't right. How did a little kid deserve that? Or the laborers in the vineyard—shouldn't the ones who worked all day get paid more than those who showed up right at the end?

I put a great value on fairness, as children do, because they are powerless and have no other protection or appeal against unjust treatment. And the story that most disturbed my sense of fairness was that of the Prodigal Son. I disapproved of him, and was glad to see him come to grief. My sympathy lay entirely with the good brother, who stuck it out at home and worked the fields all those years beside his father, keeping faith, doing his duty, while his brother lived the high life in a foreign land until his money ran out and humiliation and hunger drove him back to the farm. I knew how I would feel if I were the older brother, and my father made a big fuss over the selfish wastrel, not just taking him back but throwing a party for him—which he'd never done for me! And after my father showers favors on the prodigal, he scolds me for questioning the justice of this treatment. *Scolds me,* just as the master of the vineyard scolds his laborers for protesting the inflated wages of the latecomers, and Jesus scolds Martha for thinking her sister should help her in the kitchen instead of lazing about with him and the disciples in the living room. Not fair!

Of course my allegiance to the good brother grew from the assumption that I would have been in his shoes, not the bad brother's. Because I was a good boy then, when it was easy to be a good boy, before my body hardened and my eye began to follow, hungrily, as if on its own, the line and motion of a woman's body as she walked down the street ahead of me; before I began to prefer the company of witty, irreverent, roistering friends to that of more decorous companions; before I gave my family cause to fear for me, even, occasionally, grieve for me; before I gave myself cause for feelings of emptiness and shame; before I did the things men do to fill their emptiness and dull their shame. In other words, before I ceased to be a child, and entered the fallen world, as we all do.

Not only discovering ourselves in the fallen world but acknowledging that we are a fallen part of it is a sovereign shock cure for the habit of judgment. Unfortunately, the cure soon wears off, and must be taken again and again. At those waking moments we find ourselves much less hungry for some kind of tit-for-tat justice, blindfolded, deaf to every appeal, impersonally weighing fault against virtue. That might look good when it's someone else's faults in the scale. But once we really see where that kind of reckoning will take us, we don't want justice at all—we want mercy.

Yet mercy has sometimes seemed almost too much to hope for. Like most others of my age, and most others through the ages, I was given to understand that my life must be an unceasing preparation for a stern trial whose verdict is beyond appeal. Here the sheep will be separated from the goats, the talent-burying servant and unready bride cast into darkness, wailing and gnashing their teeth. And the list of damnable offenses seemed to grow along with me, reaching beyond the occasional impulsive transgression of youth into one's very thoughts and daydreams, even into that murk where thought and instinct inextricably mingle. The body seems to have a mind of its own, and like a runaway horse can take us where we did not think we meant to go, though that thought, the excuse of the body's power over our will, is itself a damnable offense and must not be invoked. We repent, but always in the knowledge that we will offend again, and such foreknowledge becomes nearly indistinguishable from the intention to offend again. This apprehension shadows whatever release we might gain from ritual absolution and vows of reform.

Thus we can begin to feel God's presence as surveillance, every slip noted, the charge sheet growing longer by the day. Of course we are taught, and taught sincerely, that we are loved by God, and that his mercy is infinite, but such pronouncements, as pronouncements, have little power to dispel the looming sense of our sure conviction at the bar of judgment.

But stories do have that power. In story we see the word become flesh, and recognize ourselves, and feel ourselves recognized. And just as the story of the laborers in the vineyard provoked a sense of injustice, and the situation of the hurt, uncelebrated brother stirred my sympathy, at a certain point I began to understand that my own condition was closer to that of the prodigal than to the man of reliable, steady virtue who never strayed.

I have often felt—often still feel—in a sort of exile of spirit. Self-imposed, perhaps, and self-perpetuated, but no less real for that. And like the lost brother, I have doubted my right to emerge from an exile I have brought upon myself. What is wonderful to me now in the Parable of the Prodigal Son is not just the father's forgiveness of his son but his eagerness, his joy, to have him home again: "When he was yet a great way off, his father saw him, and had compassion, and ran, and fell on his neck, and kissed him." He ran to meet him! This is beyond anything that precept can express—the image of that father, looking far down the road, recognizing his son even in the distance. He must have been longing for him all the while, hoping with all his heart for his son's return. Why else would he have been staring down that road?

And I know that this is true, because I am a father, and when my children are away I pine for them, and my greatest joy is having them with me again, back under my roof. Nothing they can do, nothing, will ever lessen the love I have for them. Even in their absence my love abides. And if I, weak and fickle as I am, can be so constant in this thing, how can I doubt the constancy, the abiding love, of the father who yearns for me? We are all a little lost, are we not? Trying, this way and that, to find our way home. The way is eased, at least for me, by this assurance—that I will be welcomed with a kiss.

The Beloved Disciple

The Book of John

Colm Tóibín

There was a crowd moving and it was difficult for him to make his way against the flow of the crowd. When he pushed his way out of the narrow street and into the broad open space that led to the baths, he noticed that people even here were moving with purpose, forcing their way past each other, leaving no room for anyone who wanted to go in the other direction. He had become alert in these months to any sign of panic or fear or aggression, but there was none here. Yet there was expectation, he could see that, but expectation without alarm or worry.

The atmosphere, however, was not bright in any way, or dreamy or cheerful. It came with an edge of seriousness and sharp intent. As more people pressed forward, he had to stand back against a wall. No one noticed him, or seemed to bother about him, and this came as a relief. He was never sure that he was not being watched and sometimes followed. He was aware that, with his blue eyes and blond hair, he stood apart from others. Now, in the crush, no one cared about anything except making their way forward.

The woman whom he guarded and protected would be, he realized, alone at home and waiting for him. She worried, she said, each time he left that he might not come back, insisting that he could easily be detained, or murdered, and then she would have no protector, no one to depend on. He knew that while he was away she would sit in the shadows of the room listening for sounds. He could imagine her there now. Even when he arrived and whispered his own name as he entered to reassure her, she would still move farther into the recesses of the house, afraid. Nothing he said could make her feel that she was safe. He wondered, as people began to call and shout, if the sound of the crowd would reach the house where she was. In that case, he dreaded returning there. She would be hiding, and it would be hard to entice her into the open space of the main room. No matter what he said, she would presume that someone was waiting close by to take her away.

This was a world of shiftings and disappearances. Nothing was fixed or simple. Even the landscape itself was not stable. The port was silting up; the river was dragging soil with it from the uplands. Soon, he thought, instead of waves hitting against cut stone, there would be flatland here, a desolate brown-colored plain. This was a place that had belonged to the old gods; he had memorized some of the strange names—Athena, Aphrodite, Asklepios, Hygeia, Eros, Demeter.

And the great mother Artemis. How was he going to explain to these people that her power had been replaced by the power of a mere man on a cross, a man who was dead, a man whose mother sat filled with fear in a small house? How could he stop them making images of the great goddess and holding them close in times of danger or when darkness fell? How could he explain that his god was not merely one among many, but the only one, and that the other gods must be dismissed, forgotten, put away? How could he make these people understand that the only god there was had come among them as a man, but that, even though he was gone, he was not gone in the same way as mortals go, and that he would not forsake them?

How could he spread the word that there was no goddess now, and that there never would be again? That the mother of the Son of God was a fearful, fretful woman, a mortal? That the oracle from now on would be silent, useless?

If he could not convince them in this city that their gods were false, then how could the battle for truth be won anywhere else? This was a place of wealth and influence and power, a power he could feel now as he began to follow the crowd, as he came to understand that they were moving toward the vast theater where some great tragedy would be enacted, a tragedy that would poison the air, fill the crowd with fright and pain. This dark illusion would be enough for their fears to be purged or lessened in some way. Their dreams would become sweeter, or less haunted, in the days after this enactment.

This was the space where he would, he knew, have to preach the truth once he had formulated words to match its majesty. He moved slowly, allowing himself to be pushed forward when more people came from a side street and merged in with the crowd. It seemed to him that he was the only one alone, and that part of the reason why it was so hard to move easily was that no one wanted to be separated from their group. The effort to keep up and not get lost was causing some to elbow others out of the way, or hold back so that some of their friends could join them. No one wanted to be in the vast theater with strangers beside them.

He began to follow a group of young men. They were too busy talking and moving ahead briskly to notice him. He would sit close to them, merge with them if he could, without having to speak to them. He did not want anyone to point him out as someone alone, an outsider, someone who had come to the city with no associates, who had arrived and taken a house in the company of a woman who could be his mother, a woman who did not venture out, not even to the market or the well.

She would be waiting for him now; she would wonder what was taking him so long. But, he thought, he must see this, he must join with the crowd in their rituals and ceremonies so that he would know what they were, so that he could have influence when the time was right, when the time came for those rituals and ceremonies to fade and be replaced by ones that were true and would lead this unthinking crowd into a realm they had never imagined possible.

By the time it was dark, the seats were full. The chatter was broken regularly by calls for silence, which spread until not a sound could be heard. The silence was unsettling; he could see how much fear and foreboding there was in the crowd. And then someone would shout and someone else would laugh, and the laughter would rise. They were, he saw, laughing as a way of keeping something else at bay. And then the chatter would resume.

It was only when the slither of a moon rose over the trees and the rocks in the distance that the crowd began to settle and grow quiet. They knew, it seemed to him, that it would begin soon.

It started with the light from torches. Figures covered in black cloth came down the steps at the side and in the center carrying burning torches. Below, more torches appeared from the sides. What was strange, he thought, was how little the torches cast light on what was around them, but rather they seemed to pull in light toward them. The flame from each torch had more white than yellow and seemed almost sculpted or shaped. The more he looked the more the torches seemed not to have a burning or even a flickering movement in them, but instead a sort of stillness, as though the flame were stable and were made of some hard substance.

For some time, nothing else happened. The crowd took in the light as those bearing the torches found positions some distance from each other and stood without moving. He wondered for a while if this might be all, if they had come here to look in awed silence at light from torches, and if this would be enough. A line came to him from the verses he had learned: "The people who sat in darkness saw great light." He shuddered as he said the line to himself until the man beside him noticed him and moved away from him, leaving a small space between them. He realized that he must do nothing that those around him did not do. He must follow them in their silence, as he would follow them later in their cries, if he heard cries.

Suddenly, below, the figures with the torches moved closer to each other and lowered the torches so that an actor dressed in white who was kneeling could be seen rising, wearing the mask of a woman. He stretched his arms out and began to speak to the oracle. The question he asked seemed like a riddle, but it made sense, or so it appeared, to the audience. The question was about light and darkness, life and death. But the question itself seemed to contain the answer, so that when the actor walked away and then turned toward the audience and howled in pain, they responded as though they understood fully what the oracle had said.

The play was about death; that much was clear to him. It was about the death of a son, and then about the death of another young man. The death of the son was, as far as he could make out, foretold, so that all the actions surrounding it seemed almost comforting to the audience. Each actor spoke as if this death was a release, or would win freedom for others, or as if the son was a hostage and it had been agreed that he would be killed for the sake of others.

But then a woman came wearing a mask of dark mourning and she began to wail and lament and cry out and demand that what was foretold be not allowed to happen. She beckoned to the figures with torches to approach, insisting that their light would obliterate the death that was about to be enacted. Each time the torches approached, however, it was only for a second; they moved away quickly as though afraid, or repelled. And then, as they retreated, the lamentation from the woman and some others began again. This happened three or four times until all the torches withdrew and the stage was in complete darkness.

In the second scene, there had been no oracle. The death of the young man, as far as he could make out, would achieve nothing, and yet it had occurred. Then the chorus appeared and spoke about futility and sorrow and the fate of those unlucky enough to be born, unlucky enough to live, unlucky enough to die. Slowly, some of the figures with torches removed what black material they were wearing on their heads. The masks they revealed were white but the expressions on the faces were blank. They began to join the chorus, until the chorus moved away in fright as the figure of a young man covered in a white cloth appeared and began to unwind the cloth.

The audience gasped and then held their breath. There was a sense that this was what they had been waiting for. All of the figures bearing torches began to move slowly and deliberately toward a point in the center. The torches were held aloft so that not one of those who had been speaking or moving could be seen.

This continued for some time, longer than any of the action or speech making that had come before. Then the figures holding the torches began to separate, and, one by one, they moved up the steps until there was less and less light. The moon had disappeared, and thus, once all the torchbearers had gone, there was no light at all. No one in the audience spoke or made a sound. After a time, however, in small groups, people made their way to the steps and then, one by one, began to ascend. There was no crush; people waited until there was space for them to leave. No one even whispered.

When he came into the house, the woman was standing in the room. She did not speak, but studied him carefully. For once, she did not seem to be afraid. He nodded to her and then went quickly toward the table where he had left the pages with the words he had been given. He added the sentences that he had thought of and memorized on his way home, tapping out the rhythm: "In him was life, and the life was the light of men. And the light shines in darkness, and the darkness comprehended it not." He moved down farther and found a larger space in the margin and he wrote the words "Yet a little while is the light with you: walk while ye have the light, lest darkness come upon you; for he that walketh in darkness, knowest not whither he goeth. While ye have light, believe in the light, that ye may be the children of light."

He was excited now and wrote quickly on the next page in case he would forget the words. "I am come a light into the world, that whoever believeth on me, should not abide in darkness." And then he looked again through the pages until he found a place where he could add some more words: "He was a burning and shining light: and ye were willing for a season to rejoice in his light." While he wrote, more words and images came to him, as though the very act of writing itself brought new unwritten, unthought-of words into being: "I am the light of the world: he that followeth me, shall not walk in darkness, but shall have the light of life." And, then, once more, moving fast, writing before the words might escape, and speaking them out loud, he wrote: "As long as I am in the world, I am the light of the world."

When he turned, he saw that she had not moved from her position in the middle of the room. She stood tall and erect, sternly observing him.

"He loved you more than the others," she said. "That is why I came here with you. You were the one whom he loved."

When he smiled, she did not smile in return. The expression on her face remained grave.

He went outside and stood looking at the stars. The crowd in the theater had watched the light, he remembered, as if it were alive, as if it had a face and a voice. But they had also watched the mask of the woman and listened to her voice. In the same way, in broad daylight, he had observed them watching the statue of Artemis with reverence and awe, but also with curiosity and wonder.

In their descriptions of the foot of the cross, the earlier writer and his helper had referred only to some followers, to no one else, no one by name. They had concentrated on the figure who was splayed against the sky, the one who was suffering until the moment when there would be no more suffering, the moment when the word . . .

He stopped for a moment and remembered how closely the crowd in the theater had listened for the sound of the oracle, waiting for its word. They had come to watch the light and hear the word, even though they knew that the word itself would not be uttered because it was already known. The word belonged within, he thought, but its power would move outward. The word had been inhaled and held in like breath, and then it would be exhaled to join the world's breath.

He went back into the room and found a small space at the top of the first page and wrote: "In the beginning was the Word, and the Word was with God, and the Word was God." As he sat rereading what he had written, he felt her presence behind him. In a firm voice, she repeated these words, even though he had not spoken them aloud. He knew that she could not read.

"How did you know those words?" he asked her.

"I have been waiting for *you* to know them," she said. "That is why I have been waiting here all this time."

When he turned and looked at her face, he saw now what he would do. He would place her, as she was, at the foot of the cross; and he would also write, so that it might be known, that he, that he himself, was the one who had been most loved.

"If I had not thought of these words," he asked her, "would you have told them to me?"

"Your question knows its answer," she replied.

"But is there something else?" he asked.

"Yes," she said, and smiled.

"The man he pulled weeping from the dead? Must that not remain a part of silence?"

"Your question knows its answer," she repeated.

In the night when he woke, he began to memorize the new words as they came to him, the words that took their bearings from the image of the figure in the theater covered with the white cloth unwinding the cloth, and the crowd watching, until the torches moved toward the center and were raised too high for anyone below them to be seen.

This is what the world is, he thought, action that seems to matter, loss and the mourning of loss, and then the light, the light rising, the light that obliterates everything that seems to matter until only the light matters, until the light, too, fades and there is nothing except a memory of words, a memory of light, and then it is time for each person to leave, to wait until there is space, and then venture alone, walk up the steps alone into the darkness.

OTHER

The Parables of Jesus of Nazareth

Rick Moody

Once upon a time, many years ago, I edited an anthology of essays about the New Testament.* The reason for this book was simple. I felt that there had once been a revolutionary cultural force that we might call the Religious Left, a cultural force that had served as the basis for the abolitionist movement, the civil rights era, and the anti–Vietnam War movement. However, this Religious Left had been much eclipsed by, overpowered by, its opposite number, the Religious Right. I believed by concentrating some attention on the New Testament—the accessible, revolutionary, and compassionate New Testament, the Gospels particularly—it might be possible to kindle anew this Religious Left, or at least its philosophical footing, and with it a politics of inclusion, equality, and class struggle.

My coeditor, Darcey Steinke, and I worked over some months to assemble this anthology, but in many cases the writers we liked and knew well turned down our earnest solicitations. There was a compelling reason for this. It is actually rather daunting to write about the Holy Bible. Why so daunting? Every day, some windbag is on the left-hand end of the FM dial in Mississippi, Alabama, Arkansas, et al., improvising on a passage in the Old Testament and finding a refuge there for his

---

*Joyful Noise: *The New Testament Revisited* was published in 1997 by Little, Brown and Company. It's still in print, I believe, if you are curious. It contains a preconversion reflection on the church by Barry Hannah, and Darcey Steinke's meditation on Mary's labor, and Ann Patchett's thoughts on Pentecostal snake handling, et cetera.

reverie of hate. Those guys do not feel any hesitation about seizing control of this open text and making it rigid, fixed, punitive. But people of a slightly more empathic cast are naturally hesitant when confronting this book, the Holy Bible, and I can well understand their hesitation. After all, it has been around now, in its canonical form, for fifteen hundred years. It is among the earliest of books, it is a foremost example of what a book is, and it has therefore acquired, over the years, its store of preconceptions.

At the time of our anthology I remember speaking to one novelist of note who said (after turning us down) that had he written the piece, he would have written about the parables of Jesus. And this got me thinking. In fact, I ended up writing the introduction to our book about the Parable of the Hidden Treasure, which in the New Revised Standard Version goes like this (Matthew 13:44, for those of you following at home): "The kingdom of heaven is like treasure hidden in a field, which someone found and hid; then in his joy he goes and sells all that he has and buys that field."

The beauty of this parable, I thought, in writing my introduction, was that it withstood close inspection, and yet remained provocative, elusive, even mysterious. There's an outlaw quality to the Parable of the Hidden Treasure, because the *someone* doing the finding and hiding is basically *conspiring* to seize the treasure in question, through legal means, perhaps, but just barely. (In the Gospel of Thomas version, the situation is a bit more transparent: "Jesus said, 'The [Father's] kingdom is like a person who had a treasure hidden in his field but did not know it. And [when] he died he left it to his [son]. The son [did] not know (about it). He took over the field and sold it. The buyer went plowing, [discovered] the treasure, and began to lend money at interest to whomever he wished.'"*) The ramifications of heaven, it seems, are such that you will do almost *anything* to attain it, once you have, accord-

---

* The Gospel of Thomas: The Hidden Sayings of Jesus, trans. Marvin Meyer (HarperSanFrancisco, 1992), p. 65.

ing to the analogy, *seen the light*. Thus buying the field for the treasure, though the treasure rightly belongs to someone else. This was the crux of my reading, which I conducted rashly, without undue recourse to the scholarship.

In this way, I came to face-to-face with the rich field that is the parabolic tradition in the Gospels, and now when I think about the mystery and beauty of the New Testament, this is one field I plow repeatedly. The parables, like few other portions of the Bible, are evocative, without being fixed, condensed, like poetry, meaningful without being labored, and story-oriented like all the best folk wisdom.

The parable, more exactly, is like the proverb, the fable, or the joke, in that it is a way that narrative can be used to a persuasive end. Its energy is in the area of analogy. But unlike in other kinds of analogies, its actors are *people* (not animals, or faeries, or sprites). Conversely, an example of the proverb can be found in *Don Quixote*, where Sancho Panza is relentless about cataloging proverbs: "I may be a fool, but I understand the proverb that says, 'It did him harm when the ant grew wings.'"* A good example of fable would be found in Aesop: "An ass, carrying a load of wood, passed through a pond. As he was crossing through the water he lost his footing, stumbled and fell, and not being able to rise on account of his load, groaned heavily. Some Frogs frequenting the pool heard his lamentation, and said, 'What would you do if you had to live here always as we do, when you make such a fuss about a mere fall into the water?'"†

The parable, like these other analogical forms, comes from a tradition of laterally achieved meanings, into which the reader must project himself or herself. And part of the way the New Testament parables invite this act of readerly substantiation is by being *oral*. The teaching of Jesus of Nazareth, that is, the instruction of Jesus of Nazareth, pre-

---

* Don Quixote, Miguel De Cervantes, trans. by Edith Grossman (Harper Perennial, 2006), p. 679.

† AesopFables.com

dates *the book*, and predates ideological systems that are book-oriented. In fact, the early teachings of Jesus of Nazareth, itinerant rabbi, were *all* oral, spoken to the apostles and the people during his ministry. They required an *actual audience*. These are stories that were spoken, heard, remembered, and only much later written down, because of their enduring value. They date to the oral tradition but survived into the era of the book (and later the era of the printing press).

According to biblical scholars, these oral fragments probably originate in a lost text of Jesus sayings called, in the commentary of the last hundred years, the Q source. The Q source accounts for the similarities of the Gospels of Matthew and Luke (and the infrequency of common parabolic material in Mark and John), and its existence is further supported by a compendium of material (a sayings gospel) in the Gospel of Thomas (which, though Gnostic, or noncanonical, shares material with Matthew and Luke). Q is the mother lode of the oral tradition of Jesus, and it contains an abundance of parables. So, in all likelihood, Jesus of Nazareth *spoke* these parables, performed them, and he believed that they were the right way to the hearts of his audience. In fact, in both Matthew (13:34: "Jesus told the crowds all these things in parables; without a parable he told them nothing") and Mark (4:34: "He did not speak to them except in parables"), it is clear that Jesus infrequently spoke to people in any other way.

There were parables of the natural world, of planting, harvesting, baking, and animal husbandry. There were parables of family, parables of slavery and servants, parables of money, parables of religious life, and parables about eschatology. (A whole host of eschatological parables, like the Parable of the Rich Fool, Luke 12:20–21: "But God said to him, 'You fool! This very night your life is being demanded of you. And the things you have prepared, whose will they be?' So it is with those who store up treasures for themselves but are not rich toward God.") There are thirty-three of these parables (a number that Dante would have favored) if you are restrictive about what a parable is. But perhaps as many more as sixty if you allow in the related figurative analogies.

Analogies, because it was hard to talk about the kingdom of heaven directly. Or: it is easier to conjure heaven with similitudes than it is to conjure heaven with description, as none of us has yet seen it. The heavenly parables (a subset of the whole) do exactly this kind of work. They use heavenly analogies. (And the heavenly parables are concerned not only with the spiritual world but can be seen in *things;* they are also about the way in which the material of daily life is in *harmony* with the spiritual world, the way the sowing of mustard seeds again reveals a larger intention.) It's a radical approach, the parabolic approach, and diabolically clever, and like unto Jesus saying that the kingdom of heaven is *at hand* (Matthew 3:2, in the King James Version, in the NRSV it has merely come *near*), which was an intervention against the idea that you had to *wait* for heaven, that heaven was *somewhere else.* It's right here, and if you can't see it, perhaps with signs, symbols, *stories,* you might *feel it.* Still, the results of these analogies were, during Jesus's ministry, mixed. Some understood, some didn't, sometimes even the apostles failed to understand, lurching around in that human fashion of theirs.

The Gospel of John, for example, which is not known for its superabundance of parables (not in the same way as the synoptic Gospels), has a good dramatization of Jesus's explicatory struggles (John 10:1–10):

> [Jesus said,] "Very truly, I tell you, anyone who does not enter the sheepfold by the gate but climbs in by another way is a thief and a bandit. The one who enters by the gate is the shepherd of the sheep. The gatekeeper opens the gate for him, and the sheep hear his voice. He calls his own sheep by name and leads them out. When he has brought out all his own, he goes ahead of them, and the sheep follow him because they know his voice. They will not follow a stranger, but they will run from him because they do not know the voice of strangers." Jesus used this figure of speech with them, but they did not understand what he was saying to them.
>
> So again Jesus said to them, "Very truly, I tell you, I am the gate

> for the sheep. All who came before me are thieves and bandits; but the sheep did not listen to them. I am the gate. Whoever enters by me will be saved, and will come in and go out and find pasture. The thief comes only to steal and kill and destroy. I came that they may have life, and have it abundantly."

The layering of possible meanings in this passage is deep! If you read only the first half of John 10, when Jesus first uncorks the Parable of the Good Shepherd, you are liable to feel that the allegorical pressures of the language are particularly heavy. You are likely to feel that you have a grip on these allegories (Jesus must be the shepherd!), but just barely, without having command of the entire thing at all. And you are not alone, apparently, because the second half of the passage concerns the apostles and their inability to follow the reasoning: "Jesus used this figure of speech with them, but they did not understand." Alas, Jesus must do what no creative writer likes to do; he must *explain the symbols*. "I am the gate," and "the thief comes only to . . . destroy."

Again, the allegory seems manifest. And yet, if the Parable of the Good Shepherd were simply about how Jesus *is the gate* (and/or the shepherd) and some fallen archangel is the thief, et cetera, then why bother to have the first half as shown earlier? Why does John include the passage in which no apostle is capable of grasping the Parable of the Good Shepherd? Partly to indicate that the parables are difficult, I suspect, and partly (despite what some exegetes might suggest) to indicate that there are multiple readings possible here. But even more, perhaps, John 10 indicates that misunderstanding and uncertainty are part of the scholarly milieu of Jesus. *You may not be able to understand the parables in the literal sense,* but only in an organic way, in the spirit, even if they are transparently narrative as good stories most often are.

They *are* narrative. See, for instance, the Parable of the Prodigal Son, or the Parable of the Good Samaritan (Luke 15:11–32 and Luke 10:25–37). In these parables, there's rising action, denouement, character, and conclusion. Narrative, in the case of these parables, is the quintessential way to make instruction memorable, rather than heavy-handed:

> If a shepherd has a hundred sheep, and one of them has gone astray, does he not leave the ninety-nine on the mountains and go in search of the one that went astray? And if he finds it, truly I tell you, he rejoices over it more than over the ninety-nine that never went astray. So it is not the will of your Father in heaven that one of these little ones should be lost. (Matthew 18:12–14)

Narrative means development, movement, change, an accrual of tension, as in the folktale, but with the additional layer of spiritual order or a divine sensibility expressing itself *through* the story as it also expresses itself *in* the story. The parables have an arc and a purpose (enlightenment), and in this way they are part of the development of story as an information storage and retrieval device. (James Joyce's emphasis on epiphany in the stories in *Dubliners*, for example, is based on a Jesuitical idea of how epiphany works in Christian parables and conversion narratives, how it indicates transformative energy.)

There are entire sections of the Holy Bible that I find tedious, and unreadable, sections that my eyes pass across only when it's that Sunday in the church calendar. The prophets, for me, are dull, because of their dense symbolic field, which is designed primarily to be read and understood by scholars and the like-minded. Revelation, the last book of the New Testament, is unreadable to me, except perhaps when I have at my side a primer for its web of psychedelic intrigues.* But the narrative sections of the New Testament, and the lovely, exceedingly literary impulse that is Jesus of Nazareth's parables, are never beyond my reach, because they pulse with life and movement.

Which means, again, that there are rules here for how to read that

* As in Elaine Pagels's recent book *Revelations: Visions, Prophecies, and Politics in the Book of Revelation* (Viking, 2012).

are being suggested to those with ears. For example, what you read may not be immediately comprehensible (as in John 10), and what you read may be rich with possibilities for interpretation, for example, Mark 4:26–29: "He also said, 'The kingdom of God is as if someone would scatter seed on the ground, and would sleep and rise night and day, and the seed would sprout and grow, he does not know how. The earth produces of itself, first the stalk, then the head, then the full grain in the head. But when the grain is ripe, at once he goes in with his sickle, because the harvest has come.'"

And so: parables are understood with your heart (to use an antique analogy), or your soul (even older!), not with your head. The atheists and intellectuals in the crowd naturally get uncomfortable when it is suggested that understanding is not merely an intellectual activity, but their worldview has its tautology, too: they use their literary brains to understand what is manifestly not well understood with brains, and then complain about the absence of brain-related logical infrastructure. The parables, with their more organic intent, are emotional in their freight, with longing for security, family, for heaven itself, for a just kingdom, for love and understanding. You can *say* that your religion trafficks in these things, that your religion brings some measure of peace, but *saying* it is less useful, it seems to me, than simply bringing about the longing *in story*, in dramatic development, and thereby embodying the epiphany, bringing its epiphany about.

Though I go to church, and take my daughter to church, and have lived a life in the church, I am in many ways a skeptic about the institutional power of the church. Few church professionals whom I have gotten to know well have avoided disappointing. Often my conviction is that sectarian Christianity is counterproductive, against the teachings that are its constitutive bedrock. But when I feel this resistance to orthodoxy and church teaching, I go back to the man, in search of what he might have *said*.

Or: a Sunday never comes to pass on which the Parable of the Prodigal Son is recounted in which I am not moved, and this despite the fact that the Prodigal Son has no easy message. The wastrel son returns home, having lost everything, and the father welcomes him: "'Quickly, bring out a robe—the best one—and put it on him; put a ring on his finger and sandals on his feet. And get the fatted calf and kill it, and let us eat and celebrate; for this son of mine was dead and is alive again; he was lost and is found!' And they began to celebrate." This while the good son, who labored his whole life, gets nothing special. What's the message? That there is no easy message? Part of the message is that *forgiveness is powerful*, and I often feel that when I am in church on a Sunday, myself a sinner in the old sense of the world, an intellectual, a person with many reasons to resist, welcomed in again despite my resistance. It's the parable that does the trick.

Some will tell you that these stories, these analogies, have *specific* meanings, that they mean one thing, and that their advertised meaning coheres with the institutional message. But I feel like it is the stories themselves, the reliance on storytelling, and performance, and improvisation, and language, and the immediacy of the teller of the tale and of the audience, that welcomes me, and I am not always so sure I *care* about the message, not as much as I want to live in the tradition of religious storytelling itself. Parables. They almost always end well—with the protagonist being admitted into the kingdom.

A Matter of Infinity

John 3:16 & Psalm 23

Clyde Edgerton

THE THREE BIGGIES

When I was a child in the 1950s, a fervent member of a Southern Baptist church in rural North Carolina, I learned that the Bible was in no way related to ambiguity. It was more of a book of rules to follow, written by God through men who had a handle on "truth." As was the custom among children in my church, I memorized several verses of scripture. Two of the most memorable were John 3:16 (King James Version):

> For God so loved the world, that he gave his only begotten Son, that whosoever believeth on him should not perish, but have everlasting life.

And the Twenty-Third Psalm:

> The Lord is my shepherd; I shall not want. He maketh me to lie down in green pastures: he leadeth me beside the still waters. He restoreth my soul: he leadeth me in the paths of righteousness for his name's sake. Yea, though I walk through the valley of the shadow of death, I will fear no evil: for thou art with me; thy rod and thy staff they comfort me. Thou preparest a table before me in the pres-

> ence of mine enemies: thou anointest my head with oil; my cup runneth over. Surely goodness and mercy shall follow me all the days of my life: and I will dwell in the house of the Lord for ever.

My beliefs about (1) God, (2) Jesus, and (3) the afterlife were firmly supported by these two pillars of scripture. Following number 3, the afterlife, was there a number 4? Something else important? Some way to live?

No. Given the fact of number 3, and my solid belief in it, solid knowledge of it, what else on earth besides God and Jesus could possibly make much of a difference about anything? Nothing.

1. God. God made the world.
2. Jesus was God's son and
3. If you "believed on" Jesus—that is, if you believed that he was God's son and came to earth to save the world, then that was that—the end; at your death you would automatically go to heaven and reside there for infinity.

Simple, reassuring. You had to do nothing beyond *believe* to be set *for eternity*. Both New and Old Testaments spoke of infinity, heaven, forever.

"Have you accepted Jesus as your Savior?" was a mantra from the pulpit at my church. I heard the question again and again. At a Friday night revival service when I was seven, I walked down the aisle and told the preacher I loved Jesus and believed in Him and wanted to accept him as my personal savior. That was how you accepted Jesus. (I've translated my salvation experience into fiction more than once, never making light of it. There remains something sacred and precious about the experience that I feel unable to exactly name.)

Heaven was on its way, no matter what. What I was to do—that is, how I was to live my life—was surely taught to me, but basically I knew that all I had to do was wait for heaven. I could even, I knew deep down, keep masturbating—against my fundamentalist mother's wishes (she was way, way more than just a fundamentalist, of course)—and, in spite of that sinful practice, I would still end up in heaven, beside her and my father and other dead Christian relatives (no Jews, Hindus, et cetera. But what about Catholics? An open question. Their elevation of Mary was blasphemous).

Presumably, there would be no need to abuse myself in heaven.

FOR EVER

If I were to face a Christian across a table today, one raised like I was, and say, "And I will dwell in the house of the Lord . . ." lift my eyebrows, and lean my head forward just a bit, I would probably hear "Forever."

Having hooked into that concept as a boy, I found myself blinded by the bright light of immortality, blinded to any Christian duty that I might commit as a Christian teenager—beyond attending church regularly, being in the youth choir, and then directing the youth choir when I was a mature teenager. I started smoking and drinking alcohol occasionally, and making out to the point of orgasm (no intercourse yet) with no major guilt. Well, no guilt that I remember. Well, maybe once or twice. Actually, it now seems that I was at times torn.

LEAVING HOME

I left home to go to college in Chapel Hill, North Carolina (a preacher at my church once preached against *the place* Chapel Hill), and things began to shift. The fact of "heaven is on the way" had been settled when I was seven, and at a university I could begin to, of all things, get excited about "ideas." My feelings about being a Christian began to change from warm toward a kind of carefree lukewarm.

I majored in English education, joined the Air Force, and became a fighter pilot, happy to kill the enemy in the presence of he who had prepared a table.

Yes, there was the Sermon on the Mount and all that "do unto your neighbor" stuff from the New Testament and "Thou shalt not kill" from the Old Testament. What Jesus had been quoted as suggesting that I might do in life for the good of all my neighbors was way back there behind me, a kind of tangential tattered flag that fluttered in the dusk of my childhood beneath a sensational sunset above which was written in the sky: FOR EVER.

After serving my country in Southeast Asia (being the Christian that I was) I went on to become a teacher and then a full-time fiction writer, playing with uncertainty in my stories—as an artist is apt to do. Religion and the human response to it became something to write stories about, and around. I became an Episcopalian, a logical next step. Now I could have real sex.

REASON

And as I grew older, I became convinced that my brain—in considering aspects of religion—was able and free to use a process called reason.

I became convinced that there were no tangible places called heaven and hell—became convinced that those places had long ago been "made up" during times when the best available nuances of reason perhaps *dictated* the existence of a heaven and hell. I will admit to times of speculation, flashbacks to my early images of standing (after my death) before a God whose finger is on a line in a ledger saying, "You actually robbed fifty cents from your fifth-grade teacher?"

But with reading and thinking and reasoning, these times of speculation became less frequent each year. I think it was something like twice last year. Maybe three, four times.

Sixteen or so years ago, a cousin of mine, John Penick (with a divinity degree and a Ph.D. in philosophy) gave me, as a gift, *The Bible: An American Translation*. John called it "the Chicago Bible" and explained that the editors, in writing down the Old Testament, had seriously studied the Hebrew language, whereas the architects of the King James

Version had relied on Greek and Latin with only a "nod" toward the Hebrew.

When I turned to the Twenty-Third Psalm in the Chicago Bible*, here's what I read:

THE GOOD SHEPHERD [A Psalm of David]

1 The LORD is my shepherd; I shall not want;
2 In green pastures he makes me lie down;
Beside refreshing waters he leads me.
3 He gives me new life; He guides me in paths of righteousness for his name's sake.
4 Even though I walk in the darkest valley, I fear no harm; for thou art with me; Thy rod and thy staff—they comfort me.
5 Thou layest a table before me in the presence of my enemies;
Thou anointest my head with oil; my cup overflows.
6 Surely goodness and kindness shall follow me all the days of my life; And I shall dwell in the house of the LORD to an old age.

STARTLING WORDS: "TO AN OLD AGE"

Could it be? Could it be that there was one grain of sand in the massive coastline that was the Bible, one grain of sand that coincided with my apostate notion of reason? My apostate notion of Christianity without heaven? Without "for ever"? Did that verse say in Hebrew "to an old age"? (The literal translation turns out to be "length of days.")

There is of course a great deal of scholarship and plain thinking wherein you or I may now find solace if we need evidence about how far back the concept of heaven exists in Christian scriptures—or scriptures that have been kidnapped from a non-Christian tradition. Had there been an early translation of the Hebrew "length of days" into the

*J. M. Powis Smith and Edgar J. Goodspeed, *The Bible: An American Translation* (University of Chicago Press, 1927).

Christian's "for ever" just to make things fit together?—to enable Christians to refer to some made-up heaven from way back when? That's my guess now.

But what about my religious thinking as a ten-year-old? What was the nature of *that* experience back when I was memorizing scripture?

I decided to talk to myself at age ten. In the following dialogue, my ten-year-old self *is in italics*. I pick up in the middle of our conversation.

Why would you say "to an old age"?

Because I believe that phrase "to an old age" makes the sentence closer to its original meaning than "for ever."

But "for ever" is in the Bible. That's what David said.

The words written in your King James Version Bible are "for ever." But—now listen carefully—I'm going to tell you something that your mama and daddy and all the people in your church don't know, or if they do, did, they never spoke of it: the first language of the Psalms was Hebrew, the language that Jews used to write most of their Bible, though Jesus probably spoke Aramaic. Jesus was a Jew, but you and I never heard much about that. When you and I heard about Jesus and Jewishness it was mostly about how "the Jews" killed Jesus. And listen—all those stories in the Old Testament were spoken at first and not written down. Like those stories you heard from your mother and aunts about Uncle Albert and Uncle Bob—you know, about Uncle Bob being on the chain gang for being in a car theft ring, and . . . Listen, some of those spoken Uncle Bob stories you are hearing are going to change because of the nature of told stories. As you get older you're going to find out some contradictory stuff about Uncle Bob. And those spoken Hebrew stories finally appeared "in stone" in the Old Testament, written down after a lot of slipping and sliding like all human stories do and then translated into Latin and Greek and slipped and slid some more until they got written down in English. The same holds true for New Testament stories that were written down in Greek and Latin. We are still slipping and sliding as we continue to translate and write new versions of the Bible, Clyde.

The Bible says that every word in it was inspired by God and if you are talking about slipping and sliding and all that you can't be talking about the Bible.

But if you—

You are not a believer, are you?

It's a little more complicated than that. You can't just— . . . A "believer"? Come on. You can't just . . . Do you know who I am?

No. But I don't think you believe in God.

Let me tell you something . . . I got some news for you . . . I'll tell you something that I know. Your brain is working like the brain of every other fundamentalist on earth: Islamists included and especially. Your way is right and other ways are wrong, and you and your big group of Fundamentalist Christians (including many gentle, good people) want all Americans and everybody to reflect your beliefs exactly. If they don't reflect your beliefs, then they go to hell. That's how you all—

I'm leaving.

Bye. You little narrow-minded fundamentalist.

At least I'm on God's side and He's on mine.

Aw, kiss my ass.

VARIOUS TRANSLATIONS

I've not kept up with Bible translations. When I was most active in church—as a youth—the King James Version was the only version I knew about, of course. I have paid some, not much, attention to new versions, which have been coming out every few years—making the solid old-fashioned language of the King James Bible a little more modern by, say, getting rid of all those *thee*s and *thou*s. The *thee*s and *thou*s never bothered me especially. New versions also use gender-neutral language. Okay with me. Good idea even. But among my favorite fiction writers, many were said to be strongly influenced by the style of the King James Version. In the process of my reading I stumbled upon some plain-out *rewrites*.

Thomas Jefferson, some of you may not know, rewrote the New Testament, creating—of all things—a book about the *teachings* of Jesus (in the main) minus the miracles, the business of heaven, et cetera. Tommy left all that out because he didn't believe it happened. And, get this: he was a *Founding Father*. Whoa! (Why, O God, will I forever argue with my people and my church of origin? Why the anger? Release me.)

Tolstoy did something similar to Jefferson's method in his book *The Gospel in Brief*—an attempt to tell the story of Jesus as pulled from the New Testament sans virgin birth, walking on water, resurrection, and other miracles. He and Jefferson figured the reports of miracles were irrelevant when placed beside Jesus's teachings.

In his book's preface, Tolstoy gets into the nature of time, not unlike the way Einstein did (and Feynman and Hawkins and others in different ways), when Einstein said, "The separation between past, present, and future is only an illusion, although a convincing one."

Well, looka here. We've arrived at an intersection of quantum physics, relativity, timelessness, belief, infinity, a subtraction of miracles, Southern Baptists, my ten-year-old self, and me. Can the question of whether it's "forever" or "to an old age" be important, really? Would Tommy and Leo say I was quibbling, dealing in mere semantics?

Maybe, maybe not.

BUT

This: I became interested a decade ago in Wittgenstein's idea of language games—of how you can't separate the meaning of a piece of language from its context, from the "game." (I oversimplify.) Surely some aspect of Wittgenstein's thoughts on that could be applied to my reasoning about heaven. I just thought of Wittgenstein because five minutes ago I discovered that he said this about Tolstoy's little twelve-chapter book: "If you are not acquainted with *The Gospel in Brief* then you cannot imagine what an effect it can have upon a person."

Wittgenstein and Tolstoy in the same bag along with Jefferson and

Einstein and Richard Feynman. The rabbit hole we find ourselves entering is perhaps about semantics and time and belief, but neither I nor my ten-year-old self will entertain the notion that we are quibbling.

What if only I could find for that ten-year-old and me, without a lot of effort, say, thirty translations into English of the Twenty-Third Psalm and see what each says in its last sentence? See what's been going on in the last fifty years or so with modern translations?

It so happens that Jeffrey D. Oldham has written a pamphlet called "Various Translations of Psalm 23," published in 2006 (theory.stanford.edu/~oldham/church/ps23-translations-2006Feb22.pdf). Let me try again with little Clyde. Show him what I found. He's still standing over against Daddy's '49 Ford.

Clyde, buddy, let me just say this. In sixty years you might just come across something in the Twenty-Third Psalm that makes you think a little about the concept of eternity. That passage may have *originally* meant something *different* than what you memorized. Here are the last lines of thirty English translations. See how they grab you. Here, read this.

1. and I will dwell in the house of the LORD for ever.
2. And I will dwell in the house of the LORD for ever.
3. And I shall dwell in the house of Jehovah for ever.
4. and I shall dwell in the house of the LORD for ever.
5. and I shall dwell in the house of the LORD my whole life long.
6. And I will dwell in the house of the LORD forever.
7. And I will dwell in the house of the LORD Forever.
8. And that I may dwell in the house of the Lord unto length of days.
9. through the long years the Lord's house shall be my dwelling-place.
10. my home, the house of Yahweh, as long as I live!
11. I make my home in the house of Yahweh for all time to come.

12. And I shall dwell in the house of the LORD for years to come.
13. And I shall dwell in the house of the LORD for ever.
14. and I shall dwell in the house of the LORD for many long years.
15. and I shall dwell in the house of the LORD my whole life long.
16. and I shall dwell in the house of the LORD throughout the years to come.
17. and through the length of my days the house of the Lord [and His presence] shall be my dwelling place.
18. and I will dwell in the house of the LORD forever.
19. and I shall dwell in the house of the LORD forever.
20. and I will live in the house of the LORD forever.
21. the Eternal's guest, within his household evermore.
22. And I shall dwell in the house of the LORD to an old age.
23. and I will have a place in the house of the Lord all my days.
24. and I shall dwell in the house of the LORD forever.
25. and your house will be my home as long as I live.
26. and I will live forever in your house, LORD.
27. and I will live in the house of the LORD forever.
28. and afterwards I will live with you forever in your home.
29. I'm back home in the house of GOD for the rest of my life.
30. and my dwelling shall be in the house of the Lord to length of days.

What do you want me to do with this?

It shows you something about ambiguity, flexibility . . . the fact that experts have come up with at least two meanings for one word, or phrase, and the difference between two of those meanings—the primary two—is infinite. *Infinite.* We're talking two translations of the same original passage and we come down to a difference as big as infinity. That's significant, don't you think?

So, I'm counting here. Give me just a minute . . .

What are you doing?

I'm seeing how many out of thirty said "forever."

Aw, don't do that. Stop. Look. Listen to something I need to say. I just read a little 150-page book called *The Story of the New Testament,* published in 1916, written by a guy named Goodspeed, a Bible translator. I want to talk to you about the last sentence of his book. I think it might be helpful when you think about scripture. He said, "Historically understood, the New Testament will still kindle in us the spirit which animated the men who wrote it, who aspired to be not the lords of our faith but the helpers of our joy."

I want to ask you to not listen closely to people who seem to want to be lords of your faith. Listen closely to those who seem to want to be helpers of your joy. That will move you into the important stuff, and away from the unimportant.

Okay. Thanks. And you should apologize for what you said to me.

I do. I apologize.

References for the thirty translations as recorded by Jeffrey D. Oldham in his 2006 pamphlet:

I. Translations in the Tyndale–King James Tradition

1. King James Version (1611)
2. Revised Version (1885)
3. American Standard Version (1901)
4. Revised Standard Version (1952)
5. New Revised Standard Version (1989)
6. New American Standard (1971)
7. New King James Version (1982)

II. Catholic Translations

8. Rheims-Douay (1610)
9. Knox (1950)

10. Jerusalem Bible (1966)
11. New Jerusalem Bible (1985)
12. New American Bible (1970)

III. Jewish Translations

13. Jewish Publication Society's Masoretic Translation (1917)
14. Tanakh (1985)

IV. British Translations

15. New English Bible (1970)
16. Revised English Bible (1989)

V. Conservative Protestant Translations

17. Amplified Bible (1965)
18. New International Version (1978)
19. English Standard Version (2001)
20. New Living Translation (1996)

VI. Modern Language and Easy-to-Read Translations

21. Moffatt (1926)
22. Smith-Goodspeed (1927)
23. Basic English Bible (1949)
24. New Berkeley Version (1969)
25. Today's English Version (1976)
26. Contemporary English Version (1995)
27. New Century Version (1991)

VII. Paraphrases

28. The Living Bible (1971)
29. The Message (2002)

VIII. Other

30. Septuagint Bible by Charles Thomson (1808)

The Beginning of the End

John 18:1-12

Paul Elie

I have never been to Jerusalem, but I have crossed the brook Kidron, and that has made all the difference. J. S. Bach, with the *St. John Passion*, conveyed me across; but I am getting ahead of the story.

Don DeLillo's novel *The Names* begins at the Acropolis, the place that for many people is the point or end of the visit to Athens:

> It daunted me, that somber rock. I preferred to wander in the modern city, imperfect, blaring. The weight and moment of those worked stones promised to make the business of seeing them a complicated one. So much converges there. It's what we've rescued from the madness. Beauty, dignity, order, proportion. There are obligations attached to such a visit.

The speaker is a risk analyst posted to Greece by an international bank, but here he speaks in the voice, a distinctive oracular-vernacular, that DeLillo has made his own. "What ambiguity there is in exalted things," he declares. "We despise them a little."

> The ruins stood above the hissing traffic like some monument to doomed expectations. I'd turn a corner, adjusting my stride among jostling shoppers, there it was, the tanned marble riding its mass of limestone and schist. I'd dodge a packed bus, there it was, at the edge of my field of vision. One night (as we enter narrative time) I was driving with friends back to Athens after a loud dinner in Piraeus and we were lost in some featureless zone when I made a sharp turn into a one-way street, the wrong way, and there it was again, directly ahead . . .

He slams on the brakes. The sudden vision of the "white fire" of the Parthenon "floating in the dark" pulls him up short. It arrests him—stops him in surprise.

That's something like what happens to us as readers when we run across the parenthetical declaration that we are entering narrative time. It's as blunt as a security broadcast at the airport. Now entering the zone of what happens next. Abandon all general truths. No oracular pronouncements past this point. Here the story begins. It happened one night.

And that's something like what happens to us at the point in the Gospel of John when Jesus and the disciples cross the brook Kidron.

The passage, at the beginning of chapter 18, is akin to what photographers after Henri Cartier-Bresson call "the decisive moment." It's the moment when the hide-glue cut-and-paste job that is this gospel enters narrative time once and for all. It's the beginning of the end, a giant step into the drama of crime and punishment whose end is the reason the story is still told.

The Gospels are exalted texts, daunting to write about. So much converges there and is shown to be complex and paradoxical. But the crossing of the brook Kidron is a piece of the action that stands alone, a slice of time as distinct as anything in the New Testament.

Who really "understands" the Gospels? I can't say that I do (though

I can't help but try). But the crossing-over into narrative time: this is something I can begin to understand. The crossing of the brook Kidron: this I can approach undaunted.

> When Jesus had spoken these words, he went forth with his disciples across the Kidron valley, where there was a garden, which he and his disciples entered. Now Judas, who betrayed him, also knew the place; for Jesus often met there with his disciples. So Judas, procuring a band of soldiers and some officers from the chief priests and the Pharisees, went there with lanterns and torches and weapons. Then Jesus, knowing all that was to befall him, came forward and said to them, "Whom do you seek?" They answered him, "Jesus of Nazareth." Jesus said to them, "I am he."

The four Gospels take up 125 pages in the zippered leather Bible I've had since college, less than a tenth of the whole. In English translation John's gospel, with its cradle-to-grave depiction of the Son of Man, is about fifteen thousand words—about the length of an old *New Yorker* profile or a new Kindle Single.

Even by gospel standards the scene at the brook Kidron is exceptionally brief. It takes up a third of a page of that zippered Bible. Jesus and his disciples cross a valley and enter a garden, and Judas musters a militia and goes after them, and Jesus puts a question to them and they reply, and he replies in turn—all this in a hundred words, in a scene lit with lanterns and torches and shadowed by the threat of violence.

The scene seems even tighter when read in sequence with what has come before. This is because what has come before is the Last Supper, and the Last Supper in John's gospel is the longest episode (nearly five chapters) and most verbose one (if you doubt it, take a look) in all of the Gospels.

"When Jesus had spoken these words . . ." That's how Chapter 18 begins. Among biblical scholars "these words" are called the Farewell

Discourses, or the Last Discourse. In the New Jerusalem Bible, they are typeset with a ragged right edge akin to poetry; they run down one page after another, a kite-tail of exhortation and prophecy. In the thirty-volume Anchor Bible—text and learned commentary—the Last Discourse is found in Volume 29A; the chief commentator, the late Catholic biblical scholar Raymond Brown, treats the Last Discourse as three "divisions," each with several units, and his commentary, polyglot and closely spaced, runs from page 545 to page 782. It's *long*.

"When Jesus had spoken these words . . .": this, then, may be a piece of wit on the part of John the evangelist or his redactors—a way of saying that even Jesus Christ tended to go on for a bit. In the beginning was the Word, and the Word refused to end.

More likely it's a structural punctuation mark: an exclamation point. George Herbert in the great poem "Prayer" calls prayer "the soul in paraphrase"; and in John's gospel "these words"—Jesus's words at the Last Supper—are the whole gospel "in paraphrase," as the Herbert poem has it. First Jesus tells the disciples what is going to happen next: one of you will betray me, and the cock will not crow till you have denied me three times. Then he tells them what they ought to do and why, in a series of epithets as consequential as any words ever spoken by anybody. And then he spells out the limits of the words he has spoken.

Few of us know all of them, but most of us know some of them and some of us know most of them and just about all of us know a few of them. Here they are in paraphrase:

Love one another as I have loved you. Keep my commandments: that is how they will know you as my disciples. I am the way, the truth, and the life: no one comes to the Father, but by me. I am the Father and the Father is in me, and he who has seen me has seen the Father. I am the true vine, and my Father is the vinedresser. Peace I leave you; my peace I give to you, but not as the world gives do I give to you. As the Father has loved me, so I have loved you; abide in me, as I abide in you. No longer do I call you servants; I call you friends, and greater love has no man than this, that he lay down his life for his friends. A little while, and you will see me no more, for the ruler of this world is coming; again a little while, and you will see me. You will weep and lament, but the world will rejoice; you will be sorrowful, but your sorrow will be turned into joy. These things I have spoken to you, that my joy may be in you, and that your joy may be full. I have said all this to you in figures; the hour is coming when I shall no longer speak to you in figures but tell you plainly of the Father.

What more was there to say? He had said enough, done all he could do in figures.

"When Jesus had spoken these words," then, he crossed the brook Kidron with the disciples—passing over to a place beyond words.

He entered narrative time, that is, and became fully a fallen creature like the rest of us.

When we think of the fall—if we think of the fall (do we think of the fall?)—we think of it as a fall into sin, or into disobedience, or into carnal life and the life of the body, or war and violence, or the realm of conscience that Flannery O'Connor, concluding her story "Everything That Rises Must Converge," called "the world of guilt and sorrow."

For St. Augustine in the *Confessions* the fall was a fall out of eternity into time. "Our hearts are restless until they rest in you." The book's famous early insight, the starting point of Augustine's *peregrinatio,* or wandering back to God, leaves unstated a conviction that was so obvious to him that he hardly needed to put it into words. It is the conviction that before he was restless, all astir in this mortal coil, he was at rest with God outside of time. The sense of that opening sentence, a sense that emerges distinctly in the course of the *Confessions,* is something like this: Once upon a time before time I rested in you. Now I no longer do. I fell away from you and into time. But I yearn to rest in you again. Meanwhile I am restless, as I try to find my way back home—back out of time.

It's a conviction shaped by the same philosophical outlook—known to us as Platonism, or Neoplatonism—that shaped John's gospel. Nothing so much as that conviction brings home just how different the outlook of the early Christians was from ours. Just as the Christian believers of late antiquity were so convinced of Jesus's divinity, so imbued with the sense of it, that they required two ecumenical councils to settle on the affirmation that Christ was not only fully divine but fully human as well, so Augustine and his contemporaries were so full of the sense of their participation in eternity that they were matter-of-factly convinced that they'd fallen out of it into human time. The question was not whether but how and why.

In the *Confessions* Augustine sets out what many modern commentators call psychological evidence for the human person's past participation in eternity. We seem to have memories of an earlier, better time. We see things transhistorically. We feel our self as a constant presence running through time. These are apt enough to remain persuasive today. Even so, that Augustine evidently felt the remnants of his pretemporal life so powerfully, and that he described them so confidently, makes him, and his outlook, strange to us.

"In my beginning is my end," T. S. Eliot wrote near the beginning of *Four Quartets*, a work that, at the end of the Christian literary era that began with St. Augustine, takes something like a Neoplatonic view of time and eternity and makes of it something new.

In John's gospel the brook Kidron is the site where eternity and time meet; and the crossing of the brook Kidron is the moment when Jesus and the disciples pass from the world of antique Neoplatonism to a world something like ours—from a world charged with the eternal to a world of space and time. The world back there is a world of immutable forms and divinity undivided. The world over here is a world of false kisses and trumped-up charges, where the clock is always ticking and the swords are kept sharp.

* * *

What happens next is like a scene out of Caravaggio:

> So Judas, procuring a band of soldiers and some officers from the chief priests and the Pharisees, went there with lanterns and torches and weapons.

It is like a scene out of Caravaggio because it *is* a scene in Caravaggio. *The Taking of Christ*, as the painting is called, is a work as powerful as anything Caravaggio ever painted, even though it hung in the refectory of the Jesuit house in Dublin for a hundred years without being recognized as his. Caravaggio's biographer Helen Langdon characterizes it as "an elaborately orchestrated tableau vivant, in which every aspect of the composition is concentrated on creating the unprecedented immediacy and reality of the figures."

Judas takes hold of Christ, pressing himself on him: arm, beard, lips. A soldier in gleaming armor goes for Christ's neck. A young man flees: John the Evangelist, it is said—the author of John's gospel, that is. A bearded man holds a lantern: Caravaggio himself, illuminating the scene, at once practicing and highlighting his technique of biblical realism.

It is the beginning of the end; and the use of light, the arrangement of the figures, the equality of attention paid to Jesus, Judas, and the band of soldiers—all these effects work together to create the sense that the taking of Christ is happening once and for all.

This isn't a decisive moment. This is a decisive instant.

The Taking of Christ derives much of its power from what is left out of the four-by-six-foot panel of the painting—all that leads up to the taking and all that leads away from it.

Johann Sebastian Bach, treating the episode, included all that surrounded that, and much more. And yet this *St. John Passion*, which runs about two hours in performance, derives its power from similar effects of excision and concision. This is clear from the very opening of the work. Following the liturgical convention of the Passion narratives—

the way they were read in churches—John's account of the Last Supper is left out. The transition at the beginning of chapter 18—"When Jesus had spoken these words"—is lopped off. In this Passion, the beginning of the end comes at the beginning.

The *St. John Passion* was a new beginning for Bach himself, and, in telling his story at a dramatic moment in a book about Bach (called *Reinventing Bach*), I tried to get behind the work's canonical authority and recover the sense of discovery that surrounded it in the beginning.

It happened this way. After serving for several years as the court musician to the prince of Cöthen, in 1723 Bach took a new job in the market city of Leipzig. The city's cantor and music director had died, and Bach had been hired to replace him. He arrived on a Saturday afternoon in two carriages with his family, following on "four wagons loaded with household goods." The role would be a step down socially, and would involve more teaching and administration than he wished. But he took it, in part because it would give him supervision of the sacred music at two grand churches and two smaller ones. These churches required programs of sacred music week in and week out. In them, through them, he would broadcast his work to a wide public.

The Thomaskirche and the Nikolaikirche are a short walk apart: the one a gray stone Gothic church with a steep roof softened by a Baroque bell tower and a baroquely remodeled interior, the other older, of brown stone, its Romanesque design highlighted by ribbed arches throughout. Bach wore a path between the two churches. As the role of cantor and music director enabled him to focus, so city life enabled him to conduct his affairs with efficiency in the shops, taverns, market square, and town hall.

His family numbered a dozen people, including a newborn daughter. He settled them in a rambling apartment in the schoolhouse, equipped with a composing room, or *Komponirstube,* which contained a large music library. There, he turned to writing music. In his first nine months in Leipzig he composed a vast body of sacred works: cantatas, motets, a radiant Magnificat—about fifty pieces of twenty minutes or more. The city churches were suddenly filled with his music. The cantatas were not all wholly new, but as music composed serially, week by week, they are astonishing.

They were exhausting, too. "The singers or instrumentalists or the composer, or indeed everyone involved including clergy," the Bach scholar Peter Williams proposes, "had found the cantor's initial efforts too taxing." Even Bach was relieved to reach the *tempus clausum*: the forty days of Lent, when liturgical music was set aside in favor of chant or silence. But he didn't rest. Lent opened up time for him to compose. In those forty days he completed the *St. John Passion* for rendition on Good Friday at the Nikolaikirche—at once taking up a form new to him, composing a work more intricate than any he had done, and dramatizing the central event of Christianity for the first time.

Given the demands of the new job, it is amazing that he composed the *St. John Passion* at all. But it may be that the chance to compose a Passion was a key reason for his move to Leipzig. In the Passion, a profound new form of sacred music was emerging, one that would allow him to deploy all his musical strengths at once.

The words of the opening chorus make his ambitions clear. As one English translation has it, they go: "O Lord, our Sovereign, Whose Glory / Is magnified in all lands, / Testify to us by Thy passion . . ." With this work Bach would see his own work magnified, so to speak—all his talents concentrated on a setting of the story of God put to the test.

The grand, doleful opening chorus; the Evangelist's plainspoken recitation; the sonorous voices of Jesus, Pilate, Peter, and the others; the crowd, wide-eyed and sharp-tongued, exultant, fierce, righteous, astonished; the rueful piety of the individual believer as expressed in a sacred aria; the chorales, softened by five centuries of Sundays; and all this over the polished stones on the streambed of the orchestra—this musical plan, this set of patterns in satisfying alternation, is so right as to seem permanent, and makes it seem as if the *St. John Passion* is a sacred work that existed "in the beginning." And yet the Passion form was substantially new to Bach. The cantatas he was writing were settings of discrete gospel passages: adages, sayings, and the like. The Passion text was a story. Where the cantatas are slices of the Christian drama, the Passion is the thing itself; where the cantatas follow the seasons of the year, the Passion (it seems) happens on a particular Friday afternoon. Composing a Passion to be heard at the Nikolaikirche in Leipzig on Good Friday—Friday, April 7, 1724—Bach entered narrative time once and for all.

It happens this way. After the opening chorus (ten minutes or so in most renditions), the singer known as the Evangelist begins, declaiming the gospel text in German in a plangent tenor voice:

> *Jesus ging mit seinen Jüngern über den Bach Kidron . . .*
> Jesus and his disciples crossed the brook Kidron . . .

In German, the word for brook is *Bach*. With the *St. John Passion* Bach created a brook of music, a work of art that fills the gap between eternity and time as a river runs through it.

Some years shy of three centuries later I crossed that brook of Bach, and did what the ancients claimed you just can't do: I stepped into the same river twice.

Holy Week began on April 1 that year, and on Palm Sunday (as we enter narrative time) I made the crossing from Brooklyn to Manhattan. Carnegie Hall was hosting a *St. John Passion* performed by a crack Baroque ensemble called Les Violons du Roy. Ian Bostridge, a celebrated tenor, would be the Evangelist. WQXR would broadcast the performance live on FM and online. Friends who were out of town gave me their tickets—an apt gift as I reached the end of the Bach book I had spent several years writing—and as I made my way down the aisle, it became evident that the tickets were for seats in the front row.

I took a front-row seat uneasily. I had heard the *St. John Passion* live and in person only once before, an evening performance on Good Friday at the Cathedral of St. John the Divine the year after I graduated from college—twenty-five years earlier. Holy Week came early that year. Winter stayed late. The midtown workday fluoresced endlessly. I had never heard Bach's sacred music performed live. I got to the cathedral after dark and claimed a rickety seat at the rear. The *St. John Passion* began: violins, harpsichord, voices by the dozens. The chill of the place, the remoteness of the sound and action, the length of the performance after a day of soul-sapping office work, the forbidding aura surrounding Bach . . .

Reader, I fell asleep during that *St. John Passion,* like a disciple in the garden. Since then I had heard it dozens of times, but always through recordings; I had come to own half a dozen CD sets of the *Johannes-Passion,* filed together in a shoe box in the small workspace in our apartment where I'd spent a thousand and one nights. Now I was here at Carnegie Hall, coaxed out of the interior castle of recordings and into the metropolis of live performance. I was in the front row, and that I was in the front row was both a gift and a challenge. I had to stay awake no matter what.

The musicians entered European-style: singers and orchestra, trailed by the soloists. There was Ian Bostridge, six foot six in formal dress but without a tie, as boyish as on the CD booklets but tall and lean to an extreme that no head shot could show. He stood diplomatically off to the side as the music director, Bernard Labadie, led the ensemble through the opening chorus: five minutes, and then another five as the whole section was repeated, concluding emphatically. The audience went as silent as 2,800 New Yorkers sitting together in a big room on West Fifty-Seventh Street can be. A spotlight followed the Evangelist. With my eyes I did likewise. I had never seen a singer this close up before.

He strode to the lip of the stage and planted his feet, in shoes black and highly polished, on a prestigious spot of hardwood. He crossed his arms at the elbows. He leaned back, like a tennis player about to serve; he opened his mouth—unscrewed it, screwed it open: that was the effect from up close—and out came the first words of recitative:

> *Jesus ging mit seinen Jüngern über den Bach Kidron . . .*
> Jesus and his disciples crossed the brook Kidron . . .

So we entered narrative time: the triple time of Bach's passions, where biblical time, the time of Bach, and what can be called "the time of this hearing" converge.

And I felt, from a cubit's distance away, the power of art, and live art in particular, to lead us across and into the far country of narrative and make us apprehend a familiar moment as if for the first time.

When he had finished those words, all together we heard all that happened next.

Resurrection

John 20

Kerry Kennedy

In John's gospel, Jesus tells Martha, Lazarus's sister, "I am the resurrection and the life. The one who believes in me will live, even though they die" (John 11:25).

Death is not the cessation of, but the beginning of, life. I witnessed the physical manifestation of that biblical promise in Haiti during Holy Week 2014.

Death swept through Haiti on January 12, 2010, when an earthquake and its aftershocks injured or killed hundreds of thousands of people, displaced 1.7 million, and reduced most of Port-au-Prince and the surrounding villages to rubble.

I visited Haiti six months after the earthquake. Even after the news videos and numerous human rights reports, I was unprepared for the horror. Port-au-Prince was a sea of tents, rough fragments of broken stone, masonry, and detritus, but also frenzied activity. Unemployment spiked from 9 percent in 2009 to over 40 percent in 2010, yet everywhere people were shoveling, building, hauling, selling, or striding with determination.

When I returned to Haiti in April 2014, the results were clear.

I was traveling with Nancy Dorsinville, a native Haitian with an M.A. from the Harvard School of Public Health whom former president Bill Clinton—the UN special envoy to Haiti—had hired to run the UN program on the ground. I asked Nancy how these people, who had lost everyone they loved and everything they owned, did not give in to despair. She said that there had been so much death and destruction that those who were spared believed God must have had a special purpose for their survival.

Port-au-Prince was bustling. The haunting remains of the Presidential Palace had given way to open green space. The scree that engulfed the city had been cleared from the major byways, and though a housing shortage persisted and too many Haitians were still living in tents, the capital was lively, verdant, and full of commotion. Where death had come with such terrifying swiftness, life had reasserted itself . . .

I went to Haiti to work at Zanmi Beni, a home for children in need. Zanmi Beni is commonly thought of as an orphanage because the parents of the sixty-four kids there will never be coming to fetch them. But in crucial ways, Zanmi Beni is not like conventional orphanages. The kids there are not up for adoption—Zanmi Beni is their home. When they introduce themselves, they give their last name as Beni ("*Bonjour, je m'appelle Peterson Beni*"). They care for and fight with (and for) one another; when they come home after school—and, eventually, after college or for Christmas or weddings—this is where they will go.

Loune Viaud, Zanmi Beni's director, explained its origins. On the day of the earthquake, Loune was attending a meeting of leaders in Haiti's public health system, including the prime minister, to devise a five-year plan to help the country recover from four hurricanes—Fay, Gustav, Hanna, and Ike—that had wiped away much of its infrastructure. The impact of the storms on the countryside was overwhelming. Ninety-eight percent of Haiti's tree cover had been deforested, setting the stage for widespread floods that displaced 8 percent of its population and leveled 70 percent of its crops. Nearly 50,000 homes were damaged, leaving nearly 200,000 people displaced or homeless. At the time, it was the costliest natural disaster in Haiti's history, a crushing financial blow for the poorest nation in the Western Hemisphere.

Seated at the head of the conference table, the prime minister was addressing the group when, without warning, the earth cracked open and swallowed the wall behind him. It was a moment of cruel irony: a meeting about recovering from one natural disaster was now interrupted by an even more destructive cataclysm. When the rumbling stopped, Loune and her best friend, Nancy Dorsinville, crawled out from beneath the conference table and ran into the street to confront the Armageddon around them. Perhaps because she was coleader of Partners in Health, the group Paul Farmer created, which helps the government of Haiti run its national health system, Loune's first instinct was to head to the General Hospital, the largest hospital in all of Haiti.

When Loune and Nancy arrived, the hospital grounds were littered with bodies, many dead, others writhing in agony. Amid the chaos they found thirty-eight kids, ranging in age from newborns to teenagers, abandoned at the General Hospital upon birth or when resources disintegrated, all physically and mentally challenged, emaciated, and near death, mostly four to a crib.

Loune told me, "The hospital's director asked me to take the children and I said yes." Loune didn't ask how she could do it or where they would live or who would pay for it all. When I asked her how she thought she could do it, she just looked to heaven and said, "I thought, He will find a way."

That is faith in action.

Since then, Loune has added twenty-six more to her brood. The latest is Micah, dropped at the hospital on Easter Sunday three years ago, a few weeks old, blind, starved, and on death's door. Today, she is thriving—impish, fun, and lively, Micah recites the entirety of the Twenty-Third Psalm ("The Lord is my shepherd; I lack nothing . . .") at daily chapel—a gift of resurrection.

Loune's is an active household, on a small farm on the outskirts of Port-au-Prince. We ate breakfast with the kids each morning at five and then read books; did calisthenics; went to the prayer service at the chapel; played wheelchair keep-away; danced; solved puzzles; ate lunch; played soccer; watched a Bible film; drew pictures; jumped in the blow-up pools; took a walk past the income-generating tilapia farm, henhouse, and restaurant; ate dinner; played Uno or checkers with the teenagers; and finally collapsed into bed.

Our days were pretty hectic. But the kids were delightful, funny, and a total inspiration.

TiJoe lost his entire family in the rubble of his home during the earthquake. He spent four days beneath the wreckage, crying for help. When he arrived at Loune's door, he didn't speak. When he finally broke his silence, it was only to repeat for days, "I'm dead. I'm dead. I'm dead." Today, TiJoe is eleven. He loves soccer and is a fierce competitor. My daughter Michaela spent hours showing him games on her laptop and practicing English with him—his third language after Creole and French.

When the Bureau of Social Services discovered that a contingent of UN soldiers deployed to Haiti to keep the peace had kidnapped Roudy and were raping him nightly as a sex slave, they brought the boy to Loune. At fifteen, Roudy's shaved head makes his egg-shaped skull distinct atop his fireplug build. He was always at the side of sweet and pretty Nephtalie, whose wheelchair he guided across the stone yard and up and down the steps. He has an easy smile and is quietly helpful, distributing books when it was time to read and sitting with Patrick, who is deaf and mute, at every meal.

At eight years old, Wendy, olive-skinned with piercing green eyes, watched his father take a stick and beat his mother to death. A few years later, his best friend died of gunshot wounds. Orphaned, despondent, homeless, lost, and defiant, he came to Loune's door. Wendy Beni is now eighteen, in ninth grade, goes to school every day, helps his brothers and sisters eat meals and play sports, and is determined to finish high school and become a master carpenter.

Carl is four. With two clubfeet, he cannot walk, but that does not slow him down. While other kids saunter, he glides across the ground on his hands, dragging his legs. With massive upper-body strength, he climbs onto the benches, and nothing makes him happier than twirling around on one of several tire swings. He will not be denied on the soccer field and whacks the ball with his entire lower body, sending the orb spinning toward the goal. When I last saw him, he was scheduled to travel to Toronto, where volunteer doctors would perform a series of operations they hoped would allow him to walk for the first time.

Every day at Zanmi Beni we went to the chapel. The kids sang and I prayed beneath the images of the Haitian Jesus and the Haitian Mary, no blond hair and blue eyes here, just reflections of the saintly people around me. Children, women, and a scattering of men who have endured unspeakable violence and anguish, loss and horror—biblical in force and nature—and have responded with unbounded love.

Redemption. Resurrection. Faith.

I left Haiti with these gifts in abundance.

Holy days, no matter the religion with which they are associated, contain lessons for all humanity. The lesson of Easter—the lesson that Jesus sought to teach—is that death is not final. The newly green lawns of Port-au-Prince, the selflessness of Loune and Nancy, the children of Zanmi Beni, smiling and laughing despite all they had endured—all of these made that lesson real for me in a way I had never before experienced.

When asked how she had endured loss, my grandmother Rose used to say, "After the storm, the birds sing. Why shouldn't we?"

The birds were certainly singing in Haiti on that Holy Week.

A Voice from Heaven

Revelation 14:13

Edwidge Danticat

I was talking to my mother when she died. She was visibly slipping away. She was no longer eating or drinking. Her body was cold. Her eyes were glazed as she drifted in and out of consciousness.

"I love you," I told her over and over, as I held her hand, kissed her face, stroked her hair. "You're a wonderful mother."

Hearing, they say, is one of the last senses to go.

My mother smiled.

I tearfully asked her, "Mommy, can you see heaven?"

She smiled again.

Then she was gone.

At her wake and funeral service, I was too scared to tell the story of how Mom had smiled her biggest smile in months when she heard the word *heaven*. I was worried people would think I'd made it up. Even though I had witnesses. There had been others in the room with me—my mother-in-law, the social worker, and the hospice nurse—and they had all confirmed that yes, my mother had smiled broadly right before taking her last breath. I was still worried that no one would believe me.

Instead I told the story to the young minister, a childhood friend, my brothers, and I asked to say the homily at my mother's wake. This young minister had known my mother his whole life. He constructed his sermon around the story. He titled his sermon "Mother Danticat's Smile."

"You could never walk away from an encounter with Mother Danticat without experiencing her smile," he said.

The young minister's sermon made me think anew about this idea of the dead smiling down on us from heaven. My mother made a powerful case for it herself with that final smile. The young minister, though, avoided the cliché. We were blessed, he said, to have enjoyed that smile while Mom was still with us.

When my mother was sick with stage 4 ovarian cancer, we had nightly devotions, just the two of us. She was visiting me from New York when she was diagnosed and had decided to stay for the treatment we hoped would gain her an undetermined amount of time. My mother was a devout Evangelical Christian and a member of a congregation of close to a thousand people in New York. In Miami, I visited many churches, but the one I attended most often met behind a grocery store and consisted of three or four families. Mom was missing the most expressive elements of her faith, the hours of sing-along worship, Bible study, and other group meetings. I tried to fill the gap.

Every night after everyone else had gone to bed, we would sing a hymn, recite or read a verse, pray, recite the Lord's Prayer, read another verse, then go to sleep. Mom had some favorites, Psalm 23 and the Beatitudes among them. The Beatitudes must have offered an extra dose of consolation. They were assurances, promises, which were about to be fulfilled, something I imagine she'd pierce the veil of heaven to tell me about now, if she could. In the Beatitudes, there was comfort both for her ("Blessed are the pure of heart, for they shall see God") and for me ("Blessed are they who mourn, for they shall be comforted"). She still had time to purify her heart. I had a lifetime to mourn.

Most of the time though Mom couldn't remember what verse she had in mind. Sometimes she'd recall a word or two and I'd go fishing in an online concordance for them.

"Syèl la," she'd say in Haitian Creole, signaling that the verse was somehow related to heaven.

When dozens of possible choices would appear, she'd ask me to pick the one closest to the top, or one we hadn't yet read. I would use different concordances, so the verses wouldn't always appear in the same order. This is how I came across Revelation 14:13 one night.

In my mother's French Bible, it read, "*Et j'entendis du ciel une voix qui disait: Ecris: Heureux dès à présent les morts qui meurent dans le Seigneur!*" Then I heard a voice from heaven say, "Write this: Blessed are the dead that die in the Lord."

I stopped reading after the equivalent of *on*.

This verse was so well suited to both my profession and my mother's circumstances that it seemed indeed like a command from heaven, not just to the Apostle John, the reported author of the Revelation, but also to me. *Write*, it said, though, as my mother's condition worsened, I was too grief stricken to even sign my name. *Write not just about living but also about dying.*

I have been writing about death for as long as I've been writing. The mother of the narrator of my first novel stabs herself seventeen times while she's pregnant. Hundreds of people drown on the high seas in my second book. My third book recounts a little-known Caribbean massacre in which thousands of people are methodically killed. While most of my work is based on actual events, I chose those subjects because I was so afraid of death that I wanted to desensitize myself to it. Many Haitian folktales begin with a death, or presume that it has already happened. Often it is the death of a mother. Most of these stories, like my mother's favorite Bible stories, offer the hope of an afterlife. Still, death remains what I most fear for the people I love, and what I most fear they'll have to not just endure but define and redefine for themselves after I'm gone.

"The death of a beloved is an amputation," C. S. Lewis writes in *A Grief Observed*.

That amputation has always terrified me.

"No one ever told me that grief felt so much like fear," Lewis wrote.

No one told me either.

I started reading C. S. Lewis's *A Grief Observed* when my mother was hospitalized for the last time and was preparing for home hospice. One never stops hoping for a miracle, but as my mother's body whittled away, it appeared less and less likely. Even the focus of my mother's prayers shifted. Rather than praying for healing, she started lingering on the part of the Lord's Prayer that says, "Thy will be done." She would repeat this line several times, as though it was now the only necessary prayer, the only one that mattered.

Ten years before, my father had made the same transition as he was dying from pulmonary fibrosis. His suffering—he was constantly coughing and out of breath—was a lot more visible than my mother's. No one had to ask him to rate his level of agony. It was always writ large on his skeletal face. His "Thy will be done" also became a plea for death.

"I didn't put myself on this earth and I can't take myself out," he'd say. "But if I could . . ."

He never allowed himself to finish the thought, but we knew he wanted out.

Mom wanted out, too, and started to withdraw. She stopped watching television and talking on the phone and no longer wanted me to read the Bible to her. It was as if the biblical conversation had now shifted to inside her head, becoming a secret dialogue from which I was suddenly barred. Instead she listened to sermons live-streamed on the Internet by a young pastor friend she'd been following since he was a teenage preacher in New York.

With my mother pulling back from our devotions, I tried to find solace in the verses and half verses she'd led me to. Reading the Bible,

I realized, was one more thing I would have to do without her after she was gone. So, I started reading *A Grief Observed* as a companion to my mother's Bible verses. I read it in the waiting rooms of diagnostic centers and in hospital rooms while she slept. Someone had given me a copy after my father died. My grief was too fresh to fully embrace it then. So I skimmed through it and put it away. Still, a few phrases stayed with me. The sentence about grief feeling like an amputation rang true. So did the one about fear, a kind of all-encompassing terror that would creep over me for months after both my parents died.

Like Mom, Lewis's wife—he calls her H. in the book—dies from cancer.

"One never meets just Cancer, or War, or Unhappiness (or Happiness)," he writes. "One only meets each hour or moment that comes."

Each moment with my mother brought a deeper understanding that she was slipping away from me, and that heaven, "Syèl la," was growing nearer and nearer. My mother had fully surrendered, but I was still flailing. Heaven did not seem like such a great place if everyone who was there had been plucked from somebody's arms. They might be blessed, those who are dead in the Lord, but what of the wretched lot of us, those they've left behind.

Lewis seemed to have had a similar thought: "His [God's] ideas of good are so very different from ours, what He calls Heaven might well be what we should call Hell . . ."

He asks his dying wife to come to him on *his* deathbed.

"Heaven would have a job to hold me," she tells him, "and as for Hell, I'd break it into bits."

Reading the Bible out of context is discouraged by all the ministers I know, but it was the only way my mother and I could read it together in the end. We only had time to zigzag through it to find what Mom wanted and needed to hear. The way we were reading it, though, led us to many comforting fragments, pockets of isolated thought, islands of ideas that, completely stripped of their context, perfectly suited us.

The Revelation, with its fiery prophecies of famines, earthquakes, plagues, and wars, is a pretty frightening book. Yet it is the one book in the Bible I kept returning to in the early days after my mother died. This felt odd, even to me, because it's also the one book I would have most hesitated to read to my mother during her last days.

The Revelation's vision of last days, all our last days, is so horrifying that it would have burdened, rather than lightened, my mother's heart.

Take for example, the beginning of Chapter 13.

> Then I saw a beast rising up out of the sea. It had seven heads and ten horns, with ten crowns on its horns. And written on each head were names that blasphemed God. This beast looked like a leopard, but it had the feet of a bear and the mouth of a lion! And the dragon gave the beast his own power and throne and great authority. (Rev. 13:1-2)

Surprisingly, I found myself relishing the descriptive and evocative, if sometimes chilling imagery of that book, the urgent stream-of-consciousness narrative, the suspenseful rollout of horrors, all of which made it seem as though my mother was lucky to have departed from a place for which this was, as she believed, a possible future.

The framing of the narrative itself seemed extravagant, to say the least. It was every writer's nightmare, being directed to jot down the orders of an enraged muse and told not to change a single commanding word. Still, nestled in the midst of all that fire and brimstone was my mother's little glacier, her own oasis, her vision of heaven.

There are other reassuring fragments from the Revelation that I now wish I'd had a chance to read to my mother, places where, after the torment and terrible suffering, everything suddenly becomes peaceful, idyllic.

In the final chapters of the Revelation, we catch a glimpse of a brand-new heaven and a new earth, where there is "no more death or mourning or crying or pain," where Eden is restored with new life and rivers flow clear as crystal, and crops bear abundant fruit and both people and nations are healed.

We are promised that:

> There will be no more night. They will not need the light of a lamp or the light of the sun, for the Lord God will give them light. And they will reign for ever and ever. (Rev. 22:5)

Maybe this is the heaven my mother wanted me to find for her as we crisscrossed the Bible. Maybe this was the heaven she was seeing when she smiled at me before taking her last breath, the type of heaven for which you have to surrender everything else, the kind of heaven that even if you could shatter the universe to bits, you would never choose to turn your back on, to return to your old life.

Living on the Ledge

Revelation 22:1–5

Lauren Slater

Then the angel showed me the river of the water of life, bright as crystal, flowing from the throne of God and of the Lamb through the middle of the street of the city; also on either side of the river, the tree of life with its twelve kinds of fruit, yielding its fruit each month. The leaves of the tree were for the healing of the nations. No longer will there be anything accursed, but the throne of God and of the Lamb will be in it, and his servants will worship him. They will see his face, and his name will be on their foreheads. And night will be no more. They will need no light of lamp or sun, for the Lord God will be their light, and they will reign for ever and ever.—Revelation 22:1–5

I have heft. The first few pounds were subtle and sneaky, making their way onto my petite frame with barely a sound, so I did not notice. The next few pounds were somewhat less subtle but still easy to ignore; however, after that the flesh began to pile up, the way sediment makes a mountain, earth upon earth, skin upon skin, my body bulging out from under the clothes I tried to conceal it with, and beneath my epidermis a breakdown began, my pancreas pooping out, so I developed diabetes, my eyesight going fuzzy, things in the distance still crystal clear but whatever was right in front of my nose impossible to decode. Diabetes takes a toll; it slows down circulation so you have to worry about your feet, which can go cold from lack of blood, sores developing, infection setting in, worst-case scenario an amputation—*not me,* I thought. And indeed my feet are fine, but the rest of me is not, most recently my kidneys starting to fail, those two lima-bean-shaped organs on either side of your torso that act, when healthy, as filters for your blood, cleansing it of toxins that make their way into you through the foods you eat, or fail to, sugars, starches, fruits sprayed with pesticides, tomatoes, bold and bright but laced with an invisible mist from the farmer trying to keep the worms from eating his harvest.

Kidney failure, like diabetes, is a quiet disease. When your appendix bursts you are blindsided by pain; an aneurysm causes a crushing headache, as if someone had thrust a spear through your open eye. Kidney failure, however, happens with barely a footfall until a critical threshold is reached, that threshold being a level of toxins your body can no longer comfortably contain. That occurred for me as I was watering my garden at the end of a hot summer day, my garden thriving in contrast to its maker, the squash plants with their huge leaves and fist-size yellow flowers, which eventually fall off, and, in their place, the rounded orbs of acorn squash that, when sliced open, reveal their firm orange flesh and neat rows of seeds slippery to the touch.

My squash plants, with their leaves the size of elephant ears, glossy, and green; my tomato plants sporting ripe red balls as cheery as Christmas ornaments, and tempting, too, biting into the side so a torrent of juice spurted from the split skin and darkened the dirt where I stood. I was barefoot, my feet alabaster white in contrast to the chocolate earth from which my garden grew; the pumpkin vines twining around the fence and lacing the lattice; tiny egg-size melons attached by the most slender of stems; eggplants, purple and black, visible beneath my verdant canopy. Barefoot, I was holding the hose while water arced out and pooled in the plants' crevices and cracks, I standing still while the wind blew the water in a sideways spray and then backwards so my face went wet, droplets falling from my eyelashes, runneling down my neck. Without a thought I reached up to swipe the spray away and was seized by a sudden cramp in a muscle I never knew I had, a muscle just beneath my lungs, a sudden seizing there, so severe it hurt to breathe for a moment, and then the moment passed and the muscle relaxed and I went back to watering, thinking nothing of it.

Later that night, however, the cramp came back, and, after it had passed, again in a mere matter of moments, my foot suddenly seized, the whole appendage balling up as the muscle clenched inward, my toes rigid, the pain severe. It was late, darkness outside my window, the moon a slender slice surrounded by speckles of stars—everything ordinary, the chapel down the street gonging out its midnight tune, the cat appearing the way she always appears, as if from out of the ether, a sudden furry swerve and she is there, leaping into your arms, curling like a living stole around your neck, her practically boneless body all purr and love. I held her in my arms, stroked her belly, noting that her nipples were more prominent than usual, twelve deeply pink protrusions, which, when squeezed, emitted a pale drop of something sweet to the taste. "Are you pregnant?" I asked our cat, knowing it was impossible as we'd bought her from the MSPCA shelter, where they spay every feline that comes their way, but then how to explain the teats, and the liquid they let out, and the uncommon roundness of her stomach, which was firm and without any motion but her breath? I held her in my arms, rocking her like a baby, and then my neck went into spasm, my whole head torqued sideways, and the pain was so severe my eyes teared up and in shock I dropped the cat, who landed effortlessly on all fours and went dancing down the stairs, I standing there with one hand on the stem that held up my head, feeling with my fingers how the muscles beneath the skin had gone grisly, kneading them hard, and harder still, trying to pound out the Gordian knots but unable to do so.

The neck is utterly essential. When it fails to operate correctly your whole body is thrown out of whack. I knew my husband was working in his study, and I tried to get down the stairs, to reach him, but I couldn't move very well what with my head at an odd angle and every bobble and bump causing excruciating pain. The children were asleep so I didn't want to call, but it was more than that. This was the third severe cramp I'd had today, all of them coming for no reason that I could see, and in addition to the physical pain a sense of foreboding was filling me now, and if I opened my mouth to call I thought I just might succumb to screaming. So I said nothing, standing as if nailed to this one spot on my bedroom floor with my fingers digging into the vertebrae at the upper end of the spine. A sudden gust of wind poured through the open window, and the curtains—white sheers—were lifted and twirled, and then, just like that, the cramp passed but not my fear; that stayed with me.

I was sweaty from pain and the effort of trying to massage my clotted knots. I sat on the edge of the bed. Three cramps, coming without warning and passing in their own time. What else? Lately I'd noticed my urine, no matter how much I drank, was so dark it was almost brown, and swirling with sediment, and with an odd, unnatural odor. And what else? Go on, say it. A thick thirst always in my mouth, my whole body calling for liquid, waking in the middle of the night soaked in a sweat for no reason that I could see, my sheets wet beneath me and my thirst driving me into the darkness and down the stairs to yank open the door of the humming fridge, my hands grasping the sides of a jar of juice and gulping it down, down—enough? No, more. And more. And when the juice was gone going to the faucet and filling not a glass but a vase with water, the glass much too small for my enormous thirst, the vase brimming with beautiful water, water with the kind of clarity you notice only when consumed by a burning thirst, you drinking as if to extinguish a conflagration inside your body, your stomach bulging and sloshing and yet the thirst still there, the throat parched, the salivary glands oddly shriveled and begging for more moisture. It was in this context that the cramps had come—strange nighttime sweats, a pervasive and all-consuming thirst, urine that was thick and darkly yellow and spare in its stream, just dribbling from my body when it should have been pouring out of me as if I were a pricked water ball—where was all the liquid going? I noticed my ankles were swollen, my legs looking large, the scrawl of veins very visible, a vinery of blues and teals just beneath the surface of my bloated skin.

These days one need not go to a doctor for a diagnosis. I knew what it was. I knew that an accumulation of toxins in the body could cause one's muscles to cramp, and that toxins accumulate in the body when your two internal filters—your kidneys—are no longer operating efficiently. I knew that drinking gallons of water a day and peeing in dark dribbles, enough to fill a lady's Victorian teacup—I knew that this was likely related to some kind of kidney malfunction as well. I typed my symptoms into WebMD and confirmed that my kidneys were the culprit, and the next day I went to my doctor and told him what was happening. Of course his phlebotomist poked me with a butterfly needle, drawing vial after vial of blood, and I was sent home with a plastic jug in which I was instructed to pee for the next twenty-four hours, after which the lab would analyze my liquid output for the presence of toxins and creatinine. Once the laboratory had finished its analysis my doctor called me in and he said, "Well, you have renal insufficiency," which I knew was a nice way of saying that my kidneys were starting to fail. "Renal insufficiency" is just another, softer way of saying that your body's filtration system is on its way out, and, on top of that, there's not much anyone can do about it; it's chronic, it's progressive, and, at the end, you have two choices: to go on dialysis or to get a kidney transplant, neither a very alluring alternative, and both simply way stations, expensive and high-tech pauses that put off for a while the ultimate end, which is complete kidney failure, your body filled to the brim with poisons you can't excrete, your muscles seizing up as if zippered shut, the heart slowing before it stops, the lobes of the lungs deflating as air leaves through the nostrils and the partly opened mouth, the end.

We all have an end, and *something* is going to cause it. All of us are going to die from *something*. We don't just expire. Our bodies, instead, betray us in some way large or small, simple or complex, and thus every death is preceded by this betrayal, and what scares us, perhaps, is not so much death itself but the betrayal that lies in wait for us. Death is rarely a peaceful passing, although occasionally it may be. Far more frequently it is a slow and painful thrashing, an exit we make with moans and morphine, the doorway we need to get through jammed shut and oh so hard to open, the line we need to cross serrated and sharp and leaving us bloodied and crying for some sort of mercy. Many people believe that on the other side of that line lies heaven, that when they finally push through that difficult door they will be greeted by twelve-foot angels and streets of pure pearl and rivers glowing brightly over rocks as precious and gorgeous as green and jade gems. My own tussle with illnesses—diabetes and now kidney disease—has led me to ponder long and hard about what follows once we leave the land. The Judeo-Christian Bible is full of descriptions, of promises, really, the bottom line being that if we are very, very good we will go to that place of pure pearl, and, if we are very, very bad we will go to a place of perpetual burn and fire.

I find, in the midst of my illnesses, the descriptions of the afterlife, specifically the descriptions of heaven, to be quite lovely, and I love to read them, in the same way I love to thumb through clothing catalogs and admire all the silks and satins I cannot in fact afford to buy. I don't mean to sound disrespectful and I know the New Testament is far more worthy than a J. Jill catalog, but that knowledge does not for a minute change my experience, my private subjective experience of reading about pure pearl and twelve-foot angels and perpetual light with a golden glow. It's not so much that I don't believe in heaven and hell—although I don't, at least as far as heaven is concerned—(hell I'm less sure about, although, if it exists, I don't think it's in the form of fire)—it's more that the concept of the afterlife, as lovely as it is, fails to comfort me, not only because I don't believe it but more importantly because the very idea in some deep and abiding way does not work for me, the same way certain movies fail to engage me, or move me, while other humans may be moved to tears by the exact same show. The Judeo-Christian heaven, for me, appears to be very pretty and thus nice to look at or contemplate for brief periods of time, but just as a clothing catalog does not fulfill my need for real and pulsing literature, so, too, heaven as it is described in the New Testament does not bring me the sort of solace I'd like to feel when contemplating my own demise. Setting aside the issue of credulity, or, better yet, assuming for the sake of it that heaven as the Bible describes it is in fact really real, what on earth, or off earth, as the case may be, are you supposed to do once you are there? I mean, quite literally, what does one do with one's time in heaven? Do you sit around and eat apples from trees perpetually ripe and red? Where, in heaven, is the conflict that gives life its kick, its edgy edge? For how long can you dance with angels before you become, inevitably, bored, and seeking, say, a steak? I assume heaven is too transcendent an experience for newspapers to be relevant, so what does one read in heaven? I suspect, if it is true, that you just sit there like you are stoned out of your mind staring into this mesmerizing golden glow, which must eventually blunt the brain, like eating too much acid.

Since my kidneys have started to fail I've been paying more attention to the afterlife as my tradition—which is Judeo-Christian—describes it, but even repeated readings don't make it into my dreams. In my dreams I am in a rocket ship specifically sized for me, a very small ship with me hunched high inside, and the ship is shooting through space, shooting through time, flying away in eternity, I utterly alone as I pass by massive planets and newborn stars and astral debris from phenomenal explosions, the atmosphere warped by gas. I am unable to sleep and have no one to talk to, ever; this infinite aloneness is my own private version of hell. I want to dream of heaven; I want the unconsciousness that comes with sleep to reveal to me how my mind truly concocts the other kind of afterlife, the good kind, but night after night I come up empty, just me in the shooting ship, and the passing stars and the planets glowing far, far away.

I think it makes sense that I don't have a heaven in my heart, because in my daily life, at my core, I'm a catastrophizer, a pessimist, poised always to believe the worst is right around the corner. For some time I went to therapy in an effort to change my mind-set, until I realized that I liked it because I was never disappointed and sometimes pleasantly surprised.

If I could design my own heaven it would be simple: a single book with a plot so pure and all consuming that your troubled teetering nattering worried rat-tat-tat mind would be totally taken up, completely quieted in blissful concentration. The book that is my heaven would be infinite of course and, freed from the bodily need for food and water, you would lie in your childhood bed and simply read, turning pages made of parchment, pages that left a faint scrim on your fingers so that when you licked them you got the tang of a taste from this big and beautiful book. Your mind would be honed to a single purposeful point, to a crescendo of concentration as you were swept up, again and again, in a denouement that never actually ended.

I will likely die of kidney failure, which is a secondary complication of my diabetes. I might die a month from now, a year from now, ten years from now, or even more; it all depends on the demise and the speed with which it happens. I'm doing what I can to keep myself here on planet earth, where my garden grows and my supposedly spayed cat has just given birth to four black kittens, who yesterday, and for the first time, opened their tiny eyes so we saw slits of ocean blue in their otherwise ebony faces. A friend suggested that I call the MSPCA and demand my adoption fee back; the $250 we paid for Amber was supposed to cover the cost of a spaying that obviously never occurred. But I'm not going to ask for my money back. The MSPCA is a fine charity and they do their best. Beyond that, is it not possible that they indeed *did* spay Amber and that these kittens are some sort of miracle, some sort of sign, a suggestion that I believe in life even when life does not believe in me? The rational side of me seriously doubts that a miracle such as the one I've just suggested could ever occur. But lately I've become a little less rational, a little more open to, shall we say, other dimensions, wacky and wayward propositions. The kittens are so small! They are no bigger than a child's fist. My husband suggests we call one of them

Fondue, and another Jallopie. My son suggests we call one of them Sun and another Moon. I like them nameless because, in such a state, they can be anything we want them to be; they can be magic; they can be miracle; they can be part of the plot of a book bigger than any of us can imagine, a book you can read with your eyes closed or open, a book that unfurls like a flower and engages with a golden hook. My heaven. There are no streets of pure pearl and thrones on which God sits and trees bearing twelve kinds of fruit. There are just infinite pages of parchment containing infinite numbers of words linked together in a way more meaningful than we here on earth can comprehend. A spayed cat has kittens. A big bang occurs. Something comes from nothing. The body disappears while the mind, unfettered and freed from the toxins that stained and maimed it, grasps concepts in a shaving of a second. In my heaven there is no end but there is always, always, a beginning.

The Bad Book

Robert Coover

In the summer of 1957, fresh out of the navy (remember the draft and the Korean War?), I rented a cabin for a month on an island in Canada just north of the Minnesota border and set out to become a writer. Like everyone else, I'd been a writer all my life, but now I was going to lay out some principles and get serious about it. I took with me all of Samuel Beckett's texts then available, some of the absurdist playwrights, a few philosophers and theologians, some dirty Olympia Press books I'd picked up in Paris, and the Bible. I decided to read the Bible straight through, front to back, to see what sort of a story it was. My grandfather had been a Bible Belt Methodist preacher, my father a Sunday school superintendent and choir soloist, and, in that postwar midwestern Hollywood era, church was a deeply ingrained family and community habit, so I was still shaking the Good Book off. I found the porn holier, Beckett wiser, and wrote a kind of Kierkegaardian response (I liked the Dane's style at the time) to the book and the dangerous institutions it spawned. I supposed that was it. Through Beckett I'd found my vocation, and I was leaving most outworn conventions behind, religion and other traditional fictions included.

But there had been a terrible Christmastime explosion in one of the coal mines near where my family lived, and, as a college kid home for the holidays, I had helped report on it for my father's newspaper. That had led to some early stories, and one of them was eventually accepted by

Saul Bellow and Keith Botsford for their celebrated literary magazine, *The Noble Savage*. Writer friends and editors, rejecting my "breakaway" fictions, urged me to attempt a book something more like the *Noble Savage* mine disaster story, and eventually I did, mainly to prove that I could. Thus, *The Origin of the Brunists*. So it could be said that the Bible helped launch my writing life, though it was less the book than the communal madness it tended to provoke that had my main attention.

Origin was about the formation of an apocalyptic cult around the bedside of a lone mine disaster survivor, and, at the time, I imagined a sequel for it, set in a time when the cult, after failed prophecies, had become an established evangelical religion. But I was no longer writing that sort of fiction, so although I took extensive notes for it through the decades that followed, a return to it seemed unlikely—until the election of young George Bush to the U.S. presidency and the rise to power with him of that swarm of crazed evangelicals. Fortunately, most of the western world has set the Bible and its savage worldview aside, but not my compatriots, who, ignoring the enlightened skepticism of the Founding Fathers, are far more likely to believe in the Devil or the virgin birth of Jesus than in evolution or global warming. So, when W declared a "crusade" against the infidels, calling up his knights in heavy armor and sending them rumbling off to Baghdad to unleash their holy shock and awe, I felt it was time for *The Brunist Day of Wrath*. Most of my eighth decade (so valuable! so gone!) was devoted to it. I thought of it as a comic work, though like the human comedy it is not always funny.

The new project forced another cover-to-cover reread of the Bible, but I had not entirely left it behind. In 1967, not long after *Origin* first appeared, I taught a reading-writing workshop at the University of Iowa called Exemplary Ancient Fictions, a course I continued to teach, off and on, over the next forty-five years, and Genesis, a kind of theologically modified folktale compilation, was usually one of the texts. Except for the *Enuma Elish* and maybe Hesiod's *Theogony*, Genesis was the least appealing of the books on the syllabus, but its tales and characters have fairy-tale status in the western world, even where not part of the catechism, and it is a good place to intrude upon a text and attempt variations.

In class, we focused on the so-called J voice, but compared his (or their) tales exemplarily to the contributions of the P voice, which were mostly negative and orthodoxly censorious: the writers versus the priestly nonwriters—those whom Sally Elliott, *The Brunist Day of Wrath*'s resident debunker, calls "a bunch of beardy guys with tight assholes." Had it not been for P, we might have had (and in class did have) stories about the stinking splendor of Leviathan, the monstrous Riz and Behemot, and the amazing Adne Sadeh, also known as Adam, the strange animal called man, a human creature fastened to the ground by his navel-string, severing it being the only way to kill him so he could be served up as an edible delicacy. We might have heard more about the rebellion of the "dark waters," about Adam's first wife, Lilith, and the curious manufacture of Eve, about Cain's nightmarish life after his exile, and about the annoyed First Man's killing of Samael's squalling son, whom he and Eve are babysitting. The damned kid keeps screaming even after he's dead, so Adam chops him up and cooks the bits and he and Eve eat them, no doubt washing them down with good wine (legend makes it clear that the fruit the serpent tempted them with was not an apple but fermented grapes). But when they lie to Samael about this, the kid pipes up from inside them and gives them away. Samael in his paternal rage is ready to kill them both, but God loves Adam and gives him the Torah as a kind of knowledge-shield. Which, in turn, makes the angels jealous and they also want to kill Adam, but the Torah is like krypton and foils their plot, so they steal it and throw it into the sea to set up future adventures. None of this adds to God's or Adam's grandeur, but at least it doesn't try to make men feel guilty for their own deaths, as the priestly version criminally does. Had these stories and the many like them got past the censors into God's handiwork, one can well imagine the scramblings of the literalists to justify them.

After Genesis, the Good Book generally falls away into a humorless

So-So Book at best, a Bad Book mostly, getting worse as it goes along, sinking into the New Testament's celebration of a deluded monomaniac, who brings the good news that the world is ending even as he speaks, thereby forming a cult around himself that shapes the world we live in now. It's no miracle. As Jesus himself says in *The Brunist Day of Wrath* (if it is he, and not a lunatic with a Christ parapathy), "Along come mad Paul, the unscrupulous evangelist scribblers, the Patmos wild man, the remote muddle-headed church fathers, so called, plus a few ruthless tyrants and you've got a powerhouse world religion." All the world's heavies, needing to hang on to what they've got while pushing their enemies' noses in it, find books like this one the perfect tool for suckering a mob.

There are a few universally acknowledged and overpraised poetic high spots in the Bible like the Song of Songs (sex—yay!), the kvetchings of Job (a conservative tale about a stubborn rich man, with a Hollywood ending), the songs and sayings anthologies (dime a dozen), and Ecclesiastes, with its ancient carpe diem message (it is, in effect, an elaboration of the alewife's message to the wayfaring Gilgamesh a millennium and a half earlier), but as my penciled-in marginalia from *Origin of the Brunists* days repeatedly bewail, it is for the most part unbearable diatribe exhibiting an appalling and infantile view of the universe, and bottoming out with Revelation, a displaced Old Testament nightmare so over the top it's almost comical, like a laughable backyard horror movie.

The Brunist books, however, are less about the Bible than about its fanatical adherents and the toxic institutions and culture they give rise to. The book can be dismissed as mere literature of disputed quality, but not its believers, who can be dangerous, not only to all nonbelievers but to the planet as well (hooray for death! bring on the apocalypse!). The human species does not need texts like this one to kill and torture others, they'd do it anyway, and with pleasure, but the texts serve conveniently as pretext. To paraphrase the old NRA slogan: the Bible doesn't kill, people do. But just as guns make it a lot easier to kill and offer up new temptations and opportunities to do so, so does the Bible make it a lot easier to justify the slaughter of nonbelievers and offer up a rationale for recklessly exploiting a world that has no future. As Sally says in *Wrath*: The world is being ruined by people with childish ideas and grown-up weapons.

Acknowledgments

In the beginning . . . there was Adam. I thank the great Mr. Gopnik for introducing this book. Profuse and profound gratitude to all of the writers in *The Good Book* for their contributions, their generosity and magnanimity. Jonathan Karp, at Simon & Schuster, is the Larry Bird of the publishing industry. He dished the proposal for this project to Trish Todd, who manifested the wisdom of Solomon, the patience of Job and more, in expertly editing and shepherding this book to publication. Her assistant, Kaitlin Olson, was an important, instrumental part of the project. Also at S&S, major thanks to Cary Goldstein, Ebony LaDelle, Amanda Lang, Richard Rhorer, Loretta Denner, Susan Brown, Ellen Sasahara, Leydiana Rodriguez, and Julius Reyes. The book would likely not exist without the ineffable, invaluable help of the wondrous Claire Dorsett. Special thanks to Elif Batuman, Harold Bloom, Joan Bingham, Anne and Georges Borchardt, Lauren Cameron, Rosanne Cash, The Collegiate School, The JBC, Jennifer Joel, Barbara Jones, Adella Ladjevardi, Katherine A. Powers, Matthew Saal, James Salter, Charles M. Schulz, Steven Shainberg, James D. Solomon, and Sheila Weisman. And to the sinners and to the saints.

About the Authors

André Aciman was born in Alexandria, Egypt, and is an American memoirist, essayist, novelist, and Distinguished Professor of Comparative Literature at the CUNY Graduate Center; he is also founder and director of The Writers' Institute and chair of The Center for the Humanities at the Graduate Center. He received his Ph.D. from Harvard University and has taught at Princeton University and Bard College. His work has appeared in *The New Yorker, The New York Review of Books, The New York Times, The New Republic,* and *Condé Nast Traveler,* as well as in many volumes of *The Best American Essays.* He is the author of *Out of Egypt: A Memoir* and the novels *Call Me by Your Name, Eight White Nights,* and *Harvard Square.* He is also the author of essay collections *False Papers* and *Alibis.* He is the editor of *The Proust Project* and *Letters of Transit.* His forthcoming books are *Enigma Variations* and *Homo Irrealis.*

Ian Caldwell is the author, most recently, of the acclaimed novel *The Fifth Gospel.* He has written previously about his Princeton experience in *The Rule of Four,* which spent forty-nine weeks on the *New York Times* bestseller list and was translated into thirty-five languages on its way to becoming one of the most successful debut novels of the decade. He has been featured on the front page of *The New York Times* and *The Washington Post,* and his novels have appeared on the covers of *The New York Review of Books* and *The New Republic.* He lives with his wife and sons in northern Virginia.

Robert Coover is the author of more than twenty books of fiction and plays, his most recent being *The Brunist Day of Wrath* and *Noir.* He has been nominated for the National Book Award and awarded numerous prizes and fellowships, including the William Faulkner First Novel Award, the Rea Lifetime Achievement Award for the Short Story, and a Lannan Foundation Literary Fellowship. His plays have been produced in New York, Los Angeles, Paris, London, and elsewhere. At Brown University, he created and directed the International Writers Project for endangered writers and taught the first workshops in creative digital writing, including Cave Writing, a writing workshop in immersive virtual reality.

Edwidge Danticat is the author of several books, including *Breath, Eyes, Memory,* an Oprah Book Club selection; *Krik? Krak!,* a National Book Award finalist; *The Farming of Bones; The Dew Breaker; Create Dangerously;* and *Claire of the Sea Light.* She is also the editor of *The Butterfly's Way: Voices from the Haitian Dyaspora in the United States, Haiti Noir* and *Haiti Noir 2,* and *The Best American Essays 2011.* She has written six books for young adults and children—*Anacaona, Behind the Mountains, Eight Days, The Last Mapou, Untwine,* and *Mama's Nightingale*—as well as a travel narrative, *After the Dance.* Her memoir, *Brother, I'm Dying,* was a 2007 finalist for the National Book Award and a 2007 winner of the National Book Critics Circle Award for autobiography. She is a 2009 MacArthur Fellow.

Lydia Davis is the author, most recently, of the story collection *Can't and Won't* (Farrar, Straus & Giroux, 2014), which followed her *Collected Stories* of 2009. She is also the translator of new versions of Flaubert's *Madame Bovary* and Proust's *Swann's Way,* as well as, in 2015, Alfred Ollivant's children's classic, *Bob, Son of Battle.* In 2014 she was awarded the Man Booker International Prize for her fiction.

Michael Eric Dyson is a Georgetown University sociology professor, ordained Baptist minister, *New York Times* contributing writer, and MSNBC political analyst. Dr. Dyson is the author of seventeen books, including *Making Malcolm: The Myth and Meaning of Malcolm X*, *Holler if You Hear Me: Searching for Tupac Shakur*, the *New York Times* bestseller *Is Bill Cosby Right? Or Has the Black Middle Class Lost Its Mind?*, and *Can You Hear Me Now? The Inspiration, Wisdom, and Insight of Michael Eric Dyson*. He has won many prestigious awards, including an American Book Award and the NAACP Image Award, and he regularly appears as a journalist on television and radio shows including *Today*, NPR's *Talk of the Nation*, *Charlie Rose*, HBO's *Def Poetry Jam*, *Meet the Press*, *Face the Nation*, *Real Time with Bill Maher*, and *The Colbert Report*. He holds a Ph.D. from Princeton University and has also taught at Brown University, the University of North Carolina at Chapel Hill, Columbia University, and the University of Pennsylvania.

Clyde Edgerton is the Thomas S. Kenan III Distinguished Professor of Creative Writing at the University of North Carolina in Wilmington. He is the author of the novels *Walking Across Egypt*, *The Floatplane Notebooks*, *Lunch at the Piccadilly*, and seven others. His last book is nonfiction: *Papadaddy's Book for New Fathers*. He lives in Wilmington with his wife and their three children.

Paul Elie is the author of *The Life You Save May Be Your Own* (2003), a group portrait of four American Catholic writers; and *Reinventing Bach* (2012), the story of the transformation of Bach's music in modern times by great musicians working with cutting-edge technology. He is a senior fellow in Georgetown University's Berkley Center for Religion, Peace, and World Affairs. He posts pieces daily to everythingthatrises.com.

Ian Frazier was born in Ohio in 1951. He writes humor and nonfiction for magazines, mainly *The New Yorker,* to which he has been contributing since 1974. His books include *Dating Your Mom, Great Plains, Family, On the Rez, Coyote v. Acme,* and *Travels in Siberia.* He lives in Montclair, New Jersey, with his wife, the novelist Jacqueline Carey.

Samuel G. Freedman is an award-winning author, columnist, and professor. A columnist for *The New York Times* and a professor at Columbia University, he is the author of seven acclaimed books, most recently *Breaking the Line: The Season in Black College Football That Transformed the Sport and Changed the Course of Civil Rights* (2013). Freedman was a staff reporter for *The New York Times* from 1981 through 1987 and currently writes the paper's column "On Religion." A tenured professor at the Columbia University Graduate School of Journalism, Freedman was named the nation's outstanding journalism educator in 1997 by the Society of Professional Journalists. In 2012 he received Columbia University's coveted Presidential Award for Excellence in Teaching. He is a board member of the Jewish Book Council and Religion News Service, and has spoken at the Smithsonian Institution, Yale University, and UCLA, among other venues, and has appeared on National Public Radio, CNN, and *The NewsHour with Jim Lehrer.* Freedman holds a bachelor's degree in journalism and history from the University of Wisconsin at Madison, which he received in May 1977. He lives in New York with his wife, Christia Chana Blomquist, and his children, Aaron and Sarah.

Adam Gopnik has been writing for *The New Yorker* since 1986. His books include *Paris to the Moon, The King in the Window, Through the Children's Gate,* and *The Table Comes First: Family, France, and the Meaning of Food.* A three-time winner of the National Magazine Award, he lives in New York with his wife and two children.

Brooks Hansen is an author, screenwriter, essayist, and teacher. He has written five novels, including *The Chess Garden* (a *Publishers Weekly* Best Book of the Year) and *John the Baptizer*, for which he received a John Simon Guggenheim Fellowship in 2005. He has also written one book for young readers, which he illustrated, and a personal memoir about infertility and adoption in the twenty-first century. He currently lives with his wife and two children in Carpinteria, California, where he teaches at Cate School.

Pico Iyer is the author of a novel that rises out of the Song of Songs, titled *Abandon*, and of many nonfiction books on migration and literature and globalism, among them *The Global Soul, The Open Road* (about the fourteenth Dalai Lama), and *The Man within My Head* (about Graham Greene). Though he has written often about Buddhism, he has been spending much of his time since 1991 in a Benedictine hermitage on the California coast, reading works such as the Song of Songs.

A. J. Jacobs is the author of four *New York Times* bestsellers, including *The Year of Living Biblically, The Know-It-All,* and *Drop Dead Healthy*. He is an editor at large at *Esquire* and a correspondent for NPR. He is currently helping to build a family tree of the entire human race and is planning a massive family reunion. You are invited. GlobalFamilyReunion.com.

Kerry Kennedy is president of Robert F. Kennedy Human Rights. She is the author of *Speak Truth to Power* and the bestseller *Being Catholic Now*. Kennedy started working in human rights in 1981, when she investigated abuses committed by U.S. immigration officials against Salvadoran refugees. Since then, her life has been devoted to the pursuit of justice and to the promotion and protection of basic rights. She established the RFK Center for Human Rights in 1988 and has led hundreds of human rights delegations across the globe. Kennedy founded RFK Speak Truth to Power, a global human rights education initiative that is taught to millions of students worldwide. In 2010 she founded RFK Compass, which convenes financial leaders to consider the impact of human rights violations, environmental degradation, and corruption on investment outcomes. Kennedy serves on the boards of directors of Human Rights First, Inter Press Service, and the United States Institute for Peace. She has three daughters, Cara, Mariah, and Michaela.

Owen King is the author of *Double Feature: A Novel.* His fiction and nonfiction have appeared in the *Los Angeles Review of Books, The New York Times Book Review, One Story,* and *Prairie Schooner* among other publications.

Jane Leavy is the author of the *New York Times* bestsellers *The Last Boy: Mickey Mantle and the End of America's Childhood* and *Sandy Koufax: A Lefty's Legacy. Entertainment Weekly* called her comic novel *Squeeze Play* "the best novel ever written about baseball."

As a staff writer for *The Washington Post* she covered baseball, tennis, the Olympics, and the Washington scene. Her work has appeared in *The New York Times* and *Sports Illustrated,* on the ESPN website *Grantland,* and in numerous anthologies, including *Jewish Jocks: An Unorthodox Hall of Fame, Damn Yankees: Twenty-Four Major League Writers on the World's Most Loved (and Hated) Team,* and *Coach: 25 Writers Reflect on People Who Made a Difference.* Her next book will be *The Big Fella: Babe Ruth and the Advent of Celebrity.*

She lives in Washington, D.C., and Truro, Massachusetts.

Lois Lowry, a children's author, was born in Honolulu, Hawaii, and has lived all over the world. She attended elementary school in Carlisle, Pennsylvania; junior high school in Tokyo; high school in New York; and went to Brown University and the University of Southern Maine. Currently she divides her time between her residence in Cambridge, Massachusetts, and an eighteenth-century farmhouse in rural Maine.

Twice the recipient of the Newbery Medal, given each year for the most distinguished contribution to children's literature by an American author, Lowry has also received the Regina Medal, the Dorothy Canfield Fisher Children's Book Award, the Mark Twain Award, the Boston Globe–Horn Book Award, the Bank Street College Award, the National Jewish Book Award, the Chicago Tribune Young Adult Fiction Award, and countless other honors for her work. She has twice been the United States nominee for the Hans Christian Andersen Award.

Her forty-plus books have been translated into over twenty languages, and in 1996 her award-winning novel *The Giver*, called in translation *Le Passeur*, was chosen by the children of Belgium and France as their favorite.

In addition, several of her books have been adapted for film and stage.

Lois Lowry has traveled around the world, speaking to children in Spain, Germany, Belgium, Luxembourg, Indonesia, Japan, New Zealand, and Australia about the importance of literature and imagination in their lives.

She is a mother and grandmother and has worked as a photojournalist as well as a writer of fiction.

Thomas Lynch is the author of five collections of poems, four books of nonfiction, and a book of stories, *Apparition & Late Fictions*. His book *The Undertaking* won the American Book Award and was a finalist for the National Book Award. His work has appeared in *The Atlantic* and *Granta*, *The New Yorker* and *Esquire*, *Poetry* and *The Paris Review*, also *The New York Times*, the *Los Angeles Times*, *The Times* of London, and

The Irish Times, and has been the subject of two documentary films, *Learning Gravity* by Cathal Black and PBS *Frontline*'s *The Undertaking*. He has taught at Wayne State University's School of Mortuary Science, University of Michigan's graduate program in creative writing, and the Candler School of Theology at Emory University. He keeps homes in Michigan and Moveen, West Clare.

Charles McGrath, formerly the deputy editor of *The New Yorker* and editor of *The New York Times Book Review*, is now a contributing writer to *The Times*.

Daniel Menaker, a former fiction editor at *The New Yorker* and later editor in chief of Random House, is also the author of six books, most recently *My Mistake: A Memoir*. He is now a professor in the MFA program at Stony Brook University and edits the online humor column "Grin & Tonic" for the *Barnes and Noble Review*.

Rick Moody is the author of five novels, three collections of stories, a memoir, and, most recently, a volume of essays, *On Celestial Music*. His forthcoming novel is *Hotels of North America*. He writes about music regularly for *The Rumpus*, *Salon*, *The Talkhouse*, and elsewhere, and plays in and writes songs for the Wingdale Community Singers.

Kathleen Norris is the author of *Dakota: A Spiritual Geography*, *The Cloister Walk*, *Amazing Grace: A Vocabulary of Faith*, *The Virgin of Bennington*, *Acedia and Me*, and several volumes of poetry. The recipient of grants from the Bush and Guggenheim Foundations, she held the Randall Chair in Christian Culture at Providence College for the 2014–15 academic year.

Jay Parini, a poet and novelist, teaches at Middlebury College. His novels include *The Last Station, Benjamin's Crossing,* and *The Passages of H.M.* He has written five volumes of poetry and biographies of Robert Frost, John Steinbeck, William Faulkner, Jesus, and Gore Vidal. He writes frequently for various newspapers and websites, including *The Guardian* and CNN.

James Parker was born in London in 1968. He is the author of *Turned On*, a biography of punk legend Henry Rollins, and writes regularly for *The Atlantic* and *The New York Times Book Review*. He edits *The Pilgrim*, a magazine featuring writing from the homeless community of downtown Boston.

Robert Pinsky's recent works include his *Selected Poems*; *PoemJazz*, a CD with Grammy-winning pianist Laurence Hobgood; and *Singing School*, an anthology manifesto. As United States poet laureate, he founded the Favorite Poem Project (www.favoritepoem.org), in which thousands of Americans—of varying backgrounds, all ages, and from every state—shared their favorite poems. Pinsky celebrates his own favorite poems in his newest anthology, *Singing School: Learning to Write (and Read) Poetry by Studying with the Masters* (2013). Pinsky teaches in the Creative Writing Program at Boston University.

Cokie Roberts is a commentator for ABC News and NPR. Her books have focused on the role of women in American history and include the national bestsellers *We Are Our Mothers' Daughters, Founding Mothers,* and *Ladies of Liberty*. Her latest book, *Capital Dames,* chronicles the women of Washington during the Civil War.

Steven V. Roberts was a *New York Times* correspondent for twenty-five years and is now the Shapiro Professor of Media and Public Affairs at George Washington University. He is also a columnist for *Bethesda* magazine and a political analyst for ABC Radio. His books include *My Fathers' Houses*, a family memoir, and *From Every End of This Earth*, an account of thirteen families that recently emigrated to America. Cokie and Steve, married for almost fifty years, have written about their interfaith union in two books, *From This Day Forward*, also a bestseller, and *Our Haggadah*.

Reverend Al Sharpton is the founder and president of the National Action Network (NAN), a not-for-profit civil rights organization headquartered in Harlem, New York, with over eighty chapters nationwide, including a Washington, D.C., bureau and regional offices from coast to coast. He is currently the host of *PoliticsNation*, a daily television show on MSNBC that analyses the top political and social news and features the country's leading newsmakers, and a nationally syndicated radio show, *Keepin' It Real*. Reverend Sharpton is the author of *The Rejected Stone: Al Sharpton and the Path to American Leadership*. He is a champion for human rights and is passionate about the key issues that involve confronting human rights violations. He says that his religious convictions are the basis for his life, and he has been at the vanguard of issues promoting equal standards and decency.

Lauren Slater is the author of eight books of both fiction and nonfiction. Her ninth book, *The Drugs That Changed Our Minds: A History of Psychiatry in Ten Treatments*, will be published in 2016. Her work has appeared seven times in Best American Essays volumes and has been translated into seventeen languages. She is the recipient of a National Endowment for the Arts Award, a finalist for the Los Angeles Times Book Award, and winner of the Bild der Wissenschaft Award for the most groundbreaking book of science. Slater lives in Harvard, Massachusetts, with her husband, two children, three horses, four cats, five hens, and her extraordinary dog.

Avi Steinberg is the author of two books, most recently *The Lost Book of Mormon: A Journey Through the Mythic Lands of Nephi, Zarahemla, and Kansas City, Missouri*. His essays appear regularly in *The New Yorker*'s "Culture Desk" section.

Colm Tóibín is the author of eight novels, including *The Master, Brooklyn*, and *Nora Webster*, and two collections of stories. His play *The Testament of Mary* was nominated for a Tony Award for Best Play in 2013. He is Irene and Sidney B. Silverman Professor of the Humanities at Columbia University.

Alec Wilkinson began writing for *The New Yorker* in 1980. Before that he was a policeman in Wellfleet, Massachusetts, and before that he was a rock and roll musician. He has published ten books—two memoirs, two collections of essays, three biographical portraits, two pieces of reporting, and one account of a historical adventure. He has been a Guggenheim Fellow, and he has won a Lyndhurst Prize and a Robert F. Kennedy Book Award.

Tobias Wolff's books include the memoirs *This Boy's Life* and *In Pharaoh's Army: Memories of the Lost War*; the short novel *The Barracks Thief*; the novel *Old School*; and four collections of short stories, *In the Garden of the North American Martyrs, Back in the World, The Night in Question*, and, most recently, *Our Story Begins: New and Selected Stories*. He has also edited several anthologies, among them *The Best American Short Stories*

1994, *A Doctor's Visit: The Short Stories of Anton Chekhov,* and *The Vintage Book of Contemporary American Short Stories.* His work is translated widely and has received numerous awards, including the PEN/Faulkner Award, the Los Angeles Times Book Award, both the PEN/Malamud Award and Rea Award for the Short Story, the Story Prize, and the Academy Award in Literature from the American Academy of Arts and Letters. A fellow of the American Academy of Arts and Sciences and the American Academy of Arts and Letters, he is the Ward W. and Priscilla B. Woods Professor of English at Stanford University.